Redwood National & State Parks
Tales, Trails, & Auto Tours

Jerry & Gisela Rohde

Illustrations by Larry Eifert

MountainHome Books
• 1994 •

Library of Congress Catalogue Number: 94-075098
International Standard Book Number: 0-9640261-0-4
Manufactured in the U. S. A. on acid-free, recycled paper by Thomson-Shore, Inc.,
    Dexter, Michigan 48130
Body text in Book Antiqua, anecdote text in CG-Omega, titles in Book Antiqua and
    Goudy Extrabold-MT

Disclaimer: The information contained in this book is meant to provide users with
    an enhanced, safe park experience. Every attempt has been made to identify po-
    tential park hazards and to urge prudent and proper planning when visiting the
    areas described. The publishers assume no responsibility for injuries, damage to
    equipment or goods, or other problems that readers of this book may encounter
    while in the parks, and the book is sold with this understanding acknowledged
    and accepted by the purchaser.

MountainHome Books
1901 Arthur Road
McKinleyville, CA 95521

Redwood National & State Parks

Tales, Trails, & Auto Tours

Also by the same authors and illustrator:

Humboldt Redwoods State Park:
The Complete Guide

Table of Contents

Section III: Hiking Trails

Section IV: A Quick Guide to the Parks

Maps:

       (individual trail maps are found with each trail)

Foreword

Experiencing the tranquility of a towering redwood grove or the peaceful grazing of elk in a golden prairie will become even more valuable to a growing population in the next century. A century ago, as the idea for creating parks was embraced, the ambitions of many to preserve redwood forests germinated, and grew into the redwood parks we appreciate today.

Publication of this guide in 1994 is timely, as California State Parks enjoy a long history of redwood park management, and Redwood National Park celebrates its 25th anniversary. This year also marks the beginning of a partnership by the national and state parks to jointly manage the parks, in order to provide maximum resource protection and the best visitor service possible into the 21st century.

With sensitivity and skill, the authors add a new insight to the visitor experience in Redwood National and State Parks. This carefully crafted guide promotes curiosity and greater exploration. Weaving historical anecdotes with modern experiences, while providing practical maps and suggestions, the authors have produced a thoroughly researched tool for those with little time, to those who enjoy the parks as a vacation destination.

Redwood National and State Parks, together a World Heritage Site and International Biosphere Reserve, protect resources cherished by citizens of many nations. We applaud Jerry and Gisela's accomplishment in bringing these outstanding parks to people in this, the first comprehensive guide.

William H. Ehorn
Superintendent
Redwood National Park

William R. Beat
Superintendent
North Coast Redwoods District
California Department of Parks
and Recreation

Acknowledgments

Many people helped the authors in preparing this book. We offer thanks to:

Larry Eifert, the "Rembrandt of the Redwoods," who has again enhanced our work with his wonderful drawings and maps.

Our editors and manuscript reviewers — Lowell "Ben" Bennion, Bob Fisk, Carolyn Mueller, Lincoln Kilian, and Matina Kilkenny, all of whom improved the text with their thoughtful comments.

Redwood National Park Superintendent Bill Ehorn and California State Parks Superintendent Bill Beat, for coauthoring the foreword and for their continuing cooperation and assistance.

Redwood National Park staff: Ann Smith, Loretta Farley, Vicki Ozaki, Sabra Steinberg, Dick Mayle, Aida Parkinson, Sue Fritzke, Art Eck, Terry Spreiter, Robin Galea, Stephen Underwood, John Wise, Sean Brannon, Norm Blair, Roy Ritchie.

California State Parks staff: Al Wilkinson, Richard Wendt, Mike Stalder, Dan Wyant, Dan Scott, Carl Knapp.

The many individuals who provided us with information, including Susie Van Kirk, Albert Gray, Mary Gray, Jackie White, Beeb White, Axel Lindgren, Charles Lindgren, Ruby McNamara, Blanche Blankenship, Thelma Hufford, Savina Barlow, Ora Leazer, Florence Kring, Janice Dore, Kenny Childs, Bill Watson, Helen Happ, Thomas Peacock, Mary Phillips Peacock, Don Andreasen, Glen Nash, Victor Crutchfield, Richard Ricklefs, Marylee Rohde, Michael Taylor, Ron Hildebrant, Ned Simmons, Dale Thornburgh, John Sawyer, Chris Peters, Loren Bommelyn.

The following institutions and agencies and their staffs: Indian Action Council Library — Darlene Magee; North Coast Redwood Interpretive Association — Barbara Wilkinson; HSU Library — Erich Schimps and Joan Berman; CalTrans — Mark Suchanek; Humboldt County Historical Society — Walt McConnell; Del Norte County

Historical Society. We also specifically acknowledge the Del Norte County Historical Society for the use of pictures which were re-done by Larry Eifert for the book. These illustrations appear on pages 32, 37, 42, 65, 203, 219, and 220.

Others who helped in various ways were Charley Manske, Bob Webster, Tom Menednhall, Gisela Haringer, Herbert Haringer, Nancy Martin, Matthew Miles, Bob Miles, Bruce Smith, and Norma Kirmmse-Borden.

A Note on the Parks

The Redwood National and State Parks area consists of four units: Redwood National Park (RNP), Prairie Creek Redwoods State Park, Del Norte Coast Redwoods State Park, and Jedediah Smith (Jed Smith) Redwoods State Park. The three state parks date from the 1920s; they were included in the 1968 legislation establishing Redwood National Park but currently remain under state operation. Additional land was added to Redwood National Park in 1978.

Park Unit	Total Acerage	Acres of Old-Growth Redwood
Redwood National Park	78,000	20,000
Prairie Creek Redwoods S. P.	14,000	13,000
Del Norte Coast Redwoods S. P.	6,400	6,000
Jedediah Smith Redwoods S. P.	10,000	9,000
Total	108,400	48,000

Redwood National Park is both a UNESCO (United Nations Educational, Scientific, and Cultural Organization) World Heritage Site and International Biosphere Reserve.

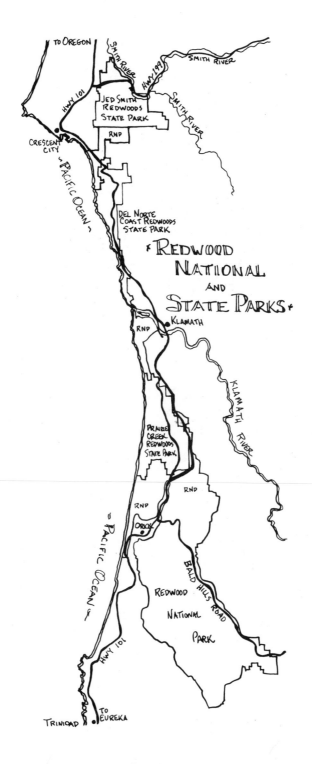

Redwood National and State Parks are located some 320 miles north of San Francisco, along California's extreme north coast. The parks are reached by the following main routes:

- from San Francsisco on U. S. Highway 101
- from Redding on State Highway 299
- from Grants Pass on U. S. Highway 199
- from the southern Oregon coast on U. S. Highway 101

Section I

* * *

History: Human and Natural

Redwoods:
Sawed and Saved

By the early 1960s, most of California's once-great redwood forest had disappeared, its many-acred, ancient stands reduced to a few far-flung fragments. A century of cutting had removed almost all the easily accessible timber, and logging crews pushed ever deeper into the distant woods. Chainsaws echoed in remote canyons as groves of old-growth giants were readied, without reservation or respite, for the mill and marketplace. Some people found the pace too fast, and worried that the few trees then protected in parks were not enough. But progress was the country's most important product, and the preservationists' pleas went unheeded. Then a magazine sent a man into the hinterlands of Humboldt County, where he discovered a treasure that stilled the saws and reprieved a redwood remnant.

Paul Zahl's Tall Tree Tale

The two men stood on a remote Georgia-Pacific logging road; G-P supervisor Casey Casebier gestured towards a stand of trees on the far side of a deep canyon: "Great timber!" he said admiringly. His companion, Paul Zahl, stared long and hard at the grove of giant redwoods and decided he would return later for a closer look.

Zahl, a naturalist with the National Geographic Society, had been sent to Humboldt County in early 1963 to study the coast redwood and its environment. His assignment took him to the logging town of Orick, which lay near the mouth of aptly named Redwood Creek. When Zahl stopped at one of the local motels, its owner, Lowell Hagood, pointed to the dense forest east of town and remarked that many woodsmen were mightily impressed by the trees there. Zahl began to investigate the claim, and now, after seeing

Casebier's stand of redwoods, he concluded that the loggers were right.

Soon Zahl was back on the G-P road, this time descending it all the way to a remote section of Redwood Creek. A century earlier, prospectors had followed a pack trail down this same slope; near the bottom they found an enormous tree some 33 feet in diameter. Now Zahl was doing some prospecting of his own, hoping to strike a lode of large-size redwoods. His boss, Society President Melville Bell Grosvenor, had told him, "Keep your eyes open. It would be wonderful to find a record-breaker," and Zahl had an inkling he might do just that.

Leaving his car, Zahl approached the stream. The grove of giant trees rose above the far bank; to the left loomed a recently logged ridge. After hiking downstream a bit, he found a shallow spot and crossed the creek. "I was immediately enveloped by deep shade," he later said. "I stopped in a small clearing, and, pivoting slowly, counted the number of trees visible from that single spot: 30 with trunks at least ten feet in diameter, some perhaps 14, even 16 feet."

Zahl returned to the location again and again, bringing along an Abney level to measure the redwoods' height. He calculated that several of the trees were about 320 feet tall, a few 335 feet. One even topped out at 350 feet.

On one trip Zahl climbed a partially cutover ridge across from the grove to take some photographs. His route up the steep slope was clogged with stumps, brambles, and debris from the logging. After rising about 300 feet above the creek, he paused to rest.

> While catching my breath, I scanned the treetops before me—then suddenly started. One particular redwood rose above the others like a giant candle. I had already measured its companions—all of them about 320 feet tall. But this great tree stood somewhat inland—and that explained my missing it earlier....[1]

Zahl hurried down the hillside and began taking measurements.

> After several readings from different points, I came to an astonishing figure. Much as I wanted to believe my rough computation, I simply could not: According to the Abney level, this was easily the world's tallest tree—about 370 feet![2]

The naturalist promptly relayed the news to Grosvenor, who soon arrived to examine the alleged record breaker. The grove was owned by the Arcata Redwood Company, and Howard A. Libbey, ARCO's President, led a party into the canyon to investigate. Among those in the group were Zahl, Grosvenor, and three local surveyors. When the men reached the grove, the surveyors took out their equipment and went to work. Meanwhile Zahl and the others stared skyward, walked around the forest...and waited.

The surveyors sighted with their instruments. They wrote some figures in their little black books. Then the three of them came together and compared their computations. Finally they approached the others.

Zahl, right, et al., measuring girth of tallest tree

Zahl's measurement had been off. The tree was only 367.8 feet tall. The surveyors were sorry, but that made it only eight and a half feet taller than the previous tallest tree instead of Zahl's estimate of ten-plus feet—would that still be all right?

Oh yes. There were also trees that measured 367.4, 364.3, and 352.3 feet tall. These would rank as the number two, three, and six trees after the new record holder...were there any other groves that Mr. Grosvenor and Mr. Libbey would like them to measure?

For over a century there had been attempts to create a national park for redwoods, but every effort had failed. Now, spurred on by the discovery of the record-breaking trees, the park movement gained new vigor. Just four years later, on a thickly forested hilltop west of the Tall Trees Grove, a delegation of dignitaries dedicated the newly established Redwood National Park. More than he ever anticipated, Zahl's zeal had paid off.

The Ancient Forest

From its beginning, the American nation built itself upon logs—Abe Lincoln's Kentucky cabin, the forts that dotted the West—the image is everywhere in the country's early history. Settlers cut their way across the land, clearing farm plots and creating building material with the same stroke of the ax. The commercial loggers soon followed; large-scale operations were busy leveling the northeastern forests by the early 1800s, and within 60 years most of the region's hardwoods and white pine were gone. The effort soon made lumbering the top manufacturing industry in the U. S.

Some of the woodsmen then headed south, cutting more pines and hardwoods. The big-tree loggers kept to the north, moving into the pineries of the Great Lakes. When Hemingway wrote his "Big Two-Hearted River" in the 1920s these forests were only a memory, the power of their vanished presence lingering like a wisp of wood smoke.

At last the loggers reached the Pacific Coast—stopped, finally, not by the ocean but by a wall of trees the likes of which were found nowhere else. In Washington and Oregon there grew huge firs and spruces that took a day or more to cut, arrayed across some of the roughest country imaginable—ridge after steep-sided ridge of slippery soil, with swirling rivers below and a gray, endlessly dripping sky above. Yet come to California and the great trees to the north faded into insignificance. Here, in the state's early days, were forests that staggered belief—filled with giants 300 feet tall and 20 feet across, their tops stretching so far skyward that the locals claimed "it took two men to look all the way to the top." These were the coast redwoods, the tallest trees on earth. Some of the smaller specimens had first sprouted when Lincoln was but a lad; trees born in the time of Columbus were just reaching their prime. The oldest went back twenty centuries, old nearly beyond imagining; nearly as old, it seemed, as the earth itself.

But that was over a hundred years ago, and time, and technology, have long exacted their toll. Choppers who cut the trees by hand gradually traded their tools for chain saws, while the mills improved their machinery to match. Grove after grove was laid flat by loggers who had nowhere else to go and were willing to take their time to deal with the biggest of the "big sticks." And time it took, but at last the tally is almost complete, and the tree cutters have taken nearly all

Humungous Humboldt redwood—
height: 300 feet; weight: 747,563 pounds

By now, more than 90 percent of the country's Pacific timberland has been logged, and the loss is even higher among the redwoods. What had once been an ancient forest of nearly two million acres has, in 1993, less than 90,000 acres of old growth left. True, much of the cutover land is currently growing a new generation of trees, but most of these stands belong to timber companies and will be cut again as soon as the profit margin dictates. The parks also contain areas of logged land, and though the trees there, with luck, will in time reach maturity, it will be centuries before they again can truly be called "ancient." For now, there are only a few great enclaves of old growth to give a hint of what the redwood forest once was—the Rockefeller Forest at Humboldt Redwoods State Park, the Tall Trees and the Lady Bird Johnson groves at Redwood National Park, the stands along upper Prairie Creek, the Stout

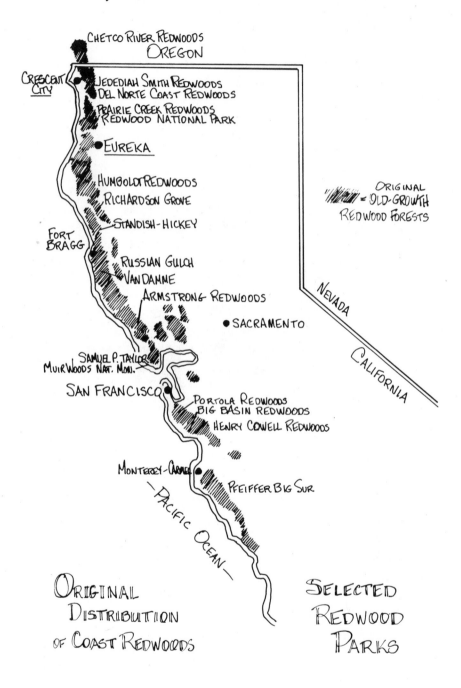

CHETCO RIVER REDWOODS
OREGON

CRESCENT CITY

JEDEDIAH SMITH REDWOODS
DEL NORTE COAST REDWOODS
PRAIRIE CREEK REDWOODS
REDWOOD NATIONAL PARK

● EUREKA

HUMBOLDT REDWOODS
RICHARDSON GROVE
STANDISH-HICKEY

FORT BRAGG

RUSSIAN GULCH
VAN DAMME
ARMSTRONG REDWOODS

● SACRAMENTO

ORIGINAL = OLD-GROWTH REDWOOD FORESTS

NEVADA

CALIFORNIA

SAMUEL P. TAYLOR
MUIR WOODS NAT. MON.

SAN FRANCISCO

PORTOLA REDWOODS
BIG BASIN REDWOODS
HENRY COWELL REDWOODS

MONTEREY-CARMEL

PFEIFFER BIG SUR

— PACIFIC OCEAN —

ORIGINAL DISTRIBUTION OF COAST REDWOODS

SELECTED REDWOOD PARKS

Grove and the corridor along lower Mill Creek at Jedediah Smith Redwoods State Park. There are no walls around these prize places, but they protect treasures more valuable than those found in any bank vault. In an era of endangered forests, the redwood parks are our Louvre and our Smithsonian, preserving a small portion of the past, carrying our hope for the future.

Coast Redwoods

Redwoods have been around a long time — tens of million years according to the best evidence. Titans of the plant world, they succeeded the big boys of the animal kingdom, the dinosaurs, after the great reptiles mysteriously faded from the scene. Then, about two million years ago, the huge trees nearly followed the dinosaurs into extinction; the last of the great ice ages swept down from the polar regions, covering much of Europe and North America and driving the redwoods from most of their former home. When the glaciers finally receded, the coast redwood *(Sequoia sempervirens)* found itself occupying only a narrow strip of land near the western coast of North America. Of a dozen or so related species, just two had survived: the giant Sequoia *(Sequoiadendron giganteum)* which grew in scattered groves in the Sierra Nevada of California, and the dawn redwood *(Metasequoia glyptostroboides),* confined to a few small areas in remotest China.

"...nature's masterpiece and unsurpassable"

So did one admiring author describe the coast redwood, and his sentiments have, over time, been more or less echoed by a host of others: "Probably the most impressive tree in N[orth] America" claims a cautious naturalist; the "wonder wood," as a lumber industry promoter would have it; "God's own flagpoles," according to an awe-struck architect.

Among its multitude of attributes, the coast redwood offers something superlative for nearly everyone. Engineers are impressed with the tree's water-drawing ability, since it is no mean feat for an organism to transport vast amounts of moisture up a 300-foot trunk and then transpire the wetness into the atmosphere at the rate of 500 gallons per day. Carpenters commend the quality of the wood, which not only resists fire and rot, but also works easily, insulates well, is good at taking paint and stain, and often contains beautiful grains and figures. Antiquarians are impressed by the age of redwoods, which routinely runs to 500 years or more for mature trees and can achieve a maximum of about 2,000 years.

Resplendent row of redwoods, Prairie Creek Redwoods State Park

But these are all merely facets of an entity that is far more than the sum of its parts, and, for that matter, more than whatever effect a single specimen can produce. It is easy to envision a lone oak, its roots embedded in some rocky hillslope, dominating the landscape with its solitary presence, but to imagine a redwood in isolation is almost impossible. The great trees are meant to grow in groves, for their shallow root system renders them susceptible to windthrow and undermining when they lack the protection of their brethren; moreover, their tall, straight trunks lend themselves to an almost architectural unity, like that of a circle of columns around some ancient temple. Enter a stand of full-sized redwoods and feel the effect—tree after tree, each adding onto the others and yet all balancing one another like a mighty organ fugue, filling the forest with a harmony beyond hearing, beyond understanding.

For thousands of years the coast redwood thrived within its reduced range, which ran from the mountains south of Big Sur to a point barely north of the Oregon border. The trees initially suffered little impact from humans. Local Indians seldom did more than convert pieces of downed redwoods into houses and various implements; if they felled a standing tree, it was chiefly to obtain a suitable section of wood for their magnificent canoes. Only with the coming of the whites were the redwoods truly put at risk.

Spanish explorers were the first Europeans to record observations of the coast redwoods. By 1776 they had not only chronicled their sightings but had also measured a sizable specimen found on the San Francisco Peninsula; Fray Pedro Font of the de Anza Expedition named it the "tall tree." The town that grew up nearby took the tree's Spanish title for its name — Palo Alto. Fray Font noted that redwood "is certainly beautiful; and I believe that it is very useful for its timber...." How useful he had no way of knowing.

Soon California's Spanish colonists were putting redwood roofbeams in their new missions and in other structures at San Francisco and San Jose. The Russians were more enthusiastic users, crafting the wood into dozens of buildings for their base at Fort Ross. It took the mid-19th-century influx of Americans to initiate heavy cutting of the great trees, however. Time and again the great gold rush port of San Francisco was swept by fire, and after each incident the loggers fanned out farther among the bayside hills to cut replacement redwoods. Within a few years much of the nearby forest had been converted into lumber, and the woodsmen went north, into Mendocino County, to log the even bigger trees produced by that area's wetter climate. Beyond lay the richest redwood lands of all, the great groves of Humboldt and Del Norte counties, but for the time being they were protected from extensive logging by the region's remoteness.

A Lexicon for the Redwood Landscape

The language used in redwood country reflects the singular setting it describes, so it is often filled with words both weird and wonderful. For example:

becket: neither the English martyr nor the Irish playwright, but a fastening device for logging cables

benchland: an elevated, generally flat area, composed of compacted streamside silt and gravel; redwoods attain their greatest size at such locations

bucker: a logger who cuts ("bucks") fallen trees into sections for transport

burl: the lumpy outgrowth on a redwood trunk, containing numerous buds; burl wood is "heavy, hard, dark...[and] figured with a fantastic grain"

cathedral trees: a circular group of redwoods that have grown around a host stump or tree to form a set of churchlike spires

chimney tree: similar to a goosepen (see below), this tree has an opening burned all the way to its top; the hollow thus created forms the "chimney"

drag saw: an early gasoline-powered saw used for felling and bucking (see above and below)

faller: a logger who cuts down (fells) the trees; when fallers used axes, they were often called "choppers"

goosepen tree: a redwood whose lower trunk has been burned out by a naturally occurring fire; the resulting opening, when fenced off, was large enough to contain a gaggle (or two) of geese

Goosepen house for humans

spiketop: a redwood whose top has died and lost its foliage due to lack of water

springboard: a narrow piece of wood, several feet long, one end of which was fitted into a precut hole in the side of a large redwood; loggers stood on planks laid across the springboards in order to cut a tree some distance above its flaring butt

widowmaker: a large broken limb that drops from a redwood and crashes to the ground, often embedding itself in the earth like a giant spike; named for its effect when it hits a married woodsman

The northern California coast retained its obscurity for decades, visited briefly by Jedediah Smith and his party in the 1820s and by precious few other whites until mid-century. Then came gold discoveries in the Salmon and Trinity mountains; to supply the mines, enterprising entrepreneurs soon established port towns at the region's three natural harbors — Crescent City and Trinidad at bays to the north and Union (later called Arcata) and Eureka on Humboldt Bay. Early on, the citizens busied themselves felling the nearby redwoods — by 1853, just three years after its founding, bustling Eureka already boasted nine sawmills. The trees were there for the cutting, rain-fed mammoths 15 or even 20 feet in diameter. The trick was to get them out of the woods easily and cut up cheaply. If the lumber could then be sent to out-of-area markets, redwood would become a big-time commodity.

Barkentine *Jane L. Sanford*
with a load of Humboldt logs

At first, none of this was easy. There were only oxen and horses to haul the huge logs from the forest, although the draft animals were gradually replaced by company railroads. Once at the mills, size was still a problem; the saws of the day were no match for the largest-diameter redwoods. When the logs finally were cut up, there was only one way for them to go anywhere—by ship, which meant a lengthy and often perilous sea voyage. The North Coast lumber industry was a bonanza waiting to happen, but it would require a greatly improved technology before it did.

The improvements came, albeit slowly. In 1869 an ingenious millwright named David Evans patented the "Evans Third Saw" that added another blade to the two already in use, thereby speeding up the cutting process. Thirteen years later, lumberman John Dolbeer designed a steam-powered "donkey" engine that could move logs by cable through the woods; by 1893 a larger version, the "bull" donkey, was hauling batches of 10 to 20 logs at once, pulling them up and down hills for distances up to a mile and doing it at a rate of 150 feet per minute. Soon the duo of steaming donkeys had done away with both horse and ox.

It took longer to improve long-haul timber transport, for while the local logging railroads gradually pushed their way over and across the most difficult terrain, it was not until 1914 that the Northwestern Pacific completed a through route between Humboldt County and San Francisco Bay. Then at last there was a relatively inexpensive and reliable way to move wood products to the waiting host of eager purchasers. It had taken more than half a century, but the lumbermen's dream had finally become reality.

Lumbermen and Land Fraud

The dream, however, was at least part nightmare. A small coterie of capitalists treated the great trees as their private preserve, reaping huge profits while their workers survived on scant wages and the forests fell before saw and ax. Dissatisfied with their level of wealth, some of the timber barons sought ways to increase their profits even further, resorting to fraud when other tactics failed. To a large part they succeeded, with the result that thousands of acres of prime timberland were taken from the public domain at a fraction of their worth. Ironically, some of the land thus acquired would be sold back to the government 80 years later for the market's highest price.

The fraud perpetrated was so enormous, so blatant, that in 1888 the House of Representatives was finally compelled to order an inquiry. The Secretary of the Interior, who had already been investigating the case, responded. He reported that

> ...a scheme was entered into by members of the firms of J. Russ & Co. and of Faulkner, Bell & Co., both of San Francisco, Cal., to obtain possession of the valuable redwood forests, situated in Humboldt County, of that State....

> Under this well-concocted scheme, boldly carried out, more than 57,000 acres were entered, and title sought to be obtained to perhaps the most valuable tract of timber land in the United States, valued, by experts of the conspirators, at $11,000,000, and worth probably much more.[3]

The plot made use of the recently enacted Timber and Stone Act, which allowed individuals to acquire 160-acre parcels of federal forestland for $2.50 per acre. The intent was for the claimants, who

Logging railroad trestle over Strawberry Creek—height: 93 feet

were called "entrymen," to gain patent to the property and obtain income by harvesting the timber found there. The conspirators circumvented this procedure by finding "dummies"—usually sailors or loggers or even local merchants—who, for a payoff of $50.00, would file claim to a particular parcel and promptly sign over the deed to the plotters. The so-called "timber ring" then sold the parcels to a capitalist syndicate based in Edinburgh, Scotland, for $7.00 per acre. After deducting the cost of the land, the entrymen's bribes, and "finder's fees" for locating the entrymen, the ring stood to make more than $300,000 on the transaction. The Scottish syndicate, meanwhile, would reap over $10 million in profits.

Knowledge of the fraud was widespread in Eureka, where the conspirators had even advertised publicly for entrymen. In an age whose motto was "the business of America is business," a corollary was that the country's hobby was fraud, and few locals seemed to begrudge either the dummy entrymen or the ring members their chance to make some small change or a small fortune.

One person who did object was Charles Keller, a Eureka butcher and member of the radical Greenback Party. In a letter to the local *Democratic Standard*, Keller described the plot and then asked:

> ...can nothing be done to stop these land thieves and this nefarious practice? If these rascalities were carried on somewhere else, say a thousand or more miles away from Eureka, we should no doubt speak about them in very bitter terms, but here, mum is the word; bread and butter depends on our remaining quiet.

Keller's words proved personally prophetic; angered locals boycotted his market, and the muckraking meat cutter left the county. Before departing, however, he collected notarized accounts of the fraud and forwarded them to the Land Office in Washington. The office duly dispatched a series of agents to investigate: the first was bought off by the timber ring, but the second, W. T. Smith, refused a bribe and reported the fraud. His superiors, however, had themselves been compromised by the conspirators; Smith's information was ignored and over 160 fraudulent patents approved. A change in Presidential administrations then invigorated the Land Office, which subsequently cancelled many of the remaining entries.[4]

In April 1886, a federal grand jury issued indictments "against eight prominent citizens of the state for subornation of perjury in a case of fraudulent entries of redwood timber land in Humboldt County...."[5] Among the indictees were two North Coast notables, Joseph Russ and David Evans. Russ was a mill operator and the largest landowner in Humboldt County; his domain extended over 50,000 acres and included 21 dairy ranches. He died later that year while serving his third term in the California legislature. Evans arrived in Eureka as a 19-year-old sailor, promptly jumped ship, and then evaded capture by hiding in a baker's oven. He later applied his ample ingenuity to sawmill inventions and gained a reputation as a first-rate timber cruiser. In 1888 the land fraud case against him was dismissed; although the *New York Times*[6] urged punishment for "[t]he bold and shameless rascals who have stolen and are stealing public land," only one member of the ring was ever convicted. Despite the episode Evans was later twice elected mayor of Eureka.

The Marshes and Their Forest

On a back shelf of the Humboldt County Recorder's office is a thick and tattered book that contains a remarkable set of entries. Written with the precise penmanship of a different century, in brown ink still vivid, is the name of David Evans; it is repeated line after line, page after page, 32 lines to the page, until it has been listed 350 consecutive times. Each entry notes the transfer of timberland to Evans from an entryman, the deeds and conveyances having been processed en masse by notaries who conspired with Evans's timber ring.

Among the conveyances are those of Harris T. Marsh and John A. Marsh, a pair of local farmers who were father and son. The elder Marsh and his wife Lena would later be recognized as Humboldt County "pioneers." Meanwhile, their son John garnered some attention in his own right.

Two years after he filed his land claim, the younger Marsh was subpoenaed by the Land Office and compelled to attend a hearing. There he testified that he was induced to file for the timberland by an agent of the conspirators, that he never saw the property he filed for nor could he describe it, and that he was paid $50.00 by the agent for his filing. Based on this information, the Land Office canceled John Marsh's entry, and his allotment reverted to the government. By then the land that Harris Marsh had filed for, which lay directly south of that claimed by his son, had already been patented; like many similar parcels, it was allowed to remain in the hands of the conspirators. These properties were later sold, at a profit of over 300 per cent, to the Hammond Lumber Company.

John Marsh's erstwhile property was eventually patented by another individual, and, years later, both his acreage and his father's were purchased by the Arcata Redwood Company. The land, which lay on a long ridgeline above the confluence of Prairie and Redwood creeks, contained a fine stand of high-elevation redwoods; when it was acquired in 1968 to become part of the new Redwood National Park, the federal government paid top dollar for it. No distinction was then made between Harris Marsh's old allotment and that of his son's, for the 80-year-old land fraud had been all but forgotten. Besides, the two parcels formed part of a single natural forest unit, one that would soon gain national attention.

On November 25, 1968, the wife of the President of the United States walked through Harris Marsh's old land, looked out over the

Second dedication at the Marshes' forest, August 27, 1969

property that had briefly belonged to Marsh's son, and then dedicated the new park. The following year, the dedicator herself was
honored when the Marshes' once-fraudulent forestland became
part of a special stand of redwoods. The name of the new site?—the
Lady Bird Johnson Grove.

The Humboldt conspirators had been caught, and although
only one of them was sent to jail, much of the land they had ille-
gally acquired was forfeited. Other fraudulent operations proved
more successful; in 1909 a report on the results of the Timber and
Stone Act concluded that over 10 million acres of "valuable timberlands" had been transferred by entrymen to corporations and other
investors. These acquisitions netted the new owners an eventual
profit of some 700 percent and sealed the fate of much of the great
western forest; the magnificent stands were about to become statistics, bandied across the boardrooms of corporate America in the
pursuit of profit.

The Preservationists and Their Parks

While the government was thus gilding the balance sheets of big
business, a few voices were raised in defense of the trees. The creation of a national redwood park was first proposed in 1852, when
California assemblyman Henry A. Crabb asked his fellow legisla-
tors to seek Congressional action prohibiting the occupation and
sale of redwood timberlands. Nothing came of Crabb's request, nor
of a similar 1879 proposal by Secretary of the Interior Carl Schurz.
Ten years later, Schurz was still at his guns, warning the American
Forestry Congress that the

> ...destruction of our forests is so fearfully rapid that if we go on at the
> same rate...we will see the day when in the United States from Maine
> to California and from the Mexican Gulf to Puget Sound, there will be
> no forest left worthy of the name.

Still nothing happened, and during the following decades tree
savers high and low continued to meet failure: in 1904 President
Theodore Roosevelt expressed approval of a plan to set aside redwoods in California for a public park, while four years later, eight
Humboldt County high school students petitioned Congress to
preserve the trees. No action was taken on either request, although

TR had the satisfaction of designating as a National Monument the recently donated, redwood-rich Muir Woods.

Other efforts to establish a federal park followed: an attempt by California Congressman John E. Raker in 1911, another led by Eureka Mayor F. W. Georgeson in 1912, yet a third by Charles Willis Ward in 1914. Ward's plan called for the purchase of 22,000 acres on the south side of the lower Klamath River; conveniently, much of the proposed acquisition was owned by Ward himself.

Nothing came of these efforts, either. Then, in 1918, a group of influential preservationists met in San Francisco and formed the Save-the-Redwoods League. Although the organization soon began considering a national redwood park, it first focused on obtaining lands that could be brought into the state system. One such area already existed—Big Basin, established in the Santa Cruz Mountains in 1901. With the League leading the way, Humboldt Redwoods became the second state redwood park in 1922. Located along the South Fork Eel River in southern Humboldt County, its development took much of the League's early energy, but by 1928 the group had added three other redwood park sites to their program: Prairie Creek, Del Norte Coast, and Mill Creek/Smith River.

Bolstered by an effective fundraising program, the League quickly acquired dramatic amounts of acreage to add to the state redwood parks, but there was still no action at the federal level. Congresswoman Helen Gahagan Douglas proposed a redwood-filled Franklin D. Roosevelt Memorial National Forest in 1946, but she was defeated for reelection the following year by Richard M. Nixon and her bill then died for lack of a sponsor.

A National Park at Last

Little more was heard on the issue until the early 1960s, when the Save-the-Redwoods League, the National Geographic Society, the Sierra Club, and other organizations revived the idea of a national redwood park. Secretary of the Interior Stewart Udall announced his plan to propose a federal park in 1963, and President Lyndon B. Johnson indicated his support the following year. Starting in early 1966, a series of hotly contested park bills was introduced in Congress, with North Coast timber companies and their sympathizers attempting to counter the growing influence of the preservationists. After much controversy, maneuvering, and appeasement, Congress finally approved the necessary legislation, and on October 2, 1968, President Johnson signed into law the act authorizing the establishment of a 58,000-acre Redwood National Park. After 116 years and the cutting of about 1,700,000 acres of redwoods, a federal park had finally become reality.

It was a reality, though, that fell far short of the preservationists' dream. Nearly half the new park's acreage was already protected, for three existing state redwood parks—Prairie Creek, Del Norte Coast, and Jedediah Smith—were included under the federal act, although they remained under state control. In addition, much of the new property was cutover land that would possess no mature forest for centuries. Worse yet, there was trouble at the Tall Trees Grove; although the record-setting redwoods now belonged to the park, it quickly became apparent that they were still at risk.

The grove was part of the "worm," a twisting, forested corridor of park property; it ran eight miles along Redwood Creek, ending just upstream from the tallest tree site. To the south was private timberland, where, according to one outraged report,[7] "the moment the park bill was signed, Arcata Redwood, Simpson Timber, and Georgia-Pacific began cutting...." Redwood Creek's tributaries were soon shorn of their protective canopies, the slopes above

"You can't see
the forest [renewal]
for the [lack of] trees."

them suddenly laid bare as "chainsaws outlined the park boundaries on the landscape." Rain rapidly transformed skid roads into gullies that carried eroded topsoil creekward. Within a short time "a plug of rocks and dirt, in some places as high as fourteen feet, moved down Redwood Creek and threatened the Tall Trees."

Preservationists demanded government action to protect the grove as the cutting upstream continued. State officials, however, failed to halt the logging, while the Department of Interior claimed its hands were tied. Congressional action proved ineffectual.

Early in 1977 Representative Phillip Burton introduced legislation to expand the park. His bill also contained provisions to rehabilitate cutover areas and to compensate timber workers who would lose their jobs as a result of the "lockup" of harvestable timberlands. Despite these benefits, local loggers were outraged by the proposal, and when Burton subsequently held hearings on the bill in Eureka, several thousand opponents took to the streets. At the meeting itself the woodsmen "pounded their axes on the wooden floor of the hall's stage and swung the wedged blades over their heads." Six weeks later a convoy of logging trucks set off on a protest ride to Washington D. C.

While North Coast timber companies and their workers continued to oppose the bill, Burton and others secured the support of organized labor, and with its backing, the controversial legislation soon passed. In March 1978 President Jimmy Carter signed a 48,000-acre park expansion act that widened the Redwood Creek corridor and extended it far up the drainage; some 39,000 acres of the acquisition were cutover lands that would require rehabilitation. The cost of the addition was over $400 million.

On March 22, 1982, Redwood National Park was dedicated as a UNESCO World Heritage Site, joining such illustrious locations as Chartres Cathedral, the Katmandu Valley, and Australia's Great Barrier Reef. The ceremony took place at the Lost Man Creek Picnic Area, where centuries-old trees tower above an abandoned logging road. Only a few years earlier timber-filled trucks had thundered past the now-quiet spot, carrying off fallen giants from the nearby hillsides. Thousands of redwoods had been lost in the upper canyon of the creek, but at the dedication site and elsewhere in the park, many others had at last been saved.

It is easy to feel sadness or even anger at the greed and short sightedness that destroyed so much of the ancient redwood forest, but it is easier still to walk through the great groves that remain, like those at Prairie Creek, or Mill Creek, or a hundred other places, and be filled with thankfulness for what has been saved. Perhaps it took the loss of so many redwoods to make us understand how precious these trees truly are—and that, even though the price has been so terribly high, is a lesson worth learning.

Sempervirens survivor,
Prairie Creek Redwoods State Park

Tribes of the Tall Trees

For its early inhabitants, the North Coast was a place of plenty, rich in nearly everything that provided comfort and contentment. Few locations on the continent were as favored, for here were not only the salmon-filled streams of the Pacific Northwest, but also the acorn-rich oak savannas that ranged across much of California. The winters were wet but the temperatures mild, and the region's many mountains and rivers often created natural tribal boundaries that helped limit territorial conflict. It was a wondrous land, protected and respected by those who dwelt within it.

The earth, for these people, was sacred, for all that lived upon it possessed a spirit. The local Native Americans walked through the forests accompanied by this awareness; they fished and hunted while carrying this knowledge within them. Every year, the North Coast Indians gathered to celebrate the world they inhabited; dressed in beautiful regalia, they performed the Feather Dance, the Jumping Dance, and the White Deerskin Dance, bringing balance and bountifulness to the forthcoming seasons. So it had been for centuries, for so long, in fact, that its beginnings had passed far beyond memory.

Then some white prospectors found gold in the mountains to the east, and nothing was ever the same again. Miners, merchants, and settlers arrived by the boatload, setting up bustling communities and cutting their way into the nearby forests. Many of the new arrivals saw the Indians as akin to the trees—obstacles to be removed from the path to profits and progress. A holocaust virtually hidden from history ensued: Native American men were often shot on sight, women raped and forced into long-term relationships, children sold as slaves or legally "indentured" to white families. Ranchers ran their stock on tribal hunting and gathering areas, while hydraulic mining debris clogged the streams and rendered them unfit for fish. Vigilantes attacked tribal villages, burning the

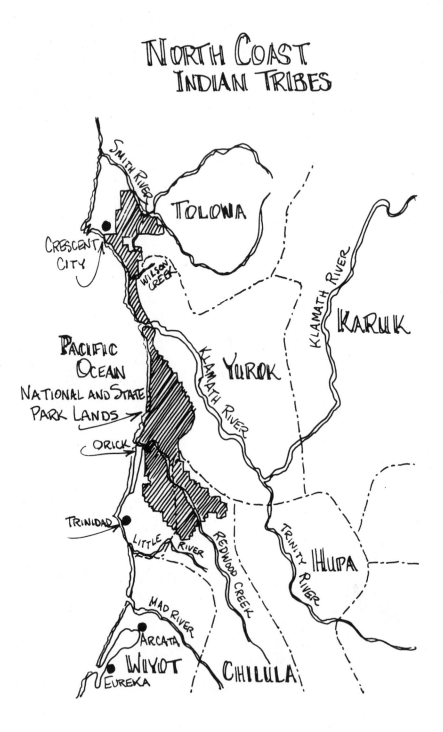

NORTH COAST
INDIAN TRIBES

buildings and massacring the inhabitants. The Indians who survived all this were forced onto reservations, places that at best were little more than prisons and at worst resembled concentration camps. Within 15 years most of the tribes had been decimated and the Indian "problem" largely solved; the whites had what they wanted, which was nearly everything, while the remaining Native Americans were left to struggle for survival as best they could.

It has been a struggle seemingly without end, continuing, in certain ways, on into the present. Over the years local Indians have suffered the loss of most of their land and much of their earlier way of life. For decades, federal law prohibited the practice of traditional tribal religions, forcing the native peoples to adopt white-based beliefs or hold their sacred ceremonies in secret. Native American children were "acculturated" at special government-run schools, where they were forbidden to speak their own language and otherwise denied their heritage. Valuable tracts of timber that had remained in Indian hands were taken by bureaucratic bullying and outright fraud. In recent years, tribes have sued to defend religious sites threatened by U. S. Forest Service logging roads.

The Indians of the North Coast have endured it all, and, amazingly, have also preserved a part of their earlier way of life; today, local Native Americans continue to participate in ceremonial dances, practice traditional crafts, learn their tribe's language, and maintain other ways of their ancestors. And although most of their land has long ago been lost, small enclaves still remain—islands of tribal territory in a sea of white real estate. The world that their forebears knew has vanished forever, but at least a fragment of its beauty and wisdom remains, kept alive by the descendants of those earlier Indians who for so long cared so well for the North Coast.

The Tolowas

Like many other North Coast tribes, the Tolowas usually lived near water—whether river or sea; they fished and found other foods in it, they travelled in their canoes on it. Their main villages were at the mouth of the Smith River and at hospitable points farther south along the coast, but there was also a string of interior settlements that ran up the Smith, with other sites on major creeks and upland prairies. The communities were formed around family groups, each governed by a "headman," whose wealth enabled him to support local activities and to gain the loyalty of other group members. Each headman served as chief of his particular "claim" or district, transacting all the legal cases and even holding the power to order death sentences. The various villages were connected by a common language (a variety of Athabascan), a shared culture, and the family bonds made by marriage.

The Tolowas were related to the Tututni and Chetco tribes of the southern Oregon coast; they also maintained close ties with the Karuks, who lived east of the Siskiyou Mountains on the Klamath River, and with Yuroks from the vicinity of Requa. The Karuk and Shasta Indians served as intermediaries in a trading system that allowed the Modocs, whose land lay even farther east, to exchange obsidian for the dentalia shells that the Tolowas acquired northward along the coast.

Makeshift Tolowa dwelling belonging to White House Charlie

Tolowa houses, like those of nearby tribes, consisted of a central pit, dug several feet into the earth, and a set of walls and roof made of redwood planks. Village headmen also constructed sweathouses that they and their male associates used for sleeping, working, and leisure.

Tracts of land for deer hunting, acorn gathering, and fishing were clearly defined as the hereditary property of a particular family claim. One site, however, was shared by the entire tribe — a communal fishing weir built each summer on the Smith River at the village of Nelechundun, downstream from today's Jedediah Smith

Redwoods State Park; the weir served as an indication of overall tribal unity and identity.

As with neighboring tribes, the Tolowas' year revolved around obtaining acorns, salmon, and other foods: each spring the people went to the Smith River for the early-year salmon run and for the subsequent harvesting of roots and berries; next they gathered shellfish and smelt at the coast, followed by a return to the river for the late summer/fall salmon run. The villagers then travelled into the mountains to gather acorns and huckleberries and to hunt game, after which they moved back to their towns for the winter. Women collected most of the plant foods, along with the shellfish and smelt; the men, using five-person canoes, hunted sea lions and whales along the coast. The Tolowas constructed at least one canoe that was considerably larger—a gigantic dugout, built and launched on the Smith River and then paddled to Humboldt Bay. Measuring 42 feet in length and more than eight feet in width, it could carry up to 24 men or five tons of freight. In the 1870s, a white observer found it "a *thing of beauty*, sitting plumb and lightly on the sea, smoothly polished, and so symmetrical that a pound's weight on either side would throw it slightly out of trim."

Male Tolowas wore only a deerskin kilt during warm weather, while females dressed with a basketry cap and a two-piece buckskin apron or a skirt made of shredded cedar or maple bark. Winter clothing included robes of deerskin or sewn rabbit skins, and, for rainy weather, hats and shawl-like coats woven from tules.

In 1850, about 2,400 Tolowas were living, as they had for centuries, in their North Coast homeland. Then the whites came.

The Destruction of the "Center of the World"

When the first white settlers arrived on the North Coast, the largest Tolowa village was Yontocket, which lay near the mouth of the Smith River. More than a community, Yontocket was also the tribe's place of greatest spiritual significance, the "Center of the World," where for millennia the Tolowas had prayed and held their religious ceremonies.

The fall of 1853 was a time for one of the great gatherings at Yontocket, as the Tolowas came together to give thanks for their summer harvest and to ask for the future well-being of their people. This was Naydosh, the "Feather Dance," which renewed the Earth Mother and honored her creation. The dancing that year began as usual, but suddenly, in the middle of the ceremony, the air was rent by gunshots:

> The whites attacked and the bullets were everywhere. Over four hundred and fifty of our people were murdered or lay dying on the ground. Then the whitemen built a huge fire and threw in our sacred ceremonial dresses, the regalia, and our feathers, and the flames grew higher. Then they threw in the babies, many of them were still alive. Some tied weights around the necks of the dead and threw them into the water.

> Two men escaped, they had been in the Sacred Sweathouse and crept down to the water's edge and hid under the Lily Pads, breathing through the reeds. The next morning they found the water red with the blood of their people.[1]

The next year, the Tolowas gathered at the village of Achulet, south of the ruins of Yontocket. Once more they were massacred, "shot down as fast as the whites could reload their guns." Hundreds more died, and then Achulet, too, was razed. Still, the ceremony had to continue, so the following year it was held at the town of Howonquet, at the mouth of the Smith River. Again the settlers attacked the Indians, this time claiming 70 lives and burning yet another village.

Yontocket, Achulet, and Howonquet were no more. The whites had shown the Tolowas what a world with no center was like.

Only after the three massacres was a "treaty" signed between the settlers and Tolowa leaders. The next Naydosh was performed without attack, but by then few Tolowas were left to participate.

Naydosh was danced until 1923, when the United States government established a policy that prohibited Indians from practicing their tribal religions. After federal agents arrested the Tolowa dance makers and confiscated their regalia, Naydosh went underground, with shortened versions staged in private homes. Not until the 1950s did the Tolowas resume public performances of the

Feather Dance. Currently, the Naydosh ceremonies are held at Nelechundun.

With their own beliefs banned, many Tolowas came to join the Indian Shaker religion, which combined Native American and Christian spiritual teachings. Led by Norman George, Frank Hostler, and Donnie Flannery, the local adherents built a church at the Smith River Rancheria that is still used today; according to a noted contemporary Tolowa leader, "[T]he Shake has become an integral part of [the] traditional Tolowa belief system."

Young Tolowas dancing Naydosh

Today there are about 950 Tolowas, a number of whom live on rancherias at Smith River and Elk Valley. A new Smith River tribal office opened in 1986, followed by a clinic the next year and a community center in 1992. Both rancherias are federally recognized tribal entities; a third group, the Tolowa Nation, is still being organized. Notable among the contemporary Tolowa leaders is Loren Bommelyn, a basket maker, story teller, tribal council member, and credentialed teacher of the Tolowa language. Bommelyn is one of only four or five tribe members who are fluent in his people's tongue; his hope is that younger Tolowas, while not becoming expert speakers, will come to "understand [the] language's view of the world." It is, according to Bommelyn, a view of wholeness and interconnectedness — truly one of the treasures of the tribe.

The Yuroks

Early-day Yuroks either lived along the Klamath or on the coast. Most members of the tribe were settled at riverside sites between the ocean and Bluff Creek, east of Weitchpec; a smaller but still sizeable number occupied coastal areas from Wilson Creek south

Yurok houses at Rek-woi

to Little River, locating near creek mouths and lagoons. Of the tribe's 54 named villages, coastal Rek-woi was the largest, but even it contained only some 25 houses. The river communities were usually situated on terraces at least a hundred feet above the stream channel; the 1861-2 flood rose nearly that high and destroyed many of the older, lower-lying villages. While no Yuroks lived year round in the mountains, many people went there regularly for hunting, gathering, and travel. South of the tribe's territory were the Wiyots, with the Chilulas, Hupas and Karuks to the east. The Yuroks are alone among North Coast Indians in speaking an Algonquian language.

Like their Tolowa neighbors to the north, the Yuroks relied on acorns and salmon as staples in their diet. They usually caught salmon with dip nets, but also used gill nets, weirs, seines, and harpoons; a single night's dip netting sometimes garnered as many as a hundred fish, which could constitute an entire winter's salmon supply. "Acorns," according to one modern-day Yurok, "were gathered, cracked, dried, peeled, ground, and leached as needed." They were "cooked using hot rocks in a cooking basket." The Yuroks generally ate only two meals a day, one shortly before midday and the other after dark.

In the mountains, several families often harvested acorns from the same stand of oaks. The men hunted while the women and children collected nuts, berries, bulbs, and other foods; temporary huts provided shelter when the people were staying at the hunting and gathering sites. On the trip back to the home village, the group carried baskets filled with the high country's bounty—acorns, wild onions and bulbs, hazelnuts, fern roots, and dried deer and elk meat.

The Yuroks were very precise in matters of property rights and general law. Unlike most Native American tribes, a Yurok individual or family often "owned" a piece of land; of these parcels, fishing places were the most important—their value was based on the number of fish they supplied. A fishing spot might be held jointly, with each owner having the use of it for a set amount of time, such as half a day, two days, etc. Use rights sometimes applied specifically to one species, allowing one man to fish for salmon and another for eels at the same spot. In other instances, the user was determined by the river's height, so that at high water a particular person could fish a site, but a different individual had access when the level was low.

Yurok law was based on payment rather than punishment; persons who were wronged had to be compensated. This required an "elaborate scale of prices for each degree of injury, from the use of ...abusive expressions on up to and including homicide." An exact reparation was necessary, and no excuses for any infraction were accepted. If an offender was unable to pay for a crime, he would often become "bound" to his victim, compelled to serve as a virtual slave unless he was somehow able to acquire enough wealth to discharge his debt.

Compensation for damages could even cross tribal lines, as it did at the conclusion of the greatest of all the Yurok wars. During the 1830s, the Hupa village of Takimitlding and the Yuroks' Rekwoi were involved in a grievous conflict; each community was attacked by the other side, both times with much destruction and many deaths. When all the participants finally felt they had been avenged, a settlement council was held and large payments made by both sides. Two great towns lay devastated, but tribal law had been followed and everyone was at last satisfied.

Marriages, too, were closely regulated economic transactions. Potential grooms had to purchase their brides from the woman's parents, and if the would-be husband could not pay the full price, he often became "half married," living with and working for his wife's parents until he had paid off the balance—a sort of matrimony on the installment plan.

Other tribes esteemed the Yurok dugout canoes. These vessels, which were similar to those of the Tolowas and Wiyots, were traded to the Hupa, Karuk, Sinkyone, Mattole, and Shasta Indians. A canoe required five to six months for construction with traditional tools—axes and wedges shaped from elk horns, malls and hammers made of granite. The wood often came from fallen trees or logs washed up on the beach, although the Yuroks also reportedly felled live redwoods for canoe making. The wood was shaped by burning, scraping, and abrading. As a log was being hollowed, a small knob was left near the stern; it was "called the heart of canoe," reported a Yurok, "and without this the canoe would be dead....[N]o Indian would use a canoe unless it had a heart left in it to make it alive...."

Illness among the Yuroks was treated by a "kegeoir," or doctor, who was almost always female. A doctor would find "pains" within the patient, which she would then suck out; the pains were material objects that were then cast away. A few Yuroks still do doctoring today.

Fanny Flounder Becomes a Doctor

Although Fanny Flounder's mother and grandmother had both been Yurok doctors, it was not expected that she would also become one. For several summers, however, she left her home at Espaᵂ and went north to dance on a hilltop that overlooked the ocean. While sleeping there one night she dreamt a strange dream. The sky was rising, and blood was dripping off its edge; the blood formed objects like icicles. Then a woman appeared, dressed in the maple bark skirt that doctors wore. The woman took one of the bloody objects and put it in Fanny's mouth. It was as cold as ice.

Fanny blacked out. She awoke to find several men holding her in the breakers near her home at Espaᵂ. They took her to one of the houses, where she was to dance, but she was so weak that the men had to take turns holding her up as they danced. For five days she danced; then she ate some crabmeat that made her nauseous and she vomited her first "pain."

She began doing some doctoring but later had a second dream on the hilltop. This time she watched as a red-tailed hawk turned into a person. Fanny received an object from this person that she swallowed; soon she lost consciousness. From then on Fanny knew that if she saw a red-tailed hawk while on her way to doctor, she would cure the patient.

Then Fanny, along with her mother, went inland to a sacred mountain known as Doctor Rock. Here she sat in a rock seat before returning to Espaᵂ. Again she danced there in the house, this time accompanied by singers. She now gained control over her second pain and became a full-fledged doctor.[2]

Pecwan Jumping Dancers, c. 1926

Along with other North Coast tribes the Yuroks performed "world renewal" dances. Preceding the dance was the narration of a long "formula," an incantation spoken before various rocks and other places of spiritual significance. It was followed by the dance itself, which lasted many days. The dancers wore regalia of great value; wealthy Yuroks lent items such as obsidian and flint blades, white deerskins, and woodpecker scalps to other members of their village, who then used them in the dance. Any man could take part, but the women were allowed only to watch. In the White Deerskin Dance and Jumping Dance, the participants formed a line abreast of each other while the chief singer, flanked by his assistants, stood in the middle. The dancers swayed or swung the stone blades in time to the dance step.

The Jumping Dance had a spectacular finish. For the one held at the mouth of the Klamath, the dancers first performed for several days at Rek-woi, just north of the river; then, on the final day, they boarded two canoes, one for the dancers from Rek-woi and the other for visiting performers from the village of Turip. With a paddler in the bow and a steersman in the stern, seven men danced in each canoe, the crafts close enough that the dancers could touch fingertips. In this way they proceeded across the river to the village of Welkwau on the southern shore. There they disembarked and resumed their dance at a traditional spot near an old spruce tree.

Rek-woi's Jumping Dance was last performed in 1904. For a time all the dances died out, but in recent years the Jumping Dance has again been held at Pecwan, on the Klamath River, while the Brush Dance is now regularly staged at several locations.

Robert Spott:
A Yurok without a Country

At the turn of the century, it was not only the Yurok dances that were dying out—the tribe itself was also still diminishing. Although the days of massacres and warfare had long passed, the local Indians had suffered decades of poverty, disruption, and disease; shunned and exploited by most of the white community, they had also been neglected by an indifferent government. The decline continued into the 1920s, when Robert Spott, a Yurok from Rek-woi, described the situation to members of San Francisco's Commonwealth Club.

"We are California Indians, from the Klamath River," Spott began, "and I am here to tell you that we are almost at the end of the road." He went on to explain that many of his tribe's hunting grounds, fishing areas, and gathering sites had been taken over by white homesteaders; his people were barred from their old lands and had few places left where they could obtain food.

There are many Indian women who are almost blind, and they only have one meal a day, because there is no one to look after them. Most of these people used to live on fish, which they cannot get, and on acorns, and they are starving. They hardly have any clothing to cover them. Many children up along the Klamath River have passed away with disease. Most of them from tuberculosis.[3]

Spott detailed the effects of the federal land allotment system, which gave the Indians small, often inferior properties but then did not deliver the livestock and tools needed to make the parcels productive. He also described the failure of the federal Indian Service to provide adequate housing and medical care for his people. In his conclusion, Spott asked: "I would like to know today if we ever will get our country back."

Only a few years earlier, Spott, although not considered a citizen under the laws of the time, had enlisted to fight in World War I. He was gassed in France, which permanently affected his lungs, and had received the Distinguished Service Cross. Ruth Roberts, a white sympathizer

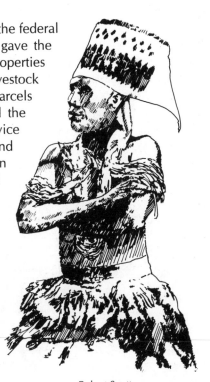

Robert Spott

from Requa, told the Commonwealth Club how nearly all the young Yurok men had enlisted in the military—that "[a]lmost to a boy...they went." Robert Spott's mother could not understand why her son had joined up. "He said he went to fight for his country," Mrs. Spott told Roberts, "but he has no country."

The federal land allotment system that Spott criticized had arbitrarily divided up Indian territory and then redistributed parts of it to individual members of the tribes, in the process dismembering villages, hunting and gathering areas, and sacred places. Some of the people chose land that kept important sites intact, but many of the allotments were later lost to timber companies; the Yuroks tell of forged papers and misrepresentation that took away parcel after parcel.

Difficulties continue to the present. Fishing rights on the Klamath have long been disputed by sport fishermen and local Indians, while residents along remote stretches of the river still live in near isolation, with few conveniences or services. Tribal politics are filled with controversy: for years the Yuroks, adhering to their traditional ways, resisted federal efforts to organize them into an officially sanctioned tribe. Then, in 1988, the Hoopa-Yurok Settlement Act divided jointly-held reservation lands between the Yuroks and Hupas while also creating a Yurok tribal government. Although many Yuroks continue to oppose this federally mandated organization, a constitution was adopted in 1993 and an elected council now provides leadership for a portion of the tribe. Some contemporary Yuroks still live on reservation lands and rancherias, while others have moved to outside communities.

Baskets and other articles, Brizard's Store on Klamath River

Despite many obstacles, several traditional Yurok crafts have survived to the present. Amy Smoker-Peters, who "worked on baskets nearly every day of her life," and Carrie Turner, with more than 80 years of basket making, carried their skills from the early 1900s into contemporary times. Axel Lindgren and George Blake are noted canoe makers; Blake, who also creates traditional dance regalia, received the National Heritage Award from the National Endowment for the Arts in 1991.

The Chilulas

The Chilulas believed that their ancestors had come out of a large, hollow redwood when the world was first created, and so they called themselves the "people within the redwood trees." Locals referred to the tribe as the "Redwood" or "Bald Hills" Indians. As these names indicate, the Chilulas lived inland; their territory started near the Tall Trees area of Redwood Creek, extended southward up the drainage, and included parts of the nearby Bald Hills. Like the Tolowas and the nearby Hupas, the Chilulas spoke an Athabascan tongue; they shared much of their culture with the Hupas, and intermarriage between the two tribes was apparently frequent.

While the Tolowas and Yuroks relied heavily on fishing, the Chilulas concentrated more on hunting and gathering, although they did catch salmon, steelhead, trout, candlefish, and lampreys in the Redwood Creek drainage; here they placed five dams during fish runs and also used dip nets, weirs, and harpoons. West of the creek, in the thick redwood forests, the Chilulas hunted elk, while they favored the prairies and oak stands to the east for deer hunting. In early fall they went to family-held "acorn grounds" on both sides of the canyon, where they harvested their other main food.

Permanent winter villages were probably located on prairieland along the Bald Hills, rather than in the redwood-crowded canyon closer to the creek. The Chilulas built plank houses typical of the region and small, square sweat houses, but they also constructed large, circular dance houses that were otherwise found only with Indians farther to the south. In winter the tribe burned areas on the northern and eastern canyon slopes and along the hilltops to promote new growth and encourage forage for game.

Although smaller in numbers, the Chilulas opposed white intrusion more actively than either the Yuroks or Tolowas. During the 1850s and early 1860s the tribe fought an ongoing guerrilla war against the settlers and packers who had invaded the Bald Hills and Redwood Creek; eventually every white was driven from the area and all their houses destroyed.

An 1864 peace treaty resulted in almost all of the tribe relocating to the Hoopa Reservation, where several Chilulas with Hupa connections were already living. By 1906, only two Chilulas remained in the tribe's northern territory—an aged man, Tom Hill, and his son, Dan. As an anthropologist subsequently noted, the Chilulas had "ceased to exist as a separate people." Nonetheless, some contemporary Indians still trace a Chilula lineage, including James Jackson, a famed story teller and ceremonial dancer.

Nature's North Coast Storehouse

In the days before the whites, both sweat lodges and family houses were common on the North Coast, but one type of building was never seen—a store. The local tribes had none because they needed none; the surrounding woods and prairies were their market, pharmacy, and fabric shop, for the forests and grasslands contained a well-established inventory of useful plants and wildlife that met nearly all of the Native Americans' requirements. The

Bah-gesh (Ellen Stanshaw),
a Tolowa basket maker

flesh, bones, skin, and feathers of various animals provided food, tools, and clothing. From the great coast redwoods came canoes, various utensils, and building materials, while a host of smaller plants also met many needs.

The Indians' larder was full and varied: meat, fish, and seafood; acorns, especially those from the tanoak and Oregon white oak; delicacies such as salmonberry shoots and bracken ferns. Other common comestibles included California laurel nuts, California hazelnuts, brodiaea and lily bulbs, and perhaps a dozen different berries. The bulbs of the soap plant made an interesting meal when roasted in a pit lined with either elderberry or skunk cabbage leaves. A favorite beverage was yerba buena tea.

Maple bark dress

Natural medicines abounded. Yarrow, either in a concoction or steamed, treated sore eyes. Inside-out flower leaves were chewed for coughs, while an infusion of cascara bark served as a cathartic. The local Native Americans also prepared plant-based poultices: wild ginger for infections, scraped trillium bulbs for burns, redwood sorrel to treat sores and swelling.

Some plants provided decoration. Pitch from the black cottonwood, mixed with soot and salmonberry juice, made the "one-eleven" tattoo, a design of three parallel lines that adorned the chins of North Coast Indian women. Wolf lichen colored the porcupine quills used in basketry work; red alder bark dyed giant chain fern fibers for the same purpose. Hazel shoots, beargrass, and five-finger fern stems provided patterns woven into the baskets.

Clothing came from both animal skins and plants. Beargrass leaves became fabric for dresses; maple bark fibers were transformed into women's skirts. When woven together, the long, narrow leaves of common cattail made raincoats.

Wood, bone, and stone were fashioned into tools and implements. Bows came from yew wood, with the string made from elk or deer sinew. Salmon spear points could be of deer horn or one of

Seis-do-tes-na (Bertha Grimes)
in Tolowa dress

several semi-hard woods. Canoe makers used granite hammers and mauls, along with elk horn axes and wedges. Elderberry shoots served as arrow shafts; iris leaves were worked into cordage. A piece of huckleberry bush became a broom, while deer fern and sword fern fronds did duty as bedding.

For toys, children stuck twig "legs" into wild cucumbers, thus turning the fruit into play animals. Youngsters also amused themselves by pressing the undersides of goldenback ferns against their faces to create a glittering design.

California laurel leaves served a special purpose; when burned inside a house, they took away bad luck.

North Coast Indians still gather and use native plants, relying, as their ancestors did, on the oldest and largest storehouse of all—the one that *nature* provides.

Then and Now

Born not long after the close of the so-called Indian "wars," Amelia Brown was a Tolowa woman whose life spanned many of her tribes' most difficult times. At the age of 104, when riding from her Del Norte home to Eureka, she surveyed the passing scenery and commented: "Used to be, I came down here in a canoe with my father. Then, nothing but Indians; now, nothing but white people." A great and tragic story was contained in those few words, which were spoken not with sadness or anger, but, as an observer put it, "good-naturedly." As a North Coast Indian, Amelia Brown had survived more than a century of hardship and harassment, but her heart, it seems, was filled only with forgiveness.

North Coast Newcomers

Whites in the Wilderness

When the early white settlers arrived on the North Coast, they plunged with little preparation into unknown country; arrayed before them was a beautiful but intimidating landscape of treacherous bays, steep-sided mountains, and nearly impenetrable forests. First off, the intrepid immigrants risked having their boats wrecked on the bar into Humboldt Bay or on the rocks near Crescent City; once ashore, they encountered poor trails, primitive living conditions, and rain by the bucketful. If they wandered too far into the redwood wilderness, they faced the possibility of tumbling over steep cliffs or languishing for days in a fastness of fallen timber and heavy undergrowth. It was the most rugged type of territory, suitable for only the most rugged individuals, and there was more than a little truth to the saying: "There's no law north of the Eel and no God north of the Klamath."

It was gold that brought the first flood of immigrants to California, and it was more gold that then enticed some of them to the state's far north. A year after the Mother Lode discovery started the stampede to the Sierras, new strikes in the mountains near the California-Oregon border brought a rush of miners to the Trinity, Salmon, and Klamath rivers. In this remote country, supplies via inland routes were hard to come by; instead, the coastal communities of Crescent City, Trinidad, Union (Arcata), and Eureka became the freighting centers for the interior. Goods were shipped by sea from San Francisco to these port towns and then transferred to pack trains for transport to the far-flung mining camps. Fortunes in gold dust were few, but the merchants and muleskinners often made a steady income providing goods to the struggling miners.

As with many of the mining operations, one of the region's first attempts at government also met with failure.

The Late, but Hardly Great, Klamath County

Of the 59 counties established by the California legislature, only one has ever been disbanded. It comprised much of what is now called the North Coast.

When it was created in 1851, Klamath County covered the entire northwestern corner of the state. It stretched southward from the Oregon border all the way to the Mad River, just above Humboldt Bay; eastward it ran to the mining camps of the Salmon and Siskiyou mountains. There were many riches within its lands, but the county's terrifying terrain daunted all but the most determined attempts at settlement. Adding to the difficulties were an almost total absence of roads and a restive resident Indian population. If ever a place needed good government, this was it.

What the new county got instead was incompetence and confusion. The first election was held so quickly after Klamath's establishment that there was neither voter registration nor printed ballots. Many voters were no doubt legitimate, but some residents along the county's northern boundary took advantage of the vague California-Oregon border by paying taxes to neither area while voting in both.

The first county seat was established at Trinidad, but by 1854 Crescent City had grown enough that Klamath's government was relocated there by the legislature. The inland miners objected to the change, and three years later Orleans Bar became the third seat of Klamath County. This proved an unfortunate choice, for the isolated mining camp lay more than 50 miles from the coast and had "no radiating roads, only a wild river and mountain trails" to connect it with the rest of the county.

By then Klamath had other problems. In 1855 its Board of Supervisors reported the county to be $25,000 in debt; additionally, the books were in disarray, and a large amount of money was unaccounted for by the sheriff. The Board levied no tax for the year, and none had been collected the previous year either. The district judge reviewed the government's operations in 1857 and found that the situation had further deteriorated: the sheriff had continued his bad habits and was now delinquent in the sum of

$32,461.27—worse yet, he was also "absent from the county," and had apparently done little work before he left, since over the last three years some 16 murders had been committed "without the least notice having been taken of any of them." The problems extended to other offices; the Crescent City newspaper earlier concluded that "we do not think...the Treasurer himself has ever had any idea how his books stood, much less been able to make any intelligible report from them." A grand jury was also baffled by the treasurer's record keeping, but did manage to determine that "the Assessor is delinquent in the sum of $39."

Klamath County, debt-ridden, sheriffless, was dying a lingering death. Other nearby counties had been nibbling away its land almost since its start, and in 1857 Crescent City was avenged when it became the seat of Del Norte County, which was carved from Klamath's far north. Klamath limped along, crippled by a steadily growing debt, until 1874, when its officials asked the legislature to end the county's misery by dissolving it. A bill was approved to that effect, with Klamath's land, assets, and debts to be divided between Humboldt and Siskiyou counties.

But Klamath was not allowed to expire in peace. A group of Siskiyou citizens, bothered by having to assume part of Klamath's

Klamath County Courthouse, reincarnated as a grammar school

encumbrances, objected to the partition. For two years the moribund county lay in a coma of "virtual anarchy" while the legislature and courts struggled with the situation. Finally, on August 14, 1876, representatives from Humboldt and Siskiyou counties met in Orleans Bar to bury Klamath and settle the estate. The commissioners found themselves dividing up a debt of $19,500 but acquiring lands that would later prove far more valuable, for they included much of today's Prairie Creek Redwoods State Park, Redwood National Park, and the Marble Mountains Wilderness.

Today the entire Klamath episode is all but forgotten. The late county's courthouse has long disappeared from Orleans, but its Humboldt counterpart in Eureka retains a few of Klamath's remaining effects. There, persistent searchers will eventually find several sets of moldering books, all bearing the sought-for inscription: "KLAMATH." Inside the mottled covers of one worn volume are a few dozen entries, and then page after page of neatly ruled, butterfly-blue paper—all empty. *Fair hopes*, the pages seem to say, but the words trail off into silence, and all that is left is the blue-tinted blankness...mute testimony to the unfulfilled future of calamitous Klamath County.

Land of the Loggers

The mining excitement cooled within a few years, and the locals then looked to lumbering as a more reliable way of life. Mineral deposits were elusive and limited in extent, but a wealth of green gold sat right at everyone's doorstep — tract upon tract of redwood forest, ready for removal. The axmen soon went to the woods, and for decades the huge trees were logged without letup. Great fortunes came to the capitalists who controlled the operations; the Carson Mansion in Eureka was merely the most opulent of a host of fancy habitations the timber barons built for themselves.

It was a different story for the lumbermen's workers. The loggers went to the woods knowing they risked life and limb on a daily basis, and those who survived into old age could look back on a career of brutally hard work and little comfort. Despite the difficulties, the men did their jobs well, for it took them barely a century to conquer the great coastal forest. The legacy they left, however, was not one of triumph; rather, it was the bitterness of boarded up mills, broken down equipment, and scarred hillsides. The time of endless trees came to an early end, and with it, the loggers' way of life.

Lumberman's luxurious lodging—Carson Mansion, Eureka

War in the Woods

Nowhere was logging more demanding than on the North Coast. It was here, in Del Norte and Humboldt counties, that stand after stand of the largest redwoods stretched skyward, crowding to capacity the fog-filled valleys and nearby canyonsides. These were titanic timberlands, and cutting them called for all the skill of the logger's art.

Ox logging

The woods had been wild enough in the days of horse and ox, when the bullwhackers in their spiked boots would sometimes walk up the backs of their oxen, singeing the air with a profanity as powerful as their beasts' bellowing breath. After steam engines supplanted the straining animals, the situation became more chaotic yet. The scene was one

> ...of trees rushing earthwards and man-made quakes, of noisy, steamy-hot, hideously dangerous donkey engines, and rigging flying through the air....[It was] a business carried on by shouting young men with nails in their boot soles, who travelled like smoke among crashing trees in a mechanical ballet whose accompaniment was the shrill music of shrieking steam whistles and the chugging of powerful engines. Civilization never before saw the likes of West Coast steam logging: only war compares to it.[1]

The comparison was apt. In 1914, soldiers in the U. S. Army were rationed a diet of 5,000 calories per day; loggers required 8,000 to get them through their daily ten-hour shifts of swinging a double-bitted ax. Moreover, casualties in the mills and woods occurred with a sickening steadiness that recalled the losses on the battlefield. Consider the following Humboldt County newspaper report for a single day, July 25, 1907:

> Yesterday was quite disastrous to woodsmen, for besides the Elk River fatality and the breaking of the leg of Bob Dunnigan at Jacoby Creek...a logger named Kane suffered a compound fracture of the left leg by being struck by a flying becket in the Vance woods.

The incidents signaled the beginning of a two-month barrage of accidents; by September 22 the carnage had killed three men and severely injured ten more. Timber workers lived at the edge of tragedy, but that was just part of the job; as one historian put it: "Men were *expected* to die when they went logging." (emphasis added)

Starting in the 1880s, steam donkeys mechanized the removal of logs from cutting sites, but it took another 50 years before power saws supplanted hand labor in the actual felling of timber. Until the first gasoline driven "drag" saws made their appearance in the 1930s, a pair of "choppers" would wield axes and crosscut saws to bring down the big trees. To avoid the flaring butt of a redwood, the men would often stand 10 feet or more above the ground on a scaffolding of planks laid across "springboards" — short timbers that had one end fitted into holes cut in the tree's trunk. Felling a 12-foot-diameter tree would take two to three days using this method. For their work, choppers in the late 1920s were paid $5.25 for a 9½-hour day, plus their meals and one bath a week.

For years, either by team or steam, every log was moved along the ground whence it fell to a cleared area, called a "landing," where it was then loaded onto a rail car for transport to the mill. This process was fraught with difficulties, for stumps, gullies, rocks, and other obstacles all threatened to impede or damage the wood on its way to the landing. By 1916 a new method of moving felled timber was in use — highlead logging — and it brought a change as dramatic as the switch from oxen to engine.

Highleading

The key to highleading was the spar tree, a 150-foot-plus speci-men selected for its sturdiness and location. It was prepared for duty by "the most spectacular forest technician of all,...the high-climber." Buckling a pair of climbing irons to his legs and attaching a safety rope, this fearless forestworker would grab his short, double-bitted ax and ascend the spar tree, cutting its limbs as he went. When he reached a point where the trunk was about 28 inches in diameter, he topped the remainder of the tree, which keeled over the cut and dropped dramatically to the ground below.

Highleading

The highclimber then rigged the spar with a collection of pulleys, beckets, and cables, which, when connected with the donkey en-gine, allowed logs from the nearby felling area to be moved through the air to the landing.

It was an operation to behold, filled with implements and work-ers who all bore strange names and performed stunning tasks:

> When the [choker] hooks had been set...[around a pair of logs,]
> the rigging slinger gave a quick look to see if all the men stood

"in the clear." Satisfied, he gave a peculiar holler, "who-ee!" The whistlepunk, who had been watching from a perch on a nearby stump, gave an immediate tug with both hands on the signal wire...which ran in all the way to the donkey engine, a half mile away and out of sight. The engineer on the yarder, in answer to the single blast on the steam whistle above his head, released the brake, "gave her friction," and began reeling in the cable. The drums began to spin, spooling the lines in and out; as the slack took up and the mainline straightened, the chokered logs leapt forward... bumping and flailing toward the spartree, plunging into the earth, leaping through the air, down again plowing rocks and dirt, traveling faster than a man could run. They gouged huge trenches along the ground and smashed smaller trees in the way, splintering and cracking them as if caught in a typhoon wind. Anyone so unfortunate as to get trapped in front of the logs coming in on the mainline, died right there.[2]

For risking his life in the tree tops, a Humboldt County high-climber in 1939 made $1.00 an hour. That same year, the hourly wage of his Del Norte counterpart was 85¢.

Forest Finale

There were ways other than logging to make a living on the North Coast, but the options were limited. Some settlers started

Hobbs, Wall & Company Mill, Crescent City

ranches, where the topography permitted — sheep in the Bald Hills, dairy cows in the bottomlands at Orick and Klamath, cattle on the bluffs above the coast north of Prairie Creek. Fishing proved profitable, and salmon canneries operated for years at Requa. Many men went out on sailing ships, for the sea was the region's roadway until the coming of the Redwood Highway in the 1920s. Still, it was timber that maintained the area, and when Hobbs, Wall & Company closed down in 1939, Del Norte County barely survived the loss of the area's largest employer and only lumbering enterprise.

Bereft of its main business, the county desperately needed to improve its condition. But the attempt it made two years later offered little chance for success.

The State of Jefferson: Not Just a Jest

The dateline read November 27, 1941, from the Siskiyou County seat of Yreka. The article bore the name of Stanton Delaplane, then a little-known staff writer for the *San Francisco Chronicle*; it breathlessly began: "Rough-shirted miners with pistols tucked in their belts barricaded the main highway north and south tonight, declared for 'patriotic independence' for their forty-ninth State...."

In actuality, Delaplane's enthralling account was only partially correct. Some of the miners wore jackets over their shirts, and they carried not pistols but Winchesters.

Rifle-toting roadblockers—Highway 99 at Yreka

The roadblocks were maintained by supporters of the new-found "State of Jefferson." A proclamation distributed to motorists indicated that "Patriotic Jeffersonians intend to secede each Thursday until further notice."

Readers from Portland to San Francisco were astounded to learn of the rural rebellion taking place along the California-Oregon border, but those who knew the area were less surprised. For years, residents of the region had complained about bad roads and poor services, chafing at the lack of concern shown by state officials. The restlessness was like a tinder-dry forest, needing only a spark before it burst into flame.

That spark had arrived a few weeks earlier in the person of Gilbert Gable, a former public relations expert who was currently mayor of Port Orford, Oregon. Accompanied by a delegation of supporters, Gable had charged into a meeting of the Curry County commissioners to demand that the county secede from Oregon and join California. It didn't matter that things were no better across the border; the idea was to get enough attention that the sluggards in the state capital would be moved to action.

Attention they got. Del Norte County, Curry's neglected California counterpart, quickly formed a "collaborative" commission, naming 78-year-old retired judge John L. Childs as a member. In mid-November Gable and Childs spoke in Yreka, where the Chamber of Commerce called for the border counties to study "the possibility of severing their present ties to form the Union's 49th state." Now malcontents from two states were talking secession.

Curry, Del Norte, and Siskiyou counties were interested, and two days later Modoc County citizens joined the movement. The *Siskiyou Daily News* then sponsored a "name the new state contest," to help stimulate secessionist sentiments; the winning entry, "Jefferson," suitably honored the main author of the Declaration of Independence. Soon residents in Lassen and Trinity counties were supporting the rising rebellion, and the pace of events accelerated. In late November, a "provisional government" was established, with Gable as its leader. He promptly announced that Jefferson would be free of sales tax, income tax, and liquor tax. Now people really began to listen.

Still, the story might have languished in the local papers had it not been for a fortuitous decision by the *Chronicle*: send that boy

Delaplane up there—it can't do any harm, and he's even willing to pay his own way.

So Delaplane departed for Yreka, hoping to find a lengthy story. He wrote his first article, which was about how the rebellion started, but, as he later said, "the second day didn't look very bright. I wanted a series out of it....I didn't want to go back to San Francisco. I mean, it was a big thing to get out of town."

Delaplane decided he would have to help the movement generate some newsworthy momentum. Early each morning, he accordingly made suggestions about such strategies as setting up roadblocks and withholding payment of the state sales tax; the secessionists eagerly agreed to implement the day's plan. Delaplane described the proposed activity in his daily story, which, to make the *Chronicle's* deadline, he wrote in the late afternoon. He'd then cross his fingers while he waited for evening, when his Jeffersonian associates would hopefully stage the event he had just reported.

To add further flavor to his accounts, Delaplane datelined them from the new state's most evocatively named locales. In quick succession he filed stories from the hinterland hamlets of Happy Camp, Hardscrabble Creek, and Pistol River.

By December 1, the Delaplane-inspired insurrection was in full swing. That night, the young reporter met with Gable in a motel room to discuss the future of Jefferson. A driving rain beat down on the roof, and the pair kept warm by drinking 150-proof Hudson Bay rum mixed with cokes. When their meeting finally finished, Gable went home and promptly died of a heart attack.

It was the first nail in the coffin of the fledgling state. Nail number two quickly followed, when Delaplane, apparently out of ideas, stopped filing stories and reluctantly returned to San Francisco. The Jeffersonians, however, were not ready to give up. The secessionists staged a huge election rally in Yreka, where "cannons boomed on the old courthouse lawn" to inaugurate Judge Childs as "governor." Childs rose to the occasion with a barrage of biblical bombast, and marchers paraded through the flag-draped streets while carrying placards proclaiming:

> **Our roads are not passable**
> **hardly jackassable;**
> **if our roads you would travel,**
> **bring your own gravel.**

Everyone eagerly awaited the forthcoming news accounts, for reporters from *Time* and *Life* magazines as well as the newsreels had covered the event.

The rally was held on the new state's weekly secession day, Thursday, which fell on December 4; that Sunday the Japanese attacked Pearl Harbor. Gone was any interest in the border rebellion, and gone, too, was Governor Childs, but not before he performed his first and only acts of office: in quick succession he declared war on California, Oregon, *and* Japan—and then dissolved, after a life of three days, the untimely State of Jefferson.

Workers still went to the woods during the war, cutting spruce for ships and clear redwood for coffins. Peace, when it came, meant millions of returning soldiers, each of whom seemed to want a new house. Logging came back bigger than ever to meet the demand; suddenly Del Norte County, so recently mill-less, had more than 25 in operation. To keep the saws running, most local lumbermen followed the destructive dictum, "cut out and get out." More mills materialized farther south, around Orick, as sawmen swarmed into the timber-rich watersheds of Prairie Creek and Redwood Creek. After the lean Depression and war years, the North Coast was suddenly living high off the log, and it was quite a heyday while it lasted.

Al Zuber log truck, Orick

Every day has its end, however, and after some 20 years of lumber-filled luminescence, twilight at last fell upon the innumerable stumps and few remaining trees. Loggers cursed the coming of Redwood National Park, which they believed took away timber from their mills and food from their dinner tables, but in truth most of the trees had already been cut, and the few thousand acres of old growth that became part of the park would have hardly satisfied the saws' enormous appetite. The great lumbering tracts had already been laid low, so there was nothing to do but wait for the trees to regenerate and the forest to heal itself. It would take a thousand years for the magnificent redwood stands to fully return, but such antiquities were now of little interest to the loggers. Profit aplenty could be had by cutting young trees hardly past their plant life's puberty, and so the timber companies set up "tree farms" to consolidate their fledgling forests, growing—and harvesting—the timber like a crop.

The early-day choppers would likely choke on their tobacco chaws if they saw the spindly second growth that is now being cut. But times change, and time, as always, is money, so the trees of today are felled as soon as they can produce a few millable boards or a profitable poundage of fiber. To find the type of timber they were once accustomed to, the loggers of yesteryear would now, ironically, have to go to the parks. Although the towering trees that thrive there could well tempt the woodsmen to again raise saw or ax, they would likely wonder at how few great redwoods now remain, and their hands would, perhaps, finally be stayed. At the very least, the men might see the old-growth preserves for what they have so quickly become—museums of the millennial forest.

Earth, Water, and Weather

> The travelling very bad, several very steep, rocky and brushy points of mountain to go up and down, with our band of horses, and a great many of them so lame and worn that we can scarce force them along...
> — from the journal of the Jedediah Smith expedition

Thus did the first white explorers describe their encounter with the formidable coastal mountains of California's far north. At the time, Smith and his companions were climbing out of the Hoopa Valley onto the eastern edge of the Bald Hills. Conditions deteriorated as they continued west; now

> The travelling [was] amazing bad; we descended one point...where it took us about six hours to get the horses down a steep place into the creek; one broke his neck....

Two days later the topography temporarily triumphed:

> We concluded that it was best to lie by today and send two men to look out a pass to travel, as the country looks awful ahead, and let our poor horses rest....

Finally, after a two-week traverse of the Bald Hills, the men, mules, and horses stumbled down to the Klamath River. Although their difficulties were not yet over, Smith and the others had already learned all they cared to about the North Coast's lamentable landscape.

From Bald Hills to Gold Bluffs: The North Coast's Tilted Terrain

The land that nearly stymied the Smith party resembles an enormous, crumpled quilt, forest green for the most part, with a few twisting threads of blue stream and several patches of pale yellow prairie. The highly visible crumpling occurred over a span of several hundred million years, as two gigantic sections of the earth's

crust, the Gorda and North American plates, collided. The Gorda
Plate was covered with marine sediments — fine-grained rock that
coated the ocean floor — and as the Gorda moved under the North
American Plate, the latter acted like a huge bulldozer blade, scraping off and piling up the sediments. The resulting collection of rock
was then folded, faulted, and severely sheared, becoming what is
today known as the Franciscan Formation, a widely distributed
mixture of ancient sandstones, siltstones, volcanic rock, and conglomerates.

Over time, further faulting uplifted the region, which was then
worn down by erosion and once again covered by the sea. Next, a
newer set of sediments washed down the ancestral Klamath River
from the inland mountains, covering part of the coastal area; rich in

The Gold Bluffs

ore, this ancient alluvium comprises much of today's Gold Bluffs. A final rise in sea level, which occurred less than 5,000 years ago, then drowned the former ocean mouths of many streams, creating the bays, lagoons, and marshy river valleys that now indent the coast.

The region's geologic foundation remains highly unstable. In the ocean southwest of Eureka is the notorious Mendocino triple junction, where the North American and Gorda plates meet a third plate, the Pacific. Disturbances centered in this region caused the devastating 7.1 earthquake of April 1992, which severely damaged several southern Humboldt communities. North of the triple junction is another area of intense instability called the Cascadia subduction zone. Locally, the last large Cascadia earthquake occurred about 300 years ago, but historic patterns suggest that another, of perhaps 8.0 magnitude or greater, will eventually hit somewhere along the northwest coast.

Heavy rainfall and steep-sloped topography add to the area's instability, which has been further increased by intensive land use. One particular activity, clearcut logging, has had an especially damaging effect.

Rehabilitating Redwood Creek

When Redwood National Park acquired the lower Redwood Creek basin, it received mostly damaged goods. Thousands of steep hillside acres had recently been shorn of their namesake redwoods and other conifers, leaving a lesion of logging roads, skid trails, and forest debris. Tremendous erosion ensued: storms washed away large sections of the mountain slopes, sending them on a sedimental journey downstream that had disastrous results for the creek and its inhabitants. The runoff ravaged fish habitat, filling pools with sediment and destroying riparian vegetation, which caused creek temperatures to increase. Streambanks eroded, causing huge redwoods to topple into the water. The Tall Trees themselves were at risk.

What to do? The park's answer was an unprecedented, 30,000-acre watershed rehabilitation program that began in 1978. Fifteen years later, more than half of the 300 miles of logging roads that crisscrossed park land had been "put to bed"—covered over and revegetated. Also being restored are some 3,000 additional miles of skid roads, scarred areas where tractors once pulled logs across steep and often unstable slopes. Prairies are again being burned to remove encroaching conifers, as they were earlier by the Chilulas and the ranchers. In the bottom of the canyon, the Tall Trees still stand high above the creekbank, but in winter the water below them runs gray with silt—the residue from logging sites that lie beyond the park in the upper drainage. The threat to the grove has lessened, but it has not ended yet.

Progress in the restoration effort will be measured in decades and even centuries, for the healing of this large landscape will not be complete until mature redwoods again cover the hillsides, herds of elk and deer again roam full-sized prairies, and the once-obvious impacts of an extractive industry have dwindled into insignificance.

Although much of the parkland is thickly covered with conifers and other plantlife, distinctive rocks and landforms are visible at several locations. Here are some sites that showcase the region's geologic underpinnings:

In the southern reaches of the parks is the Grogan Fault, which leaves the ocean at Gold Bluffs and continues southeast along the canyon of Redwood Creek; movement along the fault has brought together two of the Franciscan Formation's distinctive rock types: hillslopes to the west contain gray Redwood Creek schist, while the area east of the stream is composed mostly of sandstones and mudstones.

The Tall Trees Loop Trail descends the hillside above Redwood Creek, passing through five levels of stream terrace. Each level at one time formed a flood plain of the creek, but a series of uplifts have stacked them in their present position. The terraces are generally flat and contain rounded stream pebbles. Every major flood leaves a silt deposit on the current creekside terrace; the trunks of the Tall Trees are gradually being engulfed by this aggressive alluvium.

Probably the most famed geologic feature in the parks is the ocher-tinted escarpment known as the Gold Bluffs, whose colorful cliffs run above the beach from Redwood Creek to the Klamath River. The bluffs, which in some places rise 200 feet, are composed of cobble conglomerates, medium-grained sandstone, and siltstone. Included in the mix is enough gold to have whetted the interest of early-day miners. Several seaward-bound creeks have cut through the bluffs, creating deep gorges like Fern Canyon; coastal erosion has removed the western ends of their drainages. The shoreline to the west is dotted with occasional outcroppings, including the awesomely angular Ossagon Rocks.

Ossagon Rocks

East of the bluffs, sedimentary rock is often exposed along trails or at roadcuts, such as on the old logging road that forms the middle section of the West Ridge Trail. Near the headwaters of Prairie Creek is the northern end of the Lost Man Fault; it runs midway along the ridgeslope east of Prairie Creek before ending at Lost Man Creek.

On Highway 101 just north of RNP's Lagoon Creek picnic area, a large roadcut exposes turbidite sedimentary rock. To the west are several of the sea stacks—offshore remnant rocks composed of graywacke sandstone—that intermittently dot the coastline; Wilson Rock and the larger False Klamath Rock are two that can be seen from pullouts near the Wilson Creek Bridge.

Del Norte Coast Redwoods State Park is noted for its rocky ocean frontage, with steep sea cliffs that rise some 800 feet before rounding off at the ridgeline. Footsteps Rocks, connected to the

Rocks at False Klamath Cove

coast by a land bridge, and Sisters Rocks are two of the area's most spectacular sea stacks. Northwest of the park is a sweeping coastal plain, a recently uplifted marine-river terrace, that is highlighted by the smooth curve of beach at Crescent City. It was here, some thirty years ago, that the region's most recent geologically related disaster occurred — the result of an earthquake that happened some 1,500 miles away.

Fourth Wave Finale

At 7:36 P.M. on Good Friday, March 27, 1964, an 8.5-magnitude earthquake struck Prince William Sound in Alaska. The destruction in Anchorage and nearby areas was tremendous; buildings collapsed, cars were "tossed about like toys," and some 114 people perished. Within eight minutes, seismic waves were detected at Honolulu, Hawaii, while in Kodiak, Alaska, observers noted a wave some ten to twelve feet above normal. Officials flashed an alert to communities along the West Coast; it contained the word most feared by seaside residents: *tsunami*.

About 11 P.M. the Del Norte County sheriff's office received its first bulletin regarding the impending wave. A second warning came shortly before midnight—it indicated that the tsunami was now approaching the community. Deputies immediately went door to door in Crescent City's low-lying areas, informing residents of the situation; there was no order to evacuate.

As predicted, the first wave soon spilled across Front Street; it was about three feet high and, except for depositing a scattering of debris, did little damage. Two more waves then washed through the lower part of town, adding to the litter. After the third wave, a fire started south of town, spreading rapidly.

At the Battery Point Lighthouse Museum, Peggy and Roxy Coons, the museum's curators, saw the first three waves roll across the Crescent City harbor and into the business district; each wave was impressive, but none of them prepared the couple for the fourth. As Peggy Coons watched, the floodtide

> ...withdrew suddenly, as though someone had pulled the plug out of the basin...the water had receded far out, three fourths of a mile or more beyond the outer breakwater. We were looking down as though from a high mountain into a black abyss of rock, reefs, and shoals, never exposed even at the lowest of tides. A vast labyrinth of caves, basins, and pits undreamed of in the wildest of fantasy....
>
> Suddenly there it was, a mammoth wall of water barreling in toward us...stretching from the floor of the ocean upwards....It tossed big bundles of lumber, some splitting up with planks...flying [like matchsticks] in the air....At Citizen's Dock, the large lumber barge...came up and sat on top of the dock. The dock humped up, then relaxed right off its pilings. The fish storage houses...were dancing around in the fury. The fishing boats still at their moorings were bobbing around like corks. Some sank where they were while others came out, careened about and flew on the other side of the bay. One boat took off [up] Elk Creek as though someone were at the helm.
>
> When the Tsunami assaulted the town it was like a violent explosion....buildings, boats, lumber, everything was shifting around like crazy. The whole front of town moved, changing before our eyes. By this time the fire had raced across the water to the ruptured Texaco [b]ulk tanks: they started exploding one after the other. The whole sky lit up. It was fantastic.[1]

The event was even more exciting for those caught near the harbor when the fourth wave hit. Jackie and Dick Childs were in their home on Front Street when they heard the wave coming; gathering up their two dogs, they jumped in Dick's work vehicle and raced the water up through town. After several blocks the flow petered out behind them and the shaken couple realized they were safe.

On Second Street, Bob Ames and his family were checking on damage at their appliance store when a wall of water surged through the building, sending the Ameses scurrying for the second floor. Harry and Shirley Trehearne and their employee, Diane Pinkston, had also been driven upstairs when the wave hit their department store, and they now watched as cars and logs floated by below them; one of the vehicles belonged to Pinkston.

It was worse at Daly Brothers, another of the town's department stores. Floyd and Florence Rongstad, Dale Cleveland, and manager Cozy Collins were busy moving merchandise when they happened to look at the store's outside display windows; while they watched in horror, the wave rose rapidly behind the glass, as if someone were filling a giant aquarium. Floyd Rongstad and Cleveland attempted to hold the front doors shut, yelling at the others to "get out of here." Collins rushed to the back door, which wouldn't open; he climbed on some shelving, but it soon began to topple, forcing him to seek refuge in the freight room. As the other three raced for the mezzanine, the windows shattered, unleashing a torrent of water into the building. The Rongstads were swept through the aisles; they finally caught hold of a pillar and clung to it for dear life. Cleveland meanwhile clambered onto a wall shelf. The water quickly filled the first floor, rising until it reached the workers' chins—then the lights went out.

Fortunately for the trapped trio, the floodtide had spent itself. As the water withdrew from the store, they crawled over the debris, broke the glass in the back door, and made their exit.

It proved more difficult for manager Collins to escape. The freight room remained flooded, and when the others couldn't reach him from the outside, he was forced to dive into the water and, while submerged, locate and release the padlock on the freight door; only then could Cozy leave his all-too-cozy confines.

The Daly foursome survived the fourth wave's flood, but others were less fortunate. South of town, water poured across Highway

101, tearing buildings from their foundations and washing 10-month-old William Eugene Wright from his mother's arms as she attempted to flee; both William and his three-year-old sister, Bonita Ione, were drowned. At the Long Branch Tavern, several late-night imbibers piled into a small rowboat and attempted to outdistance the wave; the tsunami caught them, capsizing the craft and drowning all the occupants. The wave finally crested some ten feet above the normal high tide level, but it was the following outsurge that proved most destructive; officials estimated that the water withdrew from the city at an incredible 350 miles per hour.

Buckner's Auto Mart, rearranged by the tsunami

Soon Crescent City began to calculate the effects of the catastrophe. Eleven people killed; 29 blocks of the lower city destroyed. Nearly a thousand cars were wrecked, with many homes and businesses damaged by water, debris, and mud. The Childses returned to their house on Front Street to find it knocked off its foundation and split in half. After leaving their damaged store, the Trehearnes discovered their van perched atop a redwood log a hundred feet from where it had been parked. More fortunate than the Wright family, a young woman and her baby were found in a fir tree south of town—the pair was still sitting in their motel bed, which had been swept to its new resting place from across the street.

Governor Edmund G. Brown arrived to view the damage and pronounced the town "the worst disaster I've ever seen." Strong words, but nothing compared to what Peggy Coons, Cozy Collins, or any of Crescent City's other tsunami survivors could have said.

Northeast of Crescent City, the seaward-bound Smith River cuts through the coastal mountains at Jedediah Smith Redwoods State Park. One of the Smith's major tributaries, Mill Creek, has created prime redwood habitat by depositing thick layers of sediment along its stream channel. Above the eastern side of the creek rise the Little Bald Hills, a ridgeline composed chiefly of serpentine rock. This mineral base, which creates a distinctive plant community, is found in much of the Smith River drainage and also in the Kalmiopsis region of southern Oregon.

It is here that a modern traveller might conclude a geological journey through the parks—exciting enough, perhaps, but certainly lacking the cliffhanging drama of the "rocky" reconnaissance of Jedediah Smith.

The North Coast's Climactic Climate

As might be expected, the lands of the northern redwood parks are well watered, with the area's annual precipitation averaging over 70 inches per year. Summers are generally dry, as most of the moisture—some 90 percent—falls during the October-April rainy season. Seldom is there snow except on the higher ridges; the Bald Hills are sometimes besieged by blizzards that turn the prairies white for days on end.

If the region's rains are extreme, temperatures are moderate, seldom exceeding 80° except in the more inland areas, where they can reach 100°. The August average at Klamath is a refreshing 57°, while come January the mean temperature there drops only slightly, to a tolerable 47°.

While the coast is wet enough in its own right, local streams add immensely to the inundation of lowlands during stormy years. The Yuroks were well aware of the Klamath's fluctuating level, for they built their villages on slopes and terraces high above the canyon bottom. White settlers received an early lesson in the river's dynamics during the winter of 1861-2, when a historic flood swept away the suspension bridge at Martin's Ferry, which the presumably prudent J. F. Martin had placed some *ninety* feet above the low water mark. Over the years other freshets scoured the channel, but it was not until 1955 that residents received a reminder of what the river could *really* be like.

The 1955 Flood: Cleaning Out Klamath

Christmas week 1955 came up stormy on the North Coast, but that was nothing new to the locals, who were used to wet wintertime weather. Although the rain was dropping in torrents on the night of Wednesday, December 21, even out-of-towners were relaxed about the deluge; Dr. F. W. McDade and his family, en route from Canada to Los Angeles, stopped at a Klamath motel, had dinner, and then made themselves comfortable against the storm.

Their comfort, like that of everyone else in Klamath, did not have long to last. At about 1:00 A.M. Dr. McDade was to be found stumbling along the middle of the highway, barefoot, while his wife followed him in their car. McDade was attempting to lead his family to safety; he was trying to use the white line as a guide, but its visibility was impaired by water from the flooding Klamath, which already was swirling around the doctor's knees. The family finally reached higher ground, where the McDades sought refuge at the Trees of Mystery. Behind them, their "comfortable" motel was soon inundated.

Others who waited longer had more difficulty making their escape. H. B. Ranht and his family, staying at Kamp Klamath, were not warned of the rising water until 3:00 A.M. When Ranht tried driving to safety, he found the road blocked in both directions by the flood. Only the timely appearance of a rescue boat, plying the waters above what had once been the highway, saved the Ranhts from the rising river.

Many residents owed their lives to a pair of improbable heroes—two tugboats that normally hauled logs down the Klamath. The valiant vessels cruised the main street of town, plucking people from the roofs of the doomed buildings.

Meanwhile, upriver across from town, another drama was unfolding at the Fehely Mill. Clifford Whitney, his wife, his brother Ernest, and the Whitneys' son and daughter-in-law were at work in the newly constructed mill when the flood hit. All five were forced to climb to the top of the structure, from where the Whitneys saw their house trailer float down the river and break to pieces.

The group waited as the floodwaters battered the building beneath them. Finally Ernest Whitney took an air mattress and launched himself into the torrent in a desperate attempt to get help. A few minutes later bystanders saw Whitney riding the mattress down the Klamath near the Douglas Memorial Bridge; suddenly the mattress hit one of the bridge pilings, dumping Whitney into the water. He was never seen again.

Klamath, hit by
the 1955 flood

Back upriver, the situation at the mill worsened as the Klamath's continued pounding began to shake the structure apart. When a long plank washed against the building, the four Whitneys grabbed onto the timely arrival, floating away just as the mill finally gave up its fight against the flood and collapsed.

The rushing water swept the plank into a stand of trees, where the group debarked onto some conveniently placed limbs that spread above the eight-foot-deep water. There they would have to wait for help.

As the floodtide rushed by below them, the Whitneys wondered if their ordeal would ever end. Hour after hour they clung to their perch; they knew they'd been seen by people on the opposite shore, but it seemed doubtful that anyone would risk crossing the raging river to try rescuing them.

The local Yuroks had a history of saving people from the Klamath, and now a pair of them, Bill and Greely Frye, were doing just that. Maneuvering their boat through the floodborne debris, the brothers searched for survivors. They pulled one man off the top of a fence post and plucked a 92-year-old woman from her table as the water lapped at its edges; in all, they would rescue 33 people, taking them all to the shelter of the family home. Finally, nine hours after the Whitneys washed up in the tree tops, the Frye brothers brought their boat alongside and took them to safety.

Other incidents were less dramatic but nonetheless interesting. Early Wednesday morning a sodden refugee entered the Del Norte disaster center office and announced that he had forgotten to remove an intoxicated man from cabin #11 at Kamp Klamath. A boat was dispatched by radio to investigate. After a brief wait the following report was transmitted back from a sheriff's car near Klamath:

> We found him dead to the world floating around in his bed near the ceiling. Right now he is in the back of this car, smoking a cigarette and happy as a lark.

Few others were in such good spirits. Over 300 evacuees were huddled together at the Arrow Mill north of Klamath Glen, having prudently taken with them most of the local grocery store's stock. Another 300 sought shelter at the nearby Simpson mill, while about a hundred found refuge at a local ranch. A third group of 300 had managed to cross the Klamath and were crowded into the old camouflaged radar station on the hillside below Flint Ridge.

When the floodwaters finally subsided, Klamath's residents returned to what remained of their town. On the day after Christmas the *Del Norte Triplicate* reported that

> Buildings had been tossed around like matchsticks, washed from foundations and away to sea. Streets were masses of debris, where any street remained recognizable. Shops, homes and stores were smashed to bits.

The paper's headline summed it up best:

Klamath Digging
Out, But There's
Not Much Left

Still, many of the residents were willing to start over. The Whitneys, who had lost their mill, their car, and four house trailers, were among them. The family's explanation for staying was simple: "We've lived here too long and know too many people to do anything else."

While floods remain a constant worry to North Coast residents, other weather-caused disasters are seldom a threat. Once, however, one town managed to reap a whirlwind, although with something less than biblical results.

The Crescent City Cyclone

For over 70 years the ocean off Crescent City had brought both bane and bounty to the community—raging storms, log-filled floodtides, a wealth of fish, the commerce of hundreds of ships. Few of the town's residents were prepared, however, for the strange gift the sea offered up in April 1925.

Those who tracked the occurrence from its start first noticed a waterspout that had formed above the rolling Pacific. The funnel lost its moisture upon reaching the coast and entered town as a small tornado, first making itself known at Second and G streets, where it pulled off about half the shingles from the Masonic Lodge's roof and sent them swirling a thousand feet skyward into the vapor-filled air. Bounding over a couple of blocks, the tiny twister then struck the rear of the Hobbs, Wall & Company store, removing part of its roof. The next victim was Endert's Theater, which found its top story torn off and thrown into Third Street so that it obstructed the railroad track. After hitting a house and leaping over the train station, the shifty spiral attacked a hay shed on L Street; the roof and walls vanished, but nary a straw was disturbed.

Then, in the words of one witness, the turbulence "raced up the railroad track, melting the piles of lumber as it went along," twirling the timbers skyward. After bypassing the Hobbs, Wall Mill, the tempest finally blew itself out in the foothills east of town.

The effects on the city's buildings were, all things considered, quite moderate. But how had the populace fared?

Soon the reports began to trickle in. Merchant John R. Peveler had been blown to the ground and then rolled across Second Street—not his usual way of returning from the bank; Almira Francis was bruised and cut by flying glass; Mr. Ayres had his Star touring car caught in the wind and turned on edge, depositing Ayres in the street; Mr. Desjardin was picked up while walking past Endert's Theater, carried some distance through the air, and then set back down again, shaken but unharmed. It appeared that the most severely affected resident was a woman who lived two doors from the vanishing hay shed; she came out onto her front porch to see what all the excitement was about, only to have the porch roof suddenly removed from above her head. With a scream she toppled over in a dead faint and fell back inside the doorway, an unconscious casualty of Crescent City's solitary cyclone.

The 1955 deluge had, by all accounts, been the worst since the epic washout of 1861-2, and it soon became known as the "hundred-year flood." Klamath and most of the other North Coast communities rebuilt, while the water-wrought wreckage was removed from sight and, gradually, from memory. Every winter, though, residents kept a watchful eye on the river levels, knowing that sometime another big storm would hit.

They didn't have long to wait.

On December 22, 1964, torrential rains moved in from the ocean, clobbering the coast with unparalleled fury. The weather gods, it seemed, were weak at their math; it had taken just nine years, to the day, for the "hundred-year" storm to be eclipsed by the "thousand-year" flood.

In the words of one water-soaked witness, the 1955 disaster was "a picnic compared to this one." It was not an exaggeration. The Klamath River rose to 18 feet over flood stage—five feet higher than during the earlier storm—and the Douglas Memorial Bridge, battered but steadfast in 1955, washed away at 3 A.M., December 23, as awe-struck observers shone spotlights on it from the shore.

Again, the flood brought tales of terror. On the facade of Berg's Apartments in Klamath, someone painted the dramatic message:

SOS
HAVE
BABY

No one was able to respond to the plea, and so Harold Lord and his endangered family finally left the apartments in a small boat that had conveniently washed by. The current proved too powerful for Lord, who managed, however, to maneuver the boat against a building and some trees; here he lashed the craft fast, and the family spent the night covered with a canvas as the river roared past. In the morning, still unrescued, the Lords boated their own way to safety.

After the floodwaters receded, Klamath looked like a war zone. Only one of the town's buildings was still standing — Vern's Tackle Shop, and its services were not presently needed. Brizard's store, formerly a center for the community, was more typical — it looked "bombed out."

As the residents along the lower river surveyed the wreckage, a stirring story was unfolding up the coast at Crescent City.

Bahamas, the Seafaring Steer

When the storm finally subsided, the citizens of Crescent City found the shoreline littered with a collection of logs, driftwood, and debris. The bay, too, was covered with the detritus of the flood's destruction—a nearly solid mass that hid the water beneath it. As he surveyed the scene, Dave Stewart, a worker on shore, noticed something moving atop the flotsam that choked the harbor; looking more closely, he discovered to his amazement that it was a black Angus, feebly trying to raise its head. Stewart rounded up a rescue party of several men, and the group gingerly made its way across some 200 yards of tangled timber to reach the stranded steer. After digging the animal out, the men "then held him upright," according to the subsequent newspaper account, "while they lifted one foot after another from one slick water soaked log to the next until the last was conquered."

Once on shore, the steer was sick for two days, but under Stewart's constant care he finally recovered. Soon the animal's owner showed up, and the story that was then pieced together seemed beyond belief.

The Angus was called "Bahamas," and he had last been seen in his pasture at Klamath Glen before being swept away by the flood. Somehow the creature had clambered aboard a drift of debris and floated with it down the river, out to sea, and finally, some 20 miles

Bahamas back in Klamath

from home, into Crescent City's harbor. It was a feat that would have done the most legendary log-riding lumberjack proud, but it had been accomplished by a 900-pound bovine that wasn't even wearing caulked boots.

Bahamas returned home with his owners, presumably to again graze the grasslands of the Glen. The tale, however, then took a dark twist, for the seafaring survivor was slated to be sold for slaughter.

It wasn't the right ending for the steer's inspiring story, and some of the area's residents rallied to rewrite it. Soon the Klamath Chamber of Commerce became the proud possessor of the brave beast, who was put out to pasture near the new Klamath bridge. For years Bahamas was visited by friends and tourists alike, his fame increasing when North Coast author Harriet Weaver rendered his remarkable experience into a children's book. In 1981 Bahamas at last retired from his career as celebrity steer and returned to Klamath Glen, where he could be seen roaming the grassy fields not far from his original home. He finally died there in 1983, his passing having been postponed some 19 years by his wild winter ride down the Klamath's "thousand-year" floodtide.

Nature's Neighborhoods: Plant and Wildlife Communities

A stand of trees that soar skyward on massive brown trunks; grassy hillslopes, speckled with summer wildflowers and dotted with browsing elk; wide beaches that are carpeted with low, spreading plants, their colors bright with spring; a pileated woodpecker flying through the forest, its feathers flashing in the half light...scene after varied scene...all are found in the redwood parks.

But these preserves are more than mere laudable landscapes; they also protect a host of indigenous inhabitants — both plants and animals — that over time have combined to form communities of great compatibility. They do so through an omnipotent, ongoing process: fire and ice, plague and pestilence — such forces move through the ages, confronting each species with change, challenging every entity with the choice between adaptation and annihilation. The effects are ongoing, but their pace is slow; when we walk through the parklands of today we see a series of survivors who, for the most part, have long lived at their current address. They arrange themselves through some strange synthesis of inner program and outer prod, following, it seems, the demands of an ancient, unthinking wisdom — without blueprint or map does nature thus design her neighborhoods.

North Coast parklands feature four commonly found communities. They are:

Old-Growth Forest

If a stand of trees reaches middle-age maturity without undo disruption from human or natural causes, it becomes an "old-growth" forest. Such places have a presence that widens the eye and stills the voice — thick, weathered trunks that seem anchored in antiquity; a plenitude of standing dead trees (snags) which hosts birds and other wildlife; and a largess of logs that lay massively upon the forest floor, slowly returning their substance to the earth. Often the setting seems to glow in sort of half-light, the sun's rays softly filtered by the trees' thick canopy of foliage. Such forests are sometimes called "ancient," but to enter one is to go not so much *back* in time as *beyond* it, for it is here that the cycle of birth, life, and decay is present in all its stages, repeating itself in an unending, perfect rhythm — a circle of being that beckons a new way of understanding, and with it, a new knowledge.

Within the parks, the most frequently found old-growth forests are those where coast redwoods dominate. Here are statuesque sempervirens, 250 to 300 feet tall, with some reaching 350 feet or more in height; most of the trees are between 250 and 1,000 years old, although a few are even older. They grow to their largest size in the thick alluvial gravels of streamside terraces and benchlands, such as at the Tall Trees Grove on Redwood Creek, along the flats of Prairie Creek, on the benchlands above the Smith River, and in the bottomlands near Mill Creek. Stands on hillslopes and ridgetops contain somewhat smaller mature trees, although the higher-elevation giants at the Lady Bird Johnson Grove are still startlingly impressive.

Many redwood groves feature other evergreens in supporting roles: Douglas-fir, western hemlock, and Sitka spruce are the most common companion conifers; all three share space with redwoods along the James Irvine Trail near the headwaters of Godwood Creek. Tanoak, California hazel, vine maple, and cascara frequently form part of the lower level of plantlife, the understory. Closer to the ground, sword fern often occupies large areas, while wood fern sprouts from damp logs and deer fern inhabits certain bankside settings; leather fern sometimes grows on tree limbs far above the ground. Among the accompanying bushes are black and red huckleberry, salal, mock azalea, western burning bush, and — filling the hillsides with its huge blooms in June — rhododendron. Deep forest flowers include redwood sorrel, Hooker's and Smith's fairybells, redwood violet, and trillium. Partially shaded roadsides are often brightened by the blossoms of a colorful trio: leopard lily, fat false Solomon's seal, and clintonia. Poison oak entwines itself

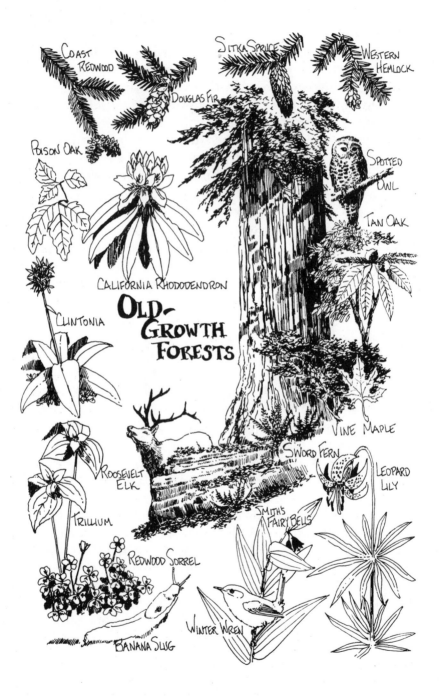

around redwood trunks, its leaves turning pale yellow and scarlet in autumn.

When they fall, mature redwoods cut a giant swath through the forest, frequently toppling neighboring trees as they crash earthward. The resultant openings are quickly colonized by various light loving plants—berry bushes, cascara, and red alder among them. In time, these leafy oases will often be shaded out by the encroaching evergreens.

Wildlife is usually difficult to observe in the darkened, foliage-filled surroundings of old-growth redwoods, but a number of species live or visit there. Steller's jay, chestnut-backed chickadee, and varied thrush are common resident birds, while Roosevelt elk, black bear, and Douglas' squirrel comprise part of the mammal contingent. Northwestern garter snakes and banana slugs are among the close-to-the-ground critters.

Threatened Species:
Why All the Fuss?

The redwood parks contain two of the most controversial creatures found on the West Coast or, for that matter, anywhere in the country. The marbled murrelet and spotted owl often dominate local news as loggers and environmentalists lock horns over how to deal with this diminishing duo of seldom-seen birds. Both species depend on old-growth forests for their survival, so the continuing destruction of their habitat by timber companies threatens their long-term existence.

More is at stake than the birds' futures, however. The complex community they live in is also home to many other entities that suffer substantially when stands of old growth are cut. The red tree vole lives only in mature conifers, feeding exclusively on the foliage found there. A number of other animals, including various bats and the Pacific giant salamander, can survive in other habitats but flourish in ancient forests. Some 79 species of birds and mammals are directly dependent on standing snags—a major old growth component—for their well-being. The dazzling pileated woodpecker, for example, bores into decaying trees to find bark beetles and other favorite foods. Heavily shaded, gravel-based streams, like those that wind through undisturbed forestland, provide ideal salmon spawning sites.

Besides the benefits they offer wildlife, old-growth forests also act to maintain the health of the surrounding environment, for they remove dust and other material from the air, filter water and control its runoff, and conserve valuable nutrients. Large-scale loss of forestland changes weather patterns, most noticeably by reducing precipitation. The reasons to preserve such ecosystems thus go far beyond protecting the marbled murrelet and the spotted owl.

And yet what of these two retiring creatures? Is their continued existence not cause enough to save the forests in which they live and breed?

A spotted owl perches in a trailside alder above Redwood Creek; perhaps a dozen passing hikers stop to stare at the gray-brown bird, who, except for an occasional blink of her eyes, remains motionless. The owl shows no fear, indicates no desire to do anything but drowse. She merely sits upon her tree limb, quietly passing the day in the mottled sunlight, content with her place in the forest.

And the marbled murrelets, of which little is known, may well spend their days like this: at a nest, high in a conifer some four or five miles from the coast, the mother murrelet removes herself from the egg and is replaced by the father; he will remain atop the egg for 24 hours, while his mate flies to the ocean to forage. Only at dawn will she return to exchange places with her partner. Later, after the egg has hatched and the young bird is ready to fledge, the parents leave their offspring alone in the nest while they search for food. The youngster preens off its down and then takes flight, travelling, on its very first trip, all the way to the sea.

Owl and murrelet are at our mercy, as are the forests which nurture them. The wonder is not that we are finally acting to provide for their protection, but that it has taken us this long to act.

In certain areas close to the coast, redwoods are restricted by the drying effects of salt air, so that Sitka spruce becomes the dominant old-growth tree species. On cutover lands, regenerating redwoods and other conifers usually form compacted contingents of thin trunked, scraggly limbed trees; only after enduring a decades-long purgatory of darkened density do the survivors begin to assume individual identities, their trunks, bark, and limbs at last developing a certain distinctiveness of color and form. All told, it can be a century or more before a specimen acquires the singularity to escape the stigma of being called "second growth."

Streamsides and Ponds

The creeks that wind their way through the parks create countless corridor communities, riparian ribbons of broadleaf plants that contrast with their conifer dominated surroundings. Prairie Creek, Lost Man Creek, and Mill Creek are good examples of this moisture filled environment, but characteristic species can also be found along the Smith River and Redwood Creek, on many smaller streams, and sometimes even in spring-fed damp spots. Still water can create similar settings, as at alder-fringed Marshall Pond, which teems with birdlife, including wood ducks, and also contains beavers.

Back from the creek and river banks, staid stands of conifers maintain an unyielding greenery, leaving it to the streamside plantlife to note the progression of the seasons. From the bleak bareness of winter, limbs sprout bright green in spring, the foliage often darkening in summer and then reaching a colorful climax in fall, when the delightfully deciduous leaves turn a dozen hues, from lemon yellow and pale bronze to reddish purple and deep gold.

Red alder, bigleaf maple, and vine maple are major streamside tree species. Coast red elderberry, salmonberry, and thimbleberry seek openings near the creeks, as does lady fern; the delicate five-finger fern clings to shaded streambanks. Monkeyflower, buttercup, and piggy-back plant are all common near creeks.

In the streams themselves swim silver and king salmon, steelhead, cutthroat and rainbow trout, and other fishes; the salmon, however, have declined drastically within the parks, and summer steelheads are in danger of extinction. Several avians, including the belted kingfisher and osprey, glean their meals from the water. Other common birds are the Swainson's thrush and Wilson's warbler. Main mammals include black-tailed deer, raccoon, and brush rabbit. Among the waterside amphibians and reptiles are various

STREAMSIDES AND PONDS

Red Alder
Red Elderberry
Bigleaf Maple
King Salmon
Steelhead
Salmonberry
Dusky-Footed Woodrat
Brush Rabbit
Dipper
Monkey Flower
California Spikenard
Osprey
Bewick's Wren
Beaver
Chestnut-Backed Chickadee
Wilson's Warbler

salamanders, newts, frogs, and toads, along with garter and ring-necked snakes.

Beaches and Dunes, Marshes and Lagoons

The seaside strand stretches for miles along the coast, its ends lost in the morning mist; sanderlings and other small birds scurry across the sand, their legs stiff and sticklike. In back of the beach are a series of low dunes, matted in places with such ground-clinging plants as sand verbena and sea rocket. Marshes and lagoons lie at canyon mouths close to the coast; they often trap the water of beach-bound creeks, creating congregations of alder, willow, rush, and sedge. Offshore, seals and sea lions share rocky sea stacks with gulls, cormorants and oystercatchers, while gray whales and river otters ply the ocean itself. Every setting is distinct, yet each exists within a short distance of the others, representatives of the seaside's several plant and wildlife habitats.

The coastal strand community features salt-tolerant flowers like beach silvertop, dune tansy, and seaside daisy, while aptly named stonecrop covers rocky outcroppings. Dead and decaying vegetation and animals continually wash ashore, as do driftwood and other debris; this fetid flotsam attracts numerous insects, who busily buzz above it. Several shorebirds come to feed on the bug and detritus melange, including sanderlings, killdeers, willets, and dowichers; they are joined by various species of gulls. Reconnoitering ravens frequently fly overhead.

Most animal activity on the beach occurs at night, for the gray fox, skunk, and bobcat favor the darkness when perusing the area for food. Roosevelt elk will sometimes swim in the ocean, perhaps to rid themselves of ticks, perhaps to imitate Mark Spitz.

Inland from the shifting beach dunes is a more stabilized zone of dune hummocks, which clump up around such plants as coyote brush, various grasses, and bush lupine. Several species of seed-eating sparrows frequent these locations, as do such insect-ingesting birds as the tree swallow, violet-green swallow, and black phoebe. Red-tailed hawks and northern harriers (marsh hawks) search the dunes for rodents, competing with weasels, coyotes, and garter snakes; their main prey are the California vole and various mice, all of which nest in the scattered driftwood.

BEACH SAND VERBENA

WESTERN SANDPIPER

BEACH SILVERTOP

KILLDEER

SEA ROCKET

DUNE TANSY

WHITE-CROWNED SPARROW

HARBOR SEAL

BEACHES AND DUNES
MARSHES AND LAGOONS

STONECROP

WESTERN GULL

BLACK OYSTERCATCHER

MARSH WREN

Beaches and dunes can be found at Freshwater Spit and the nearby area around the Redwood Information Center, along the Gold Bluffs in Redwood National Park and Prairie Creek Redwoods State Park, and at RNP's Crescent Beach.

Lagoons are home to aquatic plants like bulrush, cattail, and yellow pond-lily. Many birds populate these placid places, among them the great blue heron, green-backed heron, and red-winged blackbird. Amphibians such as the red-legged frog, Pacific tree-frog, and rough-skinned newt are often on the menu of resident river otters, minks, and other predators; pond turtles are another interesting inhabitant. Several lagoons are located in the parks; they are: at Crescent Beach, south of the beach parking area; near the mouth of Lagoon Creek, just off Highway 101 north of Trees of Mystery; Espa Lagoon, at Gold Bluffs; and Freshwater Lagoon, at the southern entrance to the parks.

Marshlands feature the animals common to the lagoons, plus elk, beaver, and an occasional mountain lion. Here, too, are coastal cutthroat trout, which come up the creeks that drain the marshes. Common birds are sora and Virginia rail. In marshy sites, thickets of willow and red alder alternate with areas of horsetail, sedges, and rushes, combining to form outposts of lush vegetation that encroach upon the sandy expanses of dune and beach. Several of the stream mouths at Gold Bluffs have, over time, created marsh areas, including those at Squashan, Home, Boat, Butler, and Ossagon creeks.

Prairies and Oak Woodlands

For all their beauty, the undiminished intensity of old-growth forests can become a bit daunting. So it is that the parks' prairies and oak woodlands provide a welcome change, offering airy openings, varied vegetation, and lots of wildlife. These are places where the vision expands, the air dries and brightens, and the verticality of tall trunks relaxes into the roundness of spreading oaks and rolling hills.

There are two types of prairies within the parks. Low-elevation grasslands are found along Prairie Creek and above the Gold Bluffs; these grassy areas are grazed regularly by the various herds of elk. The most accessible are at Elk Prairie, near the southern edge

WESTERN HOUNDS-TONGUE

CALIFORNIA BLACK OAK

PUSSY EARS

OREGON WHITE OAK

FIRECRACKER FLOWER

HARVEST BRODIAEA

BLUE DICKS

PRAIRIES AND WOODLANDS

HENDERSON'S SHOOTING STAR

INDIAN PINK

BLUE-HEADED GILIA

WOOLLY SUNFLOWER

of Prairie Creek Redwoods State Park; at Alexander Lincoln Prairie, above Fern Canyon; and on the hillside northeast of the mouth of Ossagon Creek.

Greater in extent are the ridgetop prairies found along the Little Bald Hills Trail and on Bald Hills Road. The latter area stretches for miles along the ridgeline, dropping at times far down the canyonside towards Redwood Creek. In earlier days the Tolowas (in the Little Bald Hills) and the Chilulas (in the Bald Hills) burned the upland prairies to keep them free of encroaching trees, for the grasslands provided browsing areas for deer and elk. Later, sheep ranchers like the Lyons family also ignited the hillslopes to maintain grazing lands for their flocks. Redwood National Park now has a controlled-burning program to ensure the perpetuation of the prairies, while Prairie Creek Redwoods State Park burns Elk Prairie and also cuts young trees that impinge on the grassland.

Both native and introduced grasses populate the upland prairies, to which numerous wildflowers add their seasonal coloration. Four members of the amaryllis family frequent these open expanses: harvest brodiaea, Ithuriel's spear, firecracker flower, and blue dicks. Also prominent upon the prairielands are Henderson's shooting star, woolly sunflower, blue-headed gilia, and Indian pink, while western hound's tongue wags in nearby shady spots.

The lowland prairies and those of the Little Bald Hills are encircled by conifers, while in the Bald Hills the grasslands often form savannas with Oregon white oak, California black oak, and an occasional bigleaf maple.

Both elk and black-tailed deer forage on the Bald Hills prairies, as do voles, harvest mice, and gophers, while bobcats, coyotes, and mountain lions use the area to hunt. Turkey vultures, along with raptors like the kestrel, northern harrier, and red-tailed hawk, search for food from high above.

California's Other Great Tree

The coast redwood and its cousin, the giant sequoia, are justifiably considered the celebrity trees of the golden state. But if California were to honor the tree most essential to its early cultures, most pervasive across its far-flung landscapes, and most compatible with the state's varied scenery, it would be neither of these.

It would be the oak.

From the snow-clad mountainsides of Barton Flats to the tawny hills near Santa Maria, from the grassy ridges above Petaluma to the prairies of Paradise, some type of oak spreads its limbs over the surroundings, sheltering cattle from the summer sun or shedding brown leaves upon a forest path. Oaks were once nearly everywhere in California, and, although land development and firewood cutting have long taken a great toll, many memorable woodlands remain.

Redwood National Park, of all places, is one location where oaks have found a lasting niche. Here they surround the great grasslands that stretch across the Bald Hills, rising up the flanks of Schoolhouse Peak like a leafy morning fog. For centuries, their acorns (along with those of the unrelated tanoak) were the staff of life for the Chilulas and other local tribes, and the game that inhabited oak country grew fat on the trees' bounty.

More than a dozen species of oak range across the state; two are frequently found in the Bald Hills: Oregon white oak and California black oak. Both are deciduous, the former having leaves with rounded lobes and the latter with leaf lobes that come to a prickly point. Together the two trees fringe the bald hilltops, softening the transition from low grassland to tall, canyon-bound conifers, their mid-green foliage gradating the brighter greens of the grasses and the darker hues of firs and redwoods.

No oaks grow close to the conifer-covered northern coast; to encounter them on park land requires a drive ten miles up Bald Hills Road. It's a trip few travellers now take, but one that any true tree lover will want to make.

(Lists of selected park plant and animal species are found on pages 285-292.)

Section II

* * *

Auto Tour

Riding the Redwood Highway: An Auto Tour of the North Coast Parks

For decades after the arrival of white settlers, the land that grew the tallest trees on earth hoarded its treasure, stifling the attempts of timbermen and tourists alike to either saw or see the great redwoods. The lumber barons gradually pushed their logging railroads into the forest fastness, but it was not until the 1920s that travellers were offered an uninterrupted motor route between the San Francisco Bay Area and southern Oregon. Originally called the "Redwood Highway," it now more often bills itself as federal highways 101 and 199. For over 60 years the road has run through the heart of the North Coast, offering an outstanding opportunity to observe the region's renowned redwood parks.

The 12-part tour describes both the highway and selected supplementary routes. It starts at the parks' southern entrance, on the coast below Orick, and follows the Redwood Highway northward until it leaves the parklands, near Hiouchi. Mileages for key attractions are given from the beginning of each route. The map on the reverse of this page indicates locations of the tour segments.

Key to Symbols Used at the Start of Each Tour Section:

🚗 auto route	ⓘ park visitor center	✖ food
🏃 hiking trail	🦆 picnic site-water	🛏 lodging
🚲 bicycle trail	🦆 picnic site-no water	⛽ gas station
🏇 horse trail	🚻 restroom	🚂 historic site
🛶 kayaking, boating	⛺ tent campground	📷 scenic viewpoint
🎣 fishing	🚐 trailer campground	〰 ocean access

Auto Tour

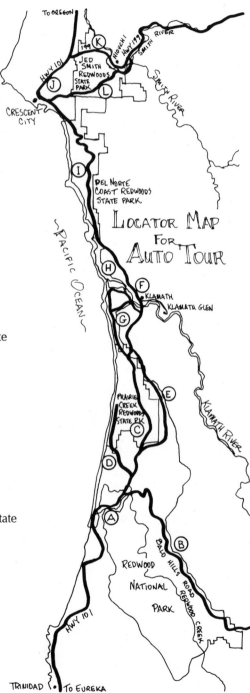

Orick Area

Running from the parks' southern boundary to the Newton B. Drury Scenic Parkway, this section of Highway 101 passes a stretch of seacoast, an old logging town, and a redwood-filled canyon along the way. The 8.3-mile route is all two-lane paved highway.

Features: (for key to symbols, see p. 89)

🚗🛶⊗🏠👤🦆≋ entrance to the parks; Freshwater Lagoon and view of the Pacific Ocean (mile 0.0)

ⓘ⊗🏠♉≋ Redwood Information Center (1.3)

🛶🦆✕🛏🏠🚂 town of Orick (2.3)

🔺⊗🏠 junction with Drydens Road; access to Redwood Creek Horse Trails (3.1)

🚗 turnoff for Bald Hills side trip (4.4)

🦆🚂≋ side road to Skunk Cabbage Section, Coastal Trail (4.8)

🚗 turnoff for Gold Bluffs side trip (5.9)

🦆🚲⊗🏠 side road to Lost Man Creek Trail, Picnic Area (6.6)

🚗 interchange for Newton B. Drury Scenic Parkway; end of route (8.3)

Some 40 miles north of Eureka, **Freshwater Lagoon** marks the **southern entrance to Redwood National and State Parks**. There are no redwoods to be seen here, however, only a long beach, a sweep of the crashing blue Pacific, and the smaller, stiller waters of the lagoon. The trees — thousands of them — will come a few miles later.

Redwood Information Center

Immediately north of the park entrance is **Freshwater Lagoon Spit**, left, a Redwood National Park (RNP) facility that offers tent

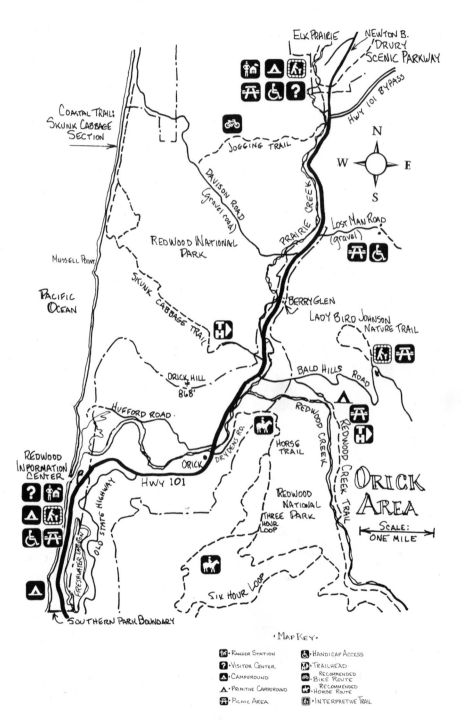

·MAP KEY·

🏠·Ranger Station   ♿·Handicap Access

❓·Visitor Center   🚶·Trailhead

🏕·Campground   🚴·Recommended Bike Route

▲·Primitive Campground   🐎·Recommended Horse Route

🏕·Picnic Area   🖼·Interpretive Trail

camping and picnicking near its southern end and RV camping to the north. The lagoon itself, right, is pinched off at its upper end by a promontory known locally as Lookout Point; the once-sharper point was blunted in 1950 by the rerouting of Highway 101. Ahead on the left, mile 1.3, is the entrance to RNP's **Redwood Creek Picnic Area** and **Redwood Information Center**, which occupy the site of one of Orick's once numerous lumber mills. The center's beachside building is a striking construction of gray and green wood that offers various interpretive features, including video programs, a small but attractive collection of Indian baskets, a captivating relief map of the park, an illustrated plant list, and a selection of books and posters. Park personnel are available to answer questions and provide brochures. At the building's entrance is a recently built Yurok dugout canoe.

Redwood Information Center

The **Wetlands Boardwalk** runs north from the center's parking lot. The wooden walkway leads a short distance to an overlook of the Redwood Creek estuary. En route are such picturesque plants as lupine, aster, dock, yarrow, and hooded ladies' tresses; birders will delight in the area's avian activity. Near here was the **Yurok village of Oreq-ʷ**, from which the present-day town derives its name.

Beyond the Information Center turnoff, Highway 101 curves east to follow the valley of Redwood Creek. The road now leaves the park and passes through private land.

At mile 2.1 is a junction, right, with the **Old State Highway**; the aging road climbs, on crumbling pavement, a mile up the hillside to reach **Lookout Point** before descending to follow the eastern side of Freshwater Lagoon. Located north of the point was once the Lookout Lunchroom, an eating establishment that provided patrons with a view of the ocean surf. A steep road led to the beach below; the lunchroom's owners, Conrad and "Pinky" Zuber, charged 25¢ for cars to use the route. Unwitting motorists often found that their vehicles could not negotiate the climb back to the highway and were forced to engage the services of an old Dodge truck, conveniently operated by Mr. Zuber, to haul them up the grade. According to a tally kept by the Zubers, the most frequent victims were Essexes and Pontiacs.

The long-gone Lookout Lunchroom

Also doing hauling from the beach was "Orick Bob," a Yurok otherwise known as Robert Johnson. Bob would attach a small sled to his horse and transport sacks of surf fish up the hillside, assessing the fishermen a small fee for the service. The elderly Indian had been born on the Klamath River, but moved to Lookout Point when he married a woman from the small Yurok settlement there. By one account, this community was started after the village of Oreq-ʷ was destroyed by a tidal wave and the residents deemed it safer to relocate to higher ground. Bob's wife was the last person from the settlement, and after her death Bob stayed on, living in a small cabin on the side of Lookout Point until he died at the approximate age of 100; he was buried in the family plot atop the ridgeslope.

Just past the old highway is the site of the "Coffin Mill," right; during World War II it produced beautiful redwood lumber for soldiers' caskets. The mill's proprietors had a less ominous name for their operation, calling it the "Knot and Rot Logging Company."

Orick

The fertile floodplain of **Redwood Creek** then opens before the highway, which at mile 2.3 enters the outskirts of **Orick**, pop. 650, elev. 26. The first business on the left displays a strange object at its front entrance. Some fifteen feet long and seven feet high, it proves, on examination, to be a wooden sculpture, somewhat constricted at its center and scored with strange patterns of cross hatching. Few observers will recall that it was once a well-travelled emblem of the embattled North Coast timber industry.

Mr. Peanut Goes to Washington

It wasn't high art, but it was an attention getter: weighing nine tons, it was the size of a small sedan and required the combined talents of a sculptor, a logger, and a sandblaster in its creation; it travelled 3,000 miles in nine days and was offered to the nation's President. The largest likeness of a legume ever created—crafted from an ancient redwood—it soon became known as "Mr. Peanut."

The idea had a touch of genius to it: distraught local loggers were planning a protest convoy to Washington, where they would pressure Congress to scrap its plan for expanding Redwood National Park. If the proposal passed, the man in the White House, Georgian Jimmy Carter, was expected to promptly approve it. They grew prize peanuts in the President's home state, so why not give him one worthy of the West Coast—an oversized replica fit to sit under a 300-foot redwood!

When the procession of timber-toting big rigs formed up for the trip, the flatbed truck bearing the giant gift was awarded the place of honor. A sign on the truck's side stated "It may be peanuts to you, but it's jobs to us." As the convoy crossed the country, bewildered bystanders saw not only a horizontal forest of very large logs, but also an odd object that only the knowledgeable and keen sighted could identify as Mr. Peanut.

The reception in Washington was not all that the loggers and their supporters had wished. Some 400 of them rallied on the Capitol's steps, their suspenders and striped shirts gaining attention from both passersby and the media. But the hoped-for climax of

Mr. Peanut on parade

their convoy came to naught, for when the woodsmen attempted to present Mr. Peanut to President Carter, their offer was refused; the White House claimed "it was not an appropriate use of redwood," which was a polite way of saying "nuts."

So the loggers and their cargo, including Mr. Peanut, returned home. The committee that had planned the convoy decided to place the rejected gift in Orick, the community most affected by the park. The town's residents sought to obtain a building in which to house the sculpture, but the effort failed; for a time Mr. Peanut ignominiously reposed in back of a local garage.

After a fierce struggle, the park expansion bill was ultimately approved. Later, at some unknown date, the peanut reappeared in public, close by the highway. The many passing motorists paid the sculpture scant heed, for they had more interesting scenery to seek, including new lands added to the now-expanded Redwood National Park.

Time has not been kind to Mr. Peanut nor to the cause he represented. Although there are plans for a sign detailing his exciting history, his exterior has long been exposed to the elements and now bears the wear of years of weathering. Meanwhile, all but one of Orick's mills have closed, and most of the embattled loggers who once made the peanut their emblem have moved on. Like the town itself, the slighted sculpture seems drained of life—a mere shell of its former self.

The "founders" of Orick were Robert Swan and George Griffin, who mined for gold along the beach at the mouth of Redwood

Creek and also ranched a short distance inland. Following Griffin's death in 1883, Swan continued the operation, gradually expanding it to include a sawmill, post office, general store, and inn, along with a ferry that crossed Redwood Creek.

Early travel through the area was mainly along the beaches, where horseback riders and even four-horse freight wagons struggled across the sand while facing fluctuating tides; Orick existed in near isolation as it often took more than a week for freighters to make the trip from Humboldt Bay. The completion of the county wagon road in 1894 allowed for easier travel between Eureka and Crescent City, and by the early 1900s Burr McConnaha had started a horse stage that linked Trinidad with Requa.

Spruce covered much of the Orick valley in its early days, but most of the trees were eventually removed. Dairy ranches took their place, thriving on the area's hospitable streamside soil, and by 1918 the town's cheese factory was processing 1,200 pounds of dairy products per day. That same year the first Orick Inn burned; its replacement was completed in 1922 and still stands as a town landmark. A favorite stop for fishermen, the inn also served such diverse luminaries as Herbert Hoover, actors Ronald Coleman and Fred MacMurray, and the famed opera singer Madame Ernestine Schuman-Heink. During World War II the building housed the Coast Guard contingent that patrolled the beaches near town. Besides using aptly named Lookout Point for a sighting area, the guardsmen also had an observation platform high in a redwood tree at what later became the Lady Bird Johnson Grove.

By 1948 the postwar housing boom and its demand for lumber had transformed Orick. Seven mills were operating in the area and the cheese factory—formerly the town's biggest business—had been converted into a logging truck repair shop.

The Orick Inn

Orick grew fast, but it had difficulty keeping up with its new-found prosperity. Electricity came only in 1940, while dial telephones didn't arrive until a decade later. Townspeople bemoaned their lack of a bank, and when a volunteer fire department was formed, its meager equipment consisted of a handcart that belonged in a museum, an old water tank, and some hoses owned by one of the residents. Despite these shortcomings, the town boasted a business district that included five restaurants, six gas stations, four bars, four garages, three churches, a barbershop, a beauty parlor, and, of all things, a detective bureau. Although logging had surpassed dairying in importance, local rancher Bruno Pialorsi proudly announced that in 1952 his grade Jersey, "#19," had produced 1,000 pounds of butterfat, a county record.

The town continued to boom as the nearby ridgeslopes were stripped of their trees. But rich in timber as the region was, the supply was rapidly shrinking, and some locals realized that the town's future in logging was limited. The community had once made much on tourism—in 1925 the Orick Inn had housed 520 guests during the first 20 days in July—and, when a national redwood park was proposed for the area, there were those who felt its presence would offer a return to those palmy, earlier days. As the controversy heated up, however, the pro-timber forces came to dominate and soon Orick was a center of anti-park sentiment.

When, after a series of compromises, the park was finally approved, its acreage included some old-growth forest but also contained considerable logged-over land; left unprotected was a substantial supply of virgin timber, and here the cutting continued unabated. Nonetheless, the available trees were eventually used up, the mills closed one by one, and Orick shrank to about a quarter of its former size. Today the town's most visible aspect is its long line of burl shops; on the adjacent highway, the procession of once-numerous log trucks has been supplanted by a stream of tourist vehicles, some with a chainsaw-sculpted redwood bear or cowboy strapped on top—decorations from a decimated timberland.

Although contemporary Orick still lacks a bank, it does have a more modern fire department and still offers the services of several businesses, including restaurants, markets, motels, gas stations, and a post office. At mile 3.1 is a junction with **Drydens Road**, right, a two-lane, paved route that runs one mile to the Orick Rodeo Grounds; located there are a small picnic site, corrals, and access to RNP's **Redwood Creek Horse Trails**, a set of rambling, interconnected routes that run across the ridges west of the creek.

Early-day Orick rodeo

The highway crosses the Redwood Creek bridge, 3.2 miles, and then passes **Hufford Road**, left, mile 3.3, which offers coastal access near the creek's mouth. At the road's end once lived Ira Dorrance, who came to Orick by auto in 1912; he parked his vehicle and never drove it again, instead making the four-mile round trip to town on foot for the next 60 years. Offshore from the creek mouth is a landmark known as **Little Girl Rock**—named, according to one account, for a legendary Yurok child who wouldn't eat her dinner and was carried to the spot by a large bird as punishment.

Lower Canyon of Prairie Creek

North of Orick at mile 4.4 is the junction with the **Bald Hills Road**, right; the route provides access to Redwood Creek, the Lady Bird Johnson Grove, the Tall Trees, and the park's Bald Hills district (see p. 108). Continuing north from the junction, the channel of Prairie Creek now runs just below the highway, right; farther to the east loom the large logs of the last active local mill, an old growth cutting facility belonging to the Arcata Redwood Company.

The marked access road to the **Skunk Cabbage Section, Coastal Trail** (see p. 261) abruptly climbs the hillside, 4.8 miles, left. After crossing Prairie Creek, the route reaches the remnants of **Berry Glen**, mile 5.6, right, site of a once-prospering business that has now all but succumbed to the vagaries of vandals, old age, and weather. Sixty years ago, however, it was a place of promise.

Berry Glen

In the summer of 1931 the Great Depression was at its height; California's dusty roads were filled with families in search of better places and better times. Among the many migrators, one group formed an improbable caravan as it crossed the sunbaked Bald Hills.

First came Jack Batrel, driving a battered Model T Ford truck whose flatbed was filled with cages of small fur bearers—minks. Then came Jack's father-in-law, "Dad" Oakes, in an equally old pickup that pulled a trailer; both of these vehicles were loaded with more cages, but this time the cargo was foxes. At the rear was the family's prize possession, a relatively new Model A driven by Jean Batrel. In the box seat were her 11-year-old daughter, Ora, and two more furry critters, Muggins and Fanny, the family dogs.

The procession was en route from Gottville, a hamlet on the middle Klamath, to the Batrels' new place next to Prairie Creek. The foxes and minks had voracious appetites, and the plan was to feed them fish and other sea food brought from the nearby ocean.

There was trouble even before the trip ended. The ride across the Bald Hills was long and grueling, and the grade down to Prairie Creek proved so steep that logs had to be tied to the rear ends of the Fords to slow their descent. The minks, traumatized by their travail, ate their young. When someone subsequently poisoned the foxes as an ill-conceived Halloween prank, the fur-bearing business came to an abrupt end.

But the Batrels were hard working and resourceful, and the family found other ways to make do in their new location. Jack went to work for the WPA, helping build bridges throughout northwestern California. The family planted strawberries and a truck garden, supplementing the blackberries and other fruit that grew wild on their wet but fertile property. Since the site was next to the recently completed Redwood Highway, the Batrels soon set up a roadside produce stand, selling to both the locals and the motor tourists who streamed by on their way to Prairie Creek Redwoods State Park and points north.

In 1938 the Batrels converted their stand into a full-fledged store. They set out tables where the patrons could eat, and Jean Batrel began selling berry pies. She would start as early as 2 A.M., baking two pies at a time on an old wood stove, sometimes making as many as 45 in a day.

About 1940 the store was enlarged to carry a full line of grocer-ies and notions; there were three mills nearby, and the workers' families saved a trip into Orick by shopping at the Batrels'. Many commodities were rationed during World War II, but Ora would go to Eureka twice a week to pick up whatever was currently avail-able. "One day it was soda pop, one day shortening," she would say, discounting the hundred-mile round trips she had to make.

The store closed in the early 1950s, and although the Batrels continued to live at Berry Glen, time gradually began to take its toll on the surroundings. When Jean Batrel died in 1984, Ora took up part-time residence in Arcata. The buildings sagged from neglect, their demise helped along by a stream of vandals drawn to the iso-lated spot. After a long series of burglaries, Ora finally removed her remaining possessions, carrying a pistol in her pocket in case she encountered any of the troublemakers.

Berry Glen in better days

Little now remains of the roadside stop. The store building near the highway is covered with a clutch of vines, and its sign, until recently visible, has fallen into the foliage. The other structures lan-guish in the ever encroaching vegetation; Ora's nursery garden, once her pride and joy, is gradually being overrun. Year by year the bushes make their inexorable progression, and soon the berries will have reclaimed Berry Glen.

Davison Road, mile 5.9, left, runs westward over the ridge to the Gold Bluffs Beach area of Prairie Creek Redwoods State Park (see p. 128). At the turnoff is a cafe parking lot that contains the region's only monument to a dead elephant.

Big Diamond: the "Prehistoric" Pachyderm of Prairie Creek

By the fall of 1927 the Eureka to Crescent City section of the Redwood Highway was nearly completed. Workers were still busy north of Orick, however, and the early season rains soon turned the unfinished roadbed into a quagmire that created great difficulties for travellers, and, in one case, death.

An article in the *Arcata Union* of October 6 described the event:

> The first casualty of the kind in Humboldt County occurred near Orick Friday when "Big Diamond," giant elephant, collapsed after several hours pushing trucks of the "Honest Bill" circus out of their mired-down positions.

> The big pachyderm fell to the ground shortly after he had landed the last circus wagon on high ground, and was unable to rise. He died the following day.

Big Diamond, the story continued, weighed approximately eight tons and was valued at $10,000. The report, perhaps confusing his age with that of the nearby redwoods, stated that the animal was 247 years old.

The tragedy had been big news in Orick. Word of the elephant's collapse spread quickly though the community, and soon more than a hundred people had arrived to see the downed beast. J. J. McConnel, the animal's trainer, stayed at his side, repeatedly saying, "come on, Diamond, it's time to start." Each time the elephant strained gallantly to get up, only to then sink back into the mud. The following day another crowd gathered, but there was no improvement. That afternoon, Big Diamond breathed his last.

Although it would have been fitting for the victim, having died in the line of duty, to be buried with full honors, such was not to be the case. It was no easy proposition to inter an eight-ton elephant, and so "Honest Bill," the circus owner, devised a plan that did no credit to his name.

Bill approached the highway contractor, W. H. Hauser, and thanked him for helping get the circus back on the road. As a token of his appreciation, Bill indicated he was willing to leave Big Diamond with Hauser. The animal's hide, Bill explained, was easily worth $2,000, and it would be Hauser's if he'd consent to bury the carcass after he'd skinned it. The contractor was agreeable, and so Honest Bill wrote up a bill of sale and soon departed with his circus.

The end of the road for Big Diamond

Hauser began to regret the arrangement almost immediately. To begin with, he had to reassign four or five men from other work to remove Big Diamond's hide; then, part way through the proceedings, it became necessary to turn the animal over—fortunately Hauser had just the thing to do it, a huge, gasoline-powered Link Belt shovel, but he had to move the ponderous machine a mile and a half down the road to lift the remains. It took three days for the men and the Link Belt to finish the job.

Now at last Big Diamond could be buried. The Link Belt dug a grave for him near where he'd fallen at Valley Green, a short distance north on the highway from Davison Road. The elephant's ample skin was rolled into a huge ball, lifted by the Link Belt onto one of Hauser's trucks, and transported to the Butler Freight Warehouse in Eureka. Hauser had meanwhile contacted a tannery in the Bay Area regarding purchase of the hide.

A number of days passed. There was no word from the tannery; the hide in the Butler warehouse began to ripen. Butler, beset by putrefying pachyderm fumes, contacted Hauser. By coincidence, the contractor had just heard from the tannery. The leather company had no use for an elephant hide and knew of no one who did; back to Orick went the skin of Big Diamond.

Out again came the lumbering Link Belt, loading the hide onto one of Hauser's trucks. The vehicle carried it down to a Redwood Creek sandbar in back of Orick; the ubiquitous Link Belt again made an appearance, a hole was dug for the hide, and, while Hauser added another debit to his books, the last remaining remains of Big Diamond were laid to rest.

It would be story enough—and travail enough for Big Diamond—were the tale to end here. The partitioned pachyderm at last had both his parts buried, but neither piece was to remain in place, and so the sad saga continues.

A few years later, two workers were hauling gravel from the bed of Redwood Creek. After a time they had dug themselves quite a pit, and, while busy within it, began to notice a remarkable odor. Day after day they dug farther into the bank and each day the smell increased. Finally, nearly overcome by the stench, they exposed a thick, many-layered object. Both men had been in the area when Big Diamond died, and they quickly recalled the burial of the animal's huge hide. Even more quickly they covered over their excavation and exited for a less historic work site.

More years passed, and the memory of Big Diamond lapsed into obscurity. It then happened that the area across from Valley Green was being prepared for a housing development. One day a work crew, digging for a foundation, uncovered some huge bones. A couple of college students were among the workers, and when they saw what looked liked the skeleton of a prehistoric mastodon or mammoth, they quickly notified one of their professors, a paleontologist at UC Berkeley. The excited academic sped northward by train that very night and was soon at the site to inspect the find. He gathered up the bones and had them shipped back to Berkeley for further study.

News of the professor's visit spread to Orick. It wasn't long before someone recalled Big Diamond's death and realized that the remains of an eight-ton elephant might be mistaken for those of a more ancient animal. The puzzled paleontologist was promptly notified that his "prehistoric" skeleton was approximately 20 years old.

What finally became of Big Diamond's bones has not been re-corded, but the incident immortalized the animal in the lore of the region. After all, it isn't everyday that a dead elephant can buffalo one of the best brains in Berkeley.[1]

A short distance beyond the Big Diamond marker, the highway passes the site of a mill that once belonged to the Geneva Lumber Company. Its construction proved to be an early-day exercise in recycling: most of the steel used for the building was war surplus plating purchased from a Eureka company that made dry docks; inside the structure, several pieces of milling equipment had an even longer history.

The "Ghost Mill" Moves up the Coast

About 1900, Neff Anderson and his two partners had big plans for the northern Mendocino woods. On a bluff above the South Fork Eel River they would erect a magnificent logging mill, utiliz-ing the finest equipment available, and begin sawing the high-qual-ity timber that grew nearby. Anderson duly bought 12,000 acres of prime forestland, a swath that stretched from the South Fork to the Pacific. An order went out to the East Coast, where a windjammer was loaded with locomotives, rails, boilers, and sawmill machin-ery. With the Panama Canal yet to be built, the vessel had to travel "around the Horn" on its way to the tiny Mendocino town of Bear Harbor. The "harbor" was extremely shallow, so the ship stood off-shore while all the equipment was transported through the air on cables. The rails were unloaded first and placed on an already pre-pared railbed; soon the shiny new locomotive was pulling the rest of the cargo over the newly christened "Bear Harbor and Eel River Railroad" to the mill site beside the South Fork. The operation there had appropriately been named "Andersonia."

At last the day for the mill's opening arrived. As the assembled onlookers watched, a beaming Neff Anderson raised his arm, giv-ing the signal to start the first log on its way to the mill platform. A moment later, as the log swung upward, a cable snapped and the log fell on Anderson, hitting him on the head.

The mill owner never knew what happened. He was carried away, unconscious, to die nine days later.

The Andersonia Lumber Company was finished before it started. With its assets tied up by litigation, the would-be workers moved away and the railroad stopped operating. The buildings quickly decayed in the damp climate, while beneath their rotting boards the mill machinery waited its first call to run.

The Andersonia Ghost Mill in 1921

For years one of the locomotives stood stranded high in the coastal mountains at the disintegrating town of Moody; finally it was moved to a display at Fort Humboldt in Eureka. In 1921 the mill machinery was relocated to another site. By then the South Fork Eel had undermined part of the old building and the head sawing rig had to be rescued from the river.

In 1946 the equipment made another migration. The head rig, edger, and resaw were moved to the Geneva Mill near Orick, more than a hundred miles north of their original location. When the saws finally started whirring, the spirit of Neff Anderson probably rested a little easier. His "Ghost Mill" was back in business.

The Hammond Lumber Company took over the Geneva Mill in 1954. With the mill came the cutting rights to nearly 300 million board feet of timber in the Lost Man Creek area to the east. Years later, hundreds of acres of prime redwoods were cut there by

Hammond's successor, Georgia-Pacific. The mill itself didn't last as long; in 1959 it was dismantled and parts of it used to build houses for the employees of the site's new owner, the Arcata Redwood Company.

Opposite the old mill site is the turnoff to **Lost Man Creek**, mile 6.6, right. Approximately one mile east on an RNP gravel road are a parking lot, picnic area, restrooms, and trailhead for the **Lost Man Creek Trail** (see p. 239) and the **Holter Ridge Bicycle Trail** (see p. 279). The lovely grove of redwoods near the trail's start was the location of the park's dedication as a World Heritage Site.

Continuing north, Highway 101 crosses the Lost Man Creek Bridge and then passes the now-closed **Prairie Creek Fish Hatchery**, mile 6.9, right, whose barn-red buildings once housed a county-operated salmon rearing facility.

The route then twists through a narrow section of the canyon; the roadside here is colored by the blue tint of Bolander's phacelia in June and the rosy hue of vine maples in fall. At mile 8.3 the tour ends at the overpass for the **Newton B. Drury Scenic Parkway** (see p. 137); an offramp just south of the overpass provides access to the parkway, which runs through the heart of Prairie Creek Redwoods State Park. Highway 101 continues straight ahead as the four-lane **Park Bypass** (see p. 152), and will reconnect with the parkway some 11 miles to the north.

Side Trip:
The Bald Hills

This scenic side trip on Bald Hills Road runs 19 miles from Highway 101 to the southeastern boundary of Redwood National Park; the road is two lanes the entire distance, paved at first and then turning to gravel. It is easily drivable by passenger car but has one very steep grade, several sections of "washboard" roadbed, is dusty in summer, and can receive snow at higher elevations in winter. *Note: the route is not recommended for trailers.*

Features: (for key to symbols, see p. 89)

    🐦⊗🏠 side road to Redwood Creek Trail (mile 0.4)

    🐦⊗🏠 Lady Bird Johnson Grove Nature Loop Trail (2.7)

    🐦🚲 Holter Ridge Bike Trail (6.3)

    ⊗🏠👀 Redwood Creek Overlook (6.7)

    🚗🐦🐴 Tall Trees Access Road (7.1)

    🐴 access to Sherman Lyons Barn (9.6)

    🐦⊗🏠🐴 side road to Dolason Prairie Trail (11.4)

    🐦🐴 side road to Lyons Ranch Historic Site (17.0)

    🐦🐴 access to Long Ridge Barn (17.7)

    🐦👀 access to Schoolhouse Peak Fire Lookout (18.0)

    🐦 access to Coyote Peak (18.7)

    🚗 park boundary; end of side trip (19.0)

Ridge above the Redwoods

Southeast of Orick a rolling ridgeline rises above the conifer-filled canyon of Redwood Creek, bursting out into a series of sloping prairies and oak woodlands—the Bald Hills—a mid-elevation

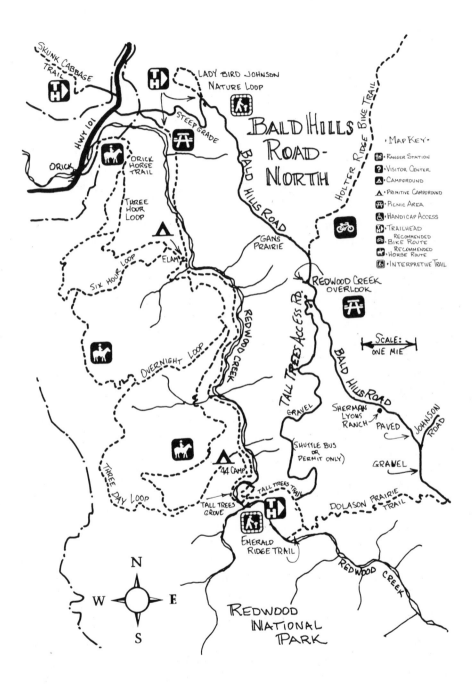

environment of high winds and hot sun that has offered both peril and promise. For centuries the land was occupied by the native Chilulas, but white ranchers and packers encroached on the area in the early 1850s, starting a series of conflicts that lasted more than a decade. Eventually, almost all the surviving Indians relocated to the Hoopa reservation, and the region's great, grassland-grazing herds of elk were replaced by flocks of prize winning sheep. Loggers came later, crisscrossing the hillsides with their skidroads as they removed the thick forests of the lower slopes. Today, the land constitutes the southeastern portion of Redwood National Park, providing visitors with a prairie and oak woodland experience not found closer to the coast.

A half mile north of Orick, the incorrectly signed "Bald Hill Road" (oldtimers, mapmakers, and RNP staff insist that the "Hill" should be plural) heads east from Highway 101. The two-lane, paved route immediately crosses Prairie Creek and then passes, mile 0.3, left, the region's only remaining lumbering operation, the Arcata Redwood Company's "A" mill. Ahead at mile 0.4, right, a paved access road leads a half mile to the **Redwood Creek Trail** (see p. 265), the **Tall Trees Shuttle Bus** pick-up stop, and a small picnic area; the road ends at the old mill site of the Orick Lumber Company, a bustling operation of the 1940s and 1950s. In addition to a tall smokestack, the mill featured a boiler salvaged from the steam schooner *Yellowstone*, which had wrecked in 1933 while trying to enter Humboldt Bay.

The main road presently ascends the thickly forested hillside, passing a vegetation-obscured roadway at mile 0.9, left; this remnant of the original Orick to Martin's Ferry route attained an intense 23 percent incline as it climbed the "four-mile mountain" to reach the ridgecrest. Construction of the current road in the 1950s ameliorated the abrupt ascent, thereby accommodating the rapidly increasing log truck traffic. The present route passes another abandoned track, 1.8 miles, left, that also connects with the older road.

Lady Bird Johnson Grove

Bald Hills Road continues its rapid rise up the mountainside; it then runs under a handsome wooden footbridge and reaches the turnoff, right, for the **Lady Bird Johnson Grove** parking lot, mile

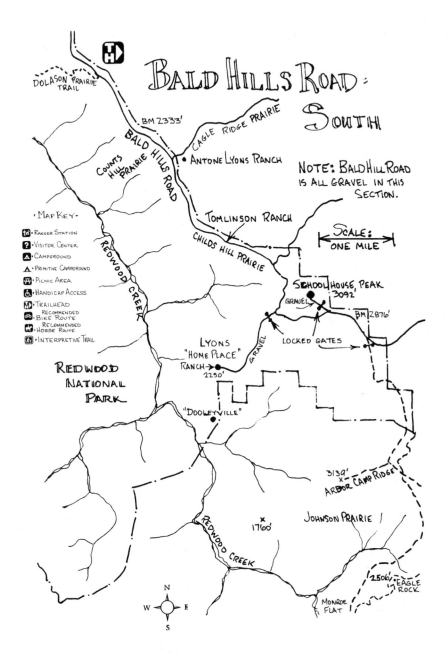

2.7. From here the **Lady Bird Johnson Grove Nature Loop Trail** (see p. 238) leads through a striking stand of hilltop redwoods; there are picnic tables and restrooms at the parking area.

At mile 2.9 is a section of ridgeline once known as "Pine Point." Massive, moss-covered Douglas-firs mark the spot, as they did when the locale received its misleading name. Early lumbermen often called these trees "Oregon pine," hoping to cash in on the pine's superior reputation as saw wood. Old-time Orickians came here by wagon to harvest the pseudonymous pines, hauling them down the great hill to a valley sawmill. They were decades ahead of other loggers, for it wasn't until the late 1940s that Douglas-fir, at last called by its rightful name, was heavily cut in California.

Gans Prairie

The road then runs through a mature mixed forest that in spring is colored by rhododendron, leopard lily, and crimson columbine. **Gans Prairie**, mile 4.9, appears downslope to the right. Yuroks from the village of Oreq-ʷ would conclude their white deerskin dance here, having danced their way up from the coast; they called the prairie Megwil Olegel—"where the elk play or dance." The Jedediah Smith party camped on the grassland in 1828, and settlers later used the location to graze sheep, raise oats and hay, and quarry rock. Over time, advancing conifers have constricted the prairie, reducing it to a fraction of its former size.

On the left at mile 6.3 is the **Holter Ridge Bike Trail** (see p. 279). The cycling route follows a hilltop logging road northward for seven miles through dense, shadowy second growth before dropping four additional miles through the increasingly attractive drainage of Lost Man Creek.

Bald Hills Road continues southeast, passing a wall of adolescent conifers, left, that marks the rim of the heavily logged Tectah Creek drainage. The **Redwood Creek Overlook**, 6.7 miles, right, provides picnic tables, a restroom, and a panoramic view of the creek canyon. The nearby hillside contains a 9,000–acre collection of old-growth redwoods, one of the largest such stands remaining.

One-lane, gravel **Tall Trees Access Road**, mile 7.1, right, follows the Arcata Redwood Company's former C-Line logging road some six miles downhill to the **Tall Trees Loop Trail** (see p. 250), a steep sloped route that not only leads to the world's tallest redwood, but also offers connections with the Redwood Creek Trail, the **Emerald Ridge Trail,** and the Dolason Prairie Trail. The access road can be travelled in summer by shuttle bus and year round by private vehicles with a permit from the Redwood Information Center south of Orick (see p. 275). A century before logging trucks first climbed the C-Line, pack mules plodded their way out of the Redwood Creek canyon on a nearby pathway.

The White Deerskin Dance

The Trinidad Trail

Established in 1850, the Trinidad Trail served as the main supply line from the coast to the Klamath gold diggings. Today the route it followed would be a hiker's dream, since it crossed a scenic creek canyon and passed a stand of magnificent redwoods; a hundred and forty years ago, however, the passage seemed like a nightmare, for the miners and mule packers who travelled it were more concerned with merely surviving the hillslopes than surveying the scenery.

John Carr was an early traverser of the trail, making the trip in 1851. After leaving the supply port of Trinidad, Carr made his way northward up the coast to Big Lagoon, where he camped on the beach. He did not have a pleasant night: "It was like lying on a bed of boulders. I could not endure my sand bed, and had to take a pick and shovel and excavate a place large enough in the side of the mountain to lay on."

Having thus had an early opportunity to practice his mining technique, Carr proceeded onto the "mountain" part of the trail, first ascending the ridge east of the lagoon, next dropping to the crossing on Redwood Creek, and then rising to the Bald Hills; a final descent to the Klamath brought him to Martin's Ferry, where

Mountainside
mule mishap

he picked up the river route that would take him upstream to the mines. It was on one of the more precipitous sections of trail that he observed an early-day traffic accident when one pack mule pushed another over the cliff. The victim

> ...did some lofty rolling and tumbling down that mountain. Sometimes his legs would be up, and sometimes the part of the pack that was on him would have the upper side. Such a scattering of plunder I never saw before. We all sat down on the bank, and there were some "tall cuss words used."[1]

The strong language proved unnecessary, for the mule was later found down the mountainside "eating grass as if nothing had happened...[the] pack saddle under his belly with part of the things still tied to it."

Despite its ruggedness, the route had its rewards, for when Carr and his companions at last reached the Bald Hills, they

> ...beheld a great sight. The prairie seemed a large one: scattered all over it were big oak trees, giving it the appearance of an old orchard in the eastern states, and, grazing quietly, were hundreds of elk, that seemed to take no more notice of us than so many tame cattle grazing in their pasture at home.[2]

In time, shorter routes were opened to the mines, and the Trinidad Trail fell into disuse; logging later obliterated much of the trailbed. A century after its heyday, however, part of the route returned to prominence when it was crisscrossed by the path to the new national park's Tall Trees Grove. Hikers now walked a tamer trail than had John Carr and his cronies; with the scenery no longer enlivened by somersaulting mules, observers had to content themselves with a more stationary sight—merely the tallest trees found anywhere on earth.

Sherman Lyons Ranch

Second-growth conifers continue to line the roadsides until mile 9.0, where a prairie opens downslope to the right. A verge of trees hides the **Lane House**, 9.6 miles, right, a building of recent vintage that is now a park ranger's residence. Nearby is a prairieside picnic area and beyond it the low form of the **Sherman Lyons Barn**, an aged structure that reposes beside a scattering of oaks. In times past

Sherman Lyons Barn

the property belonged to the pioneer Lyons family, once the region's premier sheep raisers.

A pair of metal gates, mile 10.0, right and left, marks the one-time crossing of the **K and K Road**. Formerly a sort of superhighway for huge logging trucks, the route connected Simpson Timber Company lands on the Klamath River (K#1) with the company mill at Korbel (K#2). A large segment of the road, running downhill to the right, was claimed by the 1978 Redwood National Park acquisition and is now being removed as part of the park's rehabilitation program.

The **Elk Camp Fire Station**, mile 10.1, left, is a summer outpost of the California Division of Forestry. In the 1850s another operation occupied the approximate area; it, too, was meant to provide protection, but in so doing relied on firearms instead of fire trucks.

Campaigning at Elk Camp

For the miners and packers heading inland along the Trinidad Trail, both the Redwood Creek canyon and the Bald Hills were difficult stretches of terrain—obstacles on their way to the Klamath and Salmon River mines. For the Chilula Indians, however, the prairies and forested hillsides were home, and the Chilulas chafed at the procession of outsiders that paraded through their territory. Worse yet, some of the whites chose to stay in the area, setting up small ridgeline ranches in places where the tribe had traditionally hunted and gathered its food.

There was trouble as early as 1851, when whites had been in the area for barely a year. Soon some of the newcomers constructed a blockhouse near where the trail up from Redwood Creek reached the ridgetop; here packers could wait with their mule trains until enough men had gathered to provide mutual protection for the next stage of the trip—the traverse of the Bald Hills, "where grass and water were abundant but Indians numerous and hostile." The blockhouse builders were motivated by more than a predilection for public safety; their intent was to sell meals and whiskey to the packers who sought the structure's protection.

With the blockhouse as its focus, the Elk Camp area became an outpost of white civilization during the following decade. By 1860, at least ten small ranches dotted the region, and the camp even boasted its own post office.

Meanwhile, relations between the whites and Chilulas worsened. When members of the tribe attended a peace talk in 1859, they were treacherously taken prisoner by white troops and sent to the Mendocino Reservation at Fort Bragg; the captured Chilulas later escaped, but almost all of them were killed by Lassik Indians as they attempted to make their way home. The incident only strengthened the resolve of the remaining Chilulas, who were determined to drive all the whites from the Bald Hills.

In the summer of 1862 the conflict came to a head. A Lieutenant Anderson was posted at Elk Camp with a detachment of 12 soldiers to combat the Chilulas. On June 17 a rancher named Miller arrived at the camp "in a devil of a hurry," and asked the men to capture an Indian who was asleep in his house. This the soldiers accomplished, but the prisoner subsequently escaped. No further incidents were reported until the end of July, when the Chilulas raided a ranch in the middle part of the Redwood Creek drainage. Then, two days later, a band of some 40 warriors attacked Miller's house, killing his Indian wife and their baby. The rancher, although wounded in the thigh, managed to escape to Elk Camp with his older son; along with other nearby ranchers, the pair was evacuated to Trinidad. The Indians burned Miller's house, shot his horse, and destroyed everything on the property; they also razed another dwelling in the area. In August the Chilulas swept west to burn the ranch at Redwood Camp, which sat atop the hill east of Big Lagoon and was the first stopping place on the Trinidad Trail. The following year the Redwood Camp rancher, Thomas McDonald, indicated to the county assessor that his property was *"in hostile Indian country and the owner says he cannot swear to any value."*

If the whites felt aggrieved by these attacks on their ranches, they took little notice of the effect their own actions were having on the Chilulas. In scarcely more than a decade, a progression of settlers, packers, and soldiers had first disrupted and then nearly destroyed an indigenous people who had occupied the land for centuries. The Chilulas, like so many other tribes, found themselves overrun by a white juggernaut busily manifesting its destiny.

Decimated as they were, the Chilulas nevertheless managed to regain control of their home territory. A raid in early 1863 destroyed the only house on Redwood Creek that had escaped their previous attacks, and later that year the tribe was linked with raids on the mill at Trinidad, a homestead at the mouth of Little River, and a ranch near Arcata; the Chilulas were bringing the battle of the Bald Hills all the way to the coast.

Before the end of the year, the closely related Hupas joined the Chilulas in the conflict, and other neighboring tribes became involved as well. Military authorities grew desperate; in April 1864, Colonel H. M. Black, the district commander, issued the incredible order that "all Indian men taken in battle shall be hung at once; the women and children to be humanely treated." Despite such drastic measures, some 75 armed warriors remained active the following summer. The soldiers pursued them relentlessly, but four small bands, including a Chilula group led by Curly-headed Tom, sought refuge in the caves of the New River area in Trinity County.

Curly-headed Tom had sworn he would never surrender, and he was able to keep his word, for the whites finally had enough of the fight. On August 21, 1864, the United States government concluded a treaty with the Indians that established the Hoopa Valley as a reservation for the Hupas, Chilulas, and related tribes. Along with their Hupa allies, Tom and 14 other "lonely survivors" from Redwood Creek at last laid down their arms, compromised, perhaps, but undefeated.

While the treaty was a victory of sorts for the Chilulas, it also doomed them as a separate tribe, for they now had to vacate their

> Bald Hills and Redwood Creek home country and move down to the valley of their Hupa kin. Soon, only a single Chilula family was left in the tribe's old territory, and a new wave of white ranchers swept onto the vacant land.
>
> Following the treaty, Elk Camp's blockhouse was no longer needed, and, as shorter trails were cut to the Klamath, the site dwindled further in importance. Even the camp's namesake elk, which once roamed the area by the "thousands," were at last seen no more; like the Chilulas, they had all been killed or driven off. The great oaks and grassy hillslopes remained, but Elk Camp, after its brief brush with prominence, became but another place of the past.

Just beyond the fire station is **Johnson Road**, left; the one-lane, gravel route runs northward, eventually descending to the Klamath River opposite the hamlet of Johnson. Along the way, **Hancorne Road** leads to the isolated homestead of the Hancorne family. At the turn of the century, the Hancorne children would walk a mile and a half down to the Klamath, cross the wide waterway by canoe, and then tramp another five or six miles to the Klamath school. It was good practice for Henry Hancorne, who would in later life hike 22 miles to the dances at Orick, where he'd then fox trot the night away on a pair of well-worn feet.

East of the Johnson Road junction, the surface of Bald Hills Road intermittently turns to gravel, a condition that farther on becomes permanent. The amount of dust that vehicles create in dry weather is proportionate to their speed.

Dolason Prairie descends to the right at 11.2 miles. In a stand of second growth, mile 11.4, right, an almost-hidden park road runs a hundred feet to a parking lot, picnic tables, and restroom at the beginning of the **Dolason Prairie Trail** (see p. 256). The path drops through grasslands into redwood forest, passing the picturesque **Dolason Barn** along the way; the structure's strange saltbox shape resulted from the partial removal of its east and south sides. At the trail's far end, connecting routes lead to Redwood Creek and the Tall Trees parking area. The prairie and the barn were named for James Donaldson, who ranched there in the 1860s; a later landowner inconsiderately corrupted the spelling.

Dolason
Prairie Barn

Counts Hill Prairie opens to the right at mile 12.2. Adjacent to the road is a nearly level stretch of grassland that once served as the **Bald Hills Airport**. The site was graded in 1947 by G. L. Speier, who was cutting timber in the area. For years Pierce Flying Service used the runway to bring in replacement parts for logging equipment. If workers were injured in the nearby woods, they would be lashed to metal baskets, trucked to the landing strip, and then flown to a hospital in Eureka.

Left at mile 13.4 is a private dirt road that leads to another one-time Lyons family ranch. A short distance beyond this turnoff, Bald Hills Road provides a sweeping view of the ridgetop prairieland, culminating with lookout-topped Schoolhouse Peak. The route then enters **Childs Hill Prairie**, mile 13.8, passing over sloping property once steeped in controversy.

What William Left to Willie

In the 1850s, William Childs, a young tailor from Maine, set himself up in the port town of Trinidad. He soon purchased some real estate and established a relationship with a Yurok woman who became known as Willie.

Childs was but one of many white males who lived with Indian "wives" during the early settlement days. The 1870 census found this arrangement among 15 of 17 couples in the Bald Hills-Martin's

Ferry area, while even in Trinidad, where white females were more plentiful, nine of thirty-five households were racially mixed. Of all the Indian-white couples, only three could claim marriage certificates recorded by the county clerk; the Childses were not among them.

William Childs seemed to have a knack for obtaining what he wanted; soon he'd set up a general merchandise business and acquired more property, much of it in the Bald Hills. He successfully sought public office, first becoming a road overseer, then county supervisor, and finally postmaster. Meanwhile, a son was born to William and Willie; named William Jr., he was called Billy.

Regardless of the informality of their relationship, the Childses lived together for more than 30 years as man and wife. Then, middle aged and successful, William Childs left Willie and Billy and returned east, settling in Massachusetts.

Childs then did three things that would affect his family back on the West Coast. First, he married another woman; he next arranged to have a representative pay Willie $1,000 in exchange for her agreeing to relinquish all claims to his estate; and, after this was accomplished, he sold $18,000 worth of Humboldt County property to a friend, who then transferred its title to Childs's new wife, Christina.

In November 1896, William Childs died. As a result of his earlier transactions, his eastern widow, Christina, now held the old Hopkins Ranch in the Bald Hills. Next to it was land his western son, Billy, had bought in 1883.

Perhaps Childs had thought his careful manipulations would successfully settle his estate, but if so, he'd misjudged Willie. In March of 1901 she took the property issue to court, claiming that half of the $18,000 land holdings were due her as Childs's wife. Attorneys for Christina countered that Willie lost any right to such a claim when she accepted the thousand dollars; Willie's lawyers argued that she hadn't understood the agreement. It took a week of hearings and deliberations before the jury reached a verdict.

The jurors, who in those times were of course all white males, decided that William and Willie Childs had not been married, nor had they "assumed towards each other mutual marital rights." Further, they determined that Willie Childs received a financial consideration from William and had been informed that by taking the money she gave up any claim to the property. The jury also agreed, however, that Willie did not understand the nature of the transaction when it was explained to her; despite this, the jurors found in favor of the white wife, Christina, leaving, as the headline put it, "NO MONEY FOR INDIAN WILLIE."

Even from beyond the grave, William Childs again got what he wanted. Willie, a victim of the white "justice" of the times, was left with little; only a few years later she would be found, nearly helpless, searching for food along the Trinidad beach.

Nothing more is known about the end of Willie Childs's life; after her time in the headlines, she quickly faded into the obscurity then common to most of her people. But her story, like those of all the other victimized Indians, begs for a more complete ending. The closest we can come to providing it, possibly, is through a picture of another Yurok woman, Willie's daughter-in-law, Jane.[3]

Jane Childs, with
baskets and headdress

The picture shows Jane in a Trinidad store. She stands next to a table filled with Indian baskets, while on the counter behind her rests a feathered headdress—fragments of her tribe's heritage, offered as mementos to wealthy white collectors. The objects sit close to some bolts of cloth and other goods, but they are no more a part of their surroundings than is Jane; in her long, dark dress she appears to be a presence from another world, an ancient sadness shadowing her youthful, solemn face. Her eyes stare past us, focused, it seems, on some place far beyond the confines of the store—a place untouched by the ways of William Childs and the other whites; a place, perhaps, of peace for her mother-in-law, Willie; a place that could still be found, even then, at the distant edge of memory.

Tomlinson Ranch

Bald Hills Road continues through the once-litigated grassland, at mile 14.6 passing a private dirt road, left, that leads to the old **Tomlinson Ranch**. For over 40 years the Tomlinson family ran sheep on the rolling ridgetop prairie, creating a wide-ranging operation that at times featured a sawmill, post office, library, school, and stage stop. The 18-room ranch house, built in 1919 and still standing, accommodated both the family and travellers; meals for the current day's contingent were prepared on a ten-foot-long wood stove that could cook 25 hotcakes at a time. The stove also served on laundry day to boil the sheets, all 50 of which then had to be scrubbed by hand. Freight wagons with goods bound for Orleans stopped overnight at the ranch, having travelled 18 difficult miles from Orick; the next day the drivers, fortified by Tomlinson hotcakes, would continue seven miles to French Camp, where they would meet the wagons from Orleans and exchange loads.

Lyons Ranch

The route runs east towards looming Schoolhouse Peak, passing a dirt road, mile 16.1, left, that leads out onto Williams Ridge; the house of rancher Williams was one of two burned by the Chilulas in July of 1862. Another side road at mile 16.4, left, heads toward Skookum Prairie; near the turnoff was one of several Bald Hills schools. The main road then turns south and climbs across the side of the peak, passing through a woodland of Oregon white oak. In spring the hillside brightens with giant trillium, coast delphinium, flowering currant, and white baby blue eyes, while fall brings the white fruit of snowberry. At mile 17.0 the route reaches a junction, right, where a short access road leads to the parking area for the **Lyons Ranch Historic Site**. Beyond a locked gate hikers can follow

Lyons Road (see p. 247) to the "Home Place," the earliest of the family's ranches in the Bald Hills.

The Lyonses and Their Lambs

By the late 1860s, Jonathan Lyons had travelled far and wide in a futile search for success. He'd left his Indiana home in 1850, an asthmatic 18 year old who led a party of emigrants to the Willamette Valley in Oregon Territory. Soon he reached the Salmon River gold diggings in Northern California, where he mined, freighted, and ran a travelling butcher business—"a mule was his market, with a carcass of beef slung on each side." Next Lyons relocated to Hoopa; there he acquired a ranch and took up with Amelia Misket, a local Hupa woman who would later become his wife. After the troubles between the whites and Chilulas subsided, Lyons and his family relocated to an abandoned homestead on Redwood Creek; here Jonathan tried his hand at horse ranching. He lost heavily, switched to cattle, but had little better luck. Finally, he moved down the canyon and up the hillside onto a lovely, grass-covered ridgepoint, where, running out of options, he took up sheep ranching.

It proved to be the right choice, for during the 1870s Northern California wool prices skyrocketed. While their value increased, Jonathan's flocks contentedly gobbled the grasses of the Bald Hills, unaware that they occupied some of the country's prime sheep habitat; soon Lyons was busy buying up land to expand the family business. His success was confirmed in 1900 when he received an astounding message from France—his wool had been awarded a gold medal at the Exposition Universelle de Paris.

By 1905 the Lyonses had a series of large ranches strung out along the Bald Hills—Jonathan and Amelia's "Home Place," and the properties of their sons Sherman, William, and Antonio. That same year all four locations were linked by the "ten-mile telephone," which stretched across the prairies as the family's private line.

Still, for all their affluence, the Lyonses had their difficulties. The Home Place burned down on three different occasions, and a windstorm dropped a huge redwood onto the house of a fourth son, Anderson. Predators posed another problem, often killing stock. Once Antonio had his coat consumed by a pair of panthers that couldn't find any sheep to eat, and even as late as the 1950s the family could report killing 19 bears in 19 days. Weather also rendered the remote ranches vulnerable: an epic storm in 1890 dropped *fourteen* feet of snow at Elk Camp and devastated the sheep flocks; in 1950 another heavy snow left the Lyonses and two other families without food for two weeks until supplies were air dropped to them.

Through it all the family continued to raise their sheep. Gene Lyons followed his grandfather, Jonathan, by winning a first prize at the California Wool Growers' show in 1925. Impressed

Sheep shearing

by the ranch's reputation, buyers came from as far away as Portland and Los Angeles, purchasing up to 2,000 sheep at a time. To cut the wool, the Lyonses bought an electric shearing machine and portable power plant that they moved from flock to flock; local Indians were often hired to do the shearing. One ranch hand, Henry Steinberg, trained a McNab sheep dog to open and close the ranch gates while it was herding. Bud, a collie belonging to Hattie Lyons Decker, went one better—he would go to the pasture and return with Hattie's white horse, Lottie, while riding on its back.

Gradually the Lyonses sold off their land and left the Bald Hills. Antonio was the last of Jonathan's sons to leave, moving away in 1927; always known as a "ladies' man," as a widower he remarried at age 80. Antonio's son Gene continued the ranching operation until he finally departed from the Home Place in the 1960s.

Today, most of the Lyons land is part of Redwood National Park. None of the family's ill-fated houses remain, although several of the ranch barns and shepherds' cabins still dot the peaceful hillsides. In the aging barn at the Home Place, the lambing pens have long stood silent, and it has been decades since the ring of the ten-mile telephone was last heard. Now there is only the sound of the afternoon breeze, rustling the grass as it moves across the empty ridgeslope. The family that lived here for nearly a century has vanished as completely as their prize-winning flocks, and there is little left to recall the Lyonses...or their lambs.

Downslope from the Home Place is **Dooleyville**, which consists of a collapsed barn, a lovely prairie, and a weathered cabin that dates from the 1920s. A grass-covered track descends from Lyons Road to reach the site; the route approximates part of an early trail from the Trinidad area. *Note: Hikers should check with park officials before attempting the obscure and difficult Dooleyville route.*

Coyote Creek and Coyote Peak

Bald Hills Road then turns east, moving into the Coyote Creek drainage through picturesquely sloping, oak-dappled prairieland. Unmarked **High Prairie Road**, mile 17.7, right, descends past a locked gate to the **Long Ridge Barn**, another relic of the Lyons Ranch. From the barn, a left turn on unmarked Ranch Road leads to a later Lyons structure, the **Coyote Barn**, located just west of dark **Coyote Rock**. In early summer the roadsides offer a profusion of

Rush hour at the Long Ridge Barn—
1,630 sheep plodding through the snow

Bald Hills Road, climbing Coyote Ridge

photogenic plants that includes Ithuriel's spear, woolly sunflower, blue-headed gilia, California Indian pink, and firecracker flower.

Lookout Road, mile 18.0, left, leads past another locked gate to the **Schoolhouse Peak Fire Lookout**; the route offers an invigorating half-mile climb to the hilltop viewpoint. On clear days, a full-circle panorama presents itself, encompassing the Redwood Creek drainage to the south, the Bald Hills ridgeline to the west, Williams Ridge and the distant Siskiyou Mountains to the north, the Marble Mountains to the northeast, and the Trinity Mountains and Coyote Peak to the southeast.

The main route continues east, climbing towards the Coyote Peak ridgeline. At mile 18.7 are two side roads: left leads immediately to a rock quarry; right is unmarked and gated **Coyote Peak Road**, a prairieside route that runs above a Lyons line shack and then passes around its namesake hilltop. Bald Hills Road continues uphill to mile 19.0, where it leaves Redwood National Park.

The route east of the park boundary forks in approximately two miles: French Camp Road, right, connects with the Hoopa Valley, while Bald Hills Road, left, continues to Martin's Ferry, on the Klamath River. Motorists may connect back to the coast from either destination via highways 96 and 299.

Side Trip:
The Gold Bluffs

Providing access to the coastal section of Prairie Creek Redwoods State Park, this side trip runs 7.1 miles from Highway 101 to the Fern Canyon parking area, first on Davison Road and then on Gold Bluffs Beach Road. After a short stretch of pavement, the rest of the road is one- and two-lane gravel, dusty in dry weather. State park use fees are collected midway along the route. *Note: vehicles more than eight feet wide and twenty-four feet long are prohibited.*

(for map, see p. 138)

Features: (for key to symbols, see p. 89)

🚂 Davison Ranch (0.2 miles)

🏕🚲 Jogging Trail/Bicycle Loop (2.0)

🏕 access to Gold Bluffs Environmental Camp (3.2)

🚐 🏠 Gold Bluffs Entrance Station, Prairie Creek Redwoods State Park; begin Gold Bluffs Beach Road (3.7)

🏕🚂📷 Espa Lagoon, trail to overlook (3.8)

🏕⛵🚂🌊 Skunk Cabbage Section, Coastal Trail (3.9)

⛵🚫🏠🌊 Gold Bluffs Beach Picnic Area (5.2)

⛵🏕🏠🌊 Gold Bluffs Beach Campground (5.7)

🏕🏕🚂 Miner's Ridge Trail; access to Gold Bluffs Beach Hike and Bike Camp (5.8)

🏕🚲⛵🚫🏠🚂🌊 Coastal Trail/Bicycle Loop, James Irvine Trail, Fern Canyon Trail, picnic area; end of route (7.1)

Davison Ranch

Two-lane, paved Davison Road branches left from Highway 101 at Rolf's Park Cafe. The route immediately passes through a patch

128

of prairie that often serves as elk pasture; it then crosses Prairie Creek, mile 0.2, and comes to a turnoff, right, to the former Davison Ranch. Recently acquired by RNP, the site is being developed to house various park facilities. The ranch began with land homesteaded by Arthur Davison in 1889; soon the family dairying operation was supplemented by a stopping place for travellers. Bert Reed's big Speedwell auto stage, which motored along the county road past the ranch, was so "immensely popular" that it was often "insufficient to carry all the passengers who wish[ed] to travel." In 1915, the Davisons' "inn" featured "deer and bear hunting; fine trout fishing in Prairie Creek; deep in the redwood forest."

Ahead on the left is a pair of roads that lead to the site of the Arcata Redwood Company's "B" Mill. Little remains to mark the location except for a large paved area and a rusting piece of log-moving equipment. A third turnoff, right, leads onto private land.

Davison Road now turns to gravel and starts uphill. *Note: motorists are advised to turn on their lights.* The road was constructed in 1902 by Frank Hufford, who utilized a crew of 15 workers, equipped with picks and shovels, and an early-day type of horse-drawn road grader called a "Fresno scraper." A succession of interesting individuals later lived along the route, including "Peg Leg" Jackson, who would visit the store at Berry Glen and astonish the local youngsters by jabbing a jack knife into his wooden limb; during one performance the store owner's tiny granddaughter suddenly ran away, soon to return with a Band-Aid. Another notable was Jonathan Skein, who lived about half way to the beach. Skein worked alone, cutting and then splitting redwood for shingles and other products. To fell the trees unassisted, Skein constructed a spring attachment that held the far end of his crosscut saw in place; locals called the invention "Skein's partner."

Brush rabbit

After winding uphill through somber, second-growth forest, the road crests the grade at mile 1.4 and promptly begins a long descent; numerous leopard lilies color the surroundings in early summer. The route levels briefly, mile 2.0, as the **Jogging Trail** departs to the right. The path follows an old roadbed through a stream canyon, and also forms part of the 20-mile **Prairie Creek Bike Loop Trail** (see p. 279). The bike route follows Davison Road northwestward as it rises out of the canyon.

Gold Bluffs Area

At another grade crest, mile 2.6, a side road branches left; this unused route runs about ¾ mile to the site of an old gold mining operation at the mouth of Major Creek. Davison Road then drops down switchbacks, reaching a damp, spruce-covered flat at mile 3.2. Just ahead on the right, a gated side road leads to the three-site **Gold Bluffs Environmental Camp**. The main road arrives at the **Gold Bluffs Entrance Station** to Prairie Creek Redwoods State Park, mile 3.7; day-use fees are charged to those who drive beyond this point. Here the route becomes Gold Bluffs Beach Road. To the right is a driveway that leads to a ranger's residence.

A pullout, mile 3.8, right, is for a pair of adjacent paths. The trail branching left winds uphill to an overlook of the ocean and beach; the route right leads to the edge of nearly hidden **Espa Lagoon**. At various times the versatile vicinity was occupied by a Yurok village, a mining operation, and a World War II beach patrol station.

The road then rounds a bend; ahead on the right stretch the fabled **Gold Bluffs**, a series of 200-foot-high cliffs composed of conglomerate rock that contains enough gold to have made mining it a sometimes-profitable activity. Starting in 1850, optimistic operators intermittently attempted to separate the precious metal from its accompanying minerals, but the area is now park property and mining is prohibited.

The unmarked northern end of the **Skunk Cabbage Section, Coastal Trail** begins at the locked gate for a beach access road, mile 3.9, left; the trail proceeds along the waveslope until it eventually climbs the bluffs south of Major Creek (see p. 261).

Now the route runs northward beneath the bluffs; to the right, the sound of the surf reverberates off the tall, tawny cliffs. West of

The Gold Bluffs

the road are rolling, driftwood-littered dunes and the long, sandy strand of Gold Bluffs Beach; the area lends itself to leisurely hiking, but venturing into the nearby ocean can be hazardous. Two swimmers discovered this in March, 1980, when they were suddenly swept out to sea.

Riptide Rescue

State Park Ranger Gary Strachan, responding to an emergency call at Gold Bluffs Beach, arrived to find a frightening sight: a strong riptide was running, with waves breaking six to seven feet high;

worse yet, bobbing in the water, far from shore, were the frantic forms of two men being pulled out to sea.

Strachan calculated that one man was about a hundred yards from the beach while the other was already more than 250 yards away. The water was a chilling 43° Fahrenheit, and if the pair was to be saved, there was no time to lose.

Disregarding his own safety, Strachan stripped to his underwear, plunged into the water, and headed for the more distant swimmer. After reaching the victim, the ranger struggled for several minutes but failed to bring the man closer to shore; Strachan then noticed that the second swimmer had reached safety on his own, and that a surfer was now heading out on his board to offer assistance. Almost immediately, however, the surfer was in difficulty himself. Strachan swam to the new victim and helped him cling to a floating crab pot. Taking the surfboard, the ranger returned to the swimmer. With great difficulty Strachan now managed to push the man ashore; then, nearly exhausted himself, the ranger went out and retrieved the surfer.

Against all odds, Strachan had managed to save both men. He realized that in 15 years of ocean swimming he had never come so close to death himself; as a park ranger, however, the incident was just part of his job.

Strachan was granted the Medal of Valor, the state's highest award, for his double rescue. It was a well-deserved tribute for a member of a profession that daily puts the welfare of the public—and the parks—before themselves.

Various wildflowers seasonally color the base and face of the roadside bluffs; they include Indian paintbrush, lupine, cow parsnip, and iris. At mile 4.4 a good view of the exposed cliff is enhanced by a sprinkling of seep-spring monkeyflowers. Four kinds of ferns cling to the bank: sword, five-finger, lady, and giant chain. A pullout, 5.2 miles, left, provides parking for the adjacent **Gold Bluffs Beach Picnic Area**.

The **Gold Bluffs Beach Campground** nestles in the dunes, mile 5.7, left. Its 25 sites feature metal, bear-proof food boxes and wind barriers constructed of driftwood. Ahead on the right, mile 5.8, the forest-clad **Miner's Ridge Trail** (see p. 258) initially follows the bed of an old Cal Barrel Company logging road. Near the route's start is the entrance to the **Gold Bluffs Beach Hike and Bike Camp**; the site occupies a shaded section of the bluff.

Immediately past the trail turnoff, Gold Bluffs Beach Road fords Squashan Creek. Just beyond the crossing is a gate with a sign that states "Open 9 A M—Sunset."

Fern Canyon

The road continues its course between the bluffs and beach; a picnic area, mile 6.9, lies just to the left. The route then ends in a stand of alders, 7.1 miles, that shades a turnaround, parking lot,

Foliage-filled
Fern Canyon

restrooms, and picnic area. Two trails head north across Home Creek: The route left is the continuation of the bicycle loop that now, as the **Coastal Trail**, is also a worthy hiking route. It leads along the bluffs, first to the hike and bike camp at Butler Creek and the **West Ridge Trail**, then on to a junction with the **Ossagon Trail** (see p. 249), and finally ends at Coastal Drive.

The right-hand path departing the parking area leads 50 yards to a fork: right is the picturesque **Fern Canyon Trail** (see p. 237); left is the **James Irvine Trail** (see p. 262), which connects with the Visitor Center at Elk Prairie. In a meadow just above Fern Canyon is the site of one of several blufftop mining camps.

Mining the Bluffs

In 1850, when the first whites travelled along the coast north of Trinidad, they noticed a glint to the ground at the base of the high, ocean-fronting bluffs. The glitter was indeed gold, fine grains of it, mixed with the gray and black sand of the beach. Information about the find filtered back to the south, with predictable results:

> Old hulks of steamers and sailers (sic) almost without number were at once advertised for Gold Bluff. Some hundreds were being landed at Trinidad. The vanguard rushed off pell-mell up the coast...eager to be first on the beach where the golden sands were "lying around loose" in uncounted millions.[1]

The scene at the bluffs, however, failed to equal expectations. The gold was bound so tightly to the sand that it had to be extracted with quicksilver-charged sluice boxes; further, the sand itself was only available when a wave crashed against the bluffs and dislodged a section of the bank, which tumbled to the ground below and then broke apart in the water. As a result, most of the newcomers "did not stop overnight if they arrived in time to start back."

A few of the more patient miners managed to achieve "moderate" success at the bluffs, but activity slackened until revived by a rise in gold prices during the Civil War. Several systematic operations started in the 1870s, all located near creek mouths; the mine buildings were situated safely above the ocean, atop the bluffs.

In those earlier times, the beach was much narrower than now, so that the waves washed against the bluffs at each high tide. The miners' activity revolved around this cycle: after the tide went out, the superintendent rode out to the beach, searching the base of the cliff for black sand; if he located gold in the sand, he would dispatch a messenger to the blufftop, and a string of mules, each carrying two canvas sacks, was sent down. The sand was shoveled into small piles and put in the sacks. Then,

> ...[w]ith a word from the driver each mule gravely walked up between his sacks. On their being placed on his back he would start off at a trot, for the works....When they saw a heavy breaker coming they would face the cliff like veterans, and, with firmly braced feet and drooping ears, allow the water to dash over them....[2]

Having survived the surf, the methodical mules climbed the bluff and deposited their loads in a "sand corral." The sand was later washed in sluice boxes called "long Toms," which caught the gold on copper plates charged with quicksilver. The process could garner $1,600 or more a week, and one operator, John Chapman, did well enough that he mined the bluffs for 30 years.

The beach had widened so much by the 1920s that the breakers no longer reached the bluffs. The ready supply of gold-bearing sand was thus unavailable, and, "except for a few still hopeful individuals," mining had ended.

Mining at Espa Lagoon, c. 1900

Over the following years, the elements have weathered away most signs of the miners' work. The prairie above Fern Canyon is now bare, bereft of the remains of the Pioneer Placer Mine, and the areas around Espa Lagoon, Ossagon Creek, and Butler Creek show little sign of having once been mining sites. Only at two places are traces of the activity still evident: one is above Carruther's Cove, where the long-dry flume for Anthony Johnston's placer mine still cuts across the hillside. The other is on the knoll above Major Creek; here a few boards and bits of rust mark the headquarters of Chapman's Union Gold Bluff Mine. Both locations lie off infrequently used trails, and the only people likely to find them are a handful of modern-day treasure seekers—attracted not by the glint of precious metal, but merely by the ghostly glimmer of the past.

Prairie Creek Redwoods State Park

The park is traversed by two-lane, paved Newton B. Drury Scenic Parkway, which leaves Highway 101 some five miles north of Orick and reconnects with the highway 9.3 miles later. *Warning: watch for elk, bicyclists, pedestrians, and slow-moving vehicles.*

Features: (for key to symbols, see p. 89)

🅿️ 🚴 access to Jogging Trail/Bicycle Loop (mile 0.2)

🚗 🅿️ 📷 entrance to Prairie Creek Redwoods State Park; Elk Prairie and Elk Prairie Trail (0.4)

🅿️ 🚴 ⓘ 🚻 🏪 ⛺ 🐾 🚂 turnoff to entrance station, Elk Prairie Visitor Center, and campground; trail access (1.1)

🚗 🅿️ junction with Cal Barrel Road; trail access (1.5)

🅿️ 🏪 📷 turnoff to Big Tree; trail access (1.9)

🅿️ Big Tree–Prairie Creek Trailhead (2.1)

🅿️ 📷 trail to Corkscrew Tree (2.4)

🅿️ South Fork–Prairie Creek Trailhead (2.9)

🅿️ Rhododendron–Zig Zag #2 Trailhead (4.5)

🅿️ unnamed trail at Moorman Grove (5.0)

🅿️ Little Creek Trail (5.9)

🅿️ 🚴 〰️ Hope Creek–Ossagon Trailhead (6.8)

🚗 junction with Ah Pah Road (7.7)

🚗 turnoff for Coastal Drive side trip (8.3)

🚗 interchange with Highway 101; end of route (9.3)

The **Newton B. Drury Scenic Parkway**, until recently a segment of the historic Redwood Highway, runs through an elk-inhabited

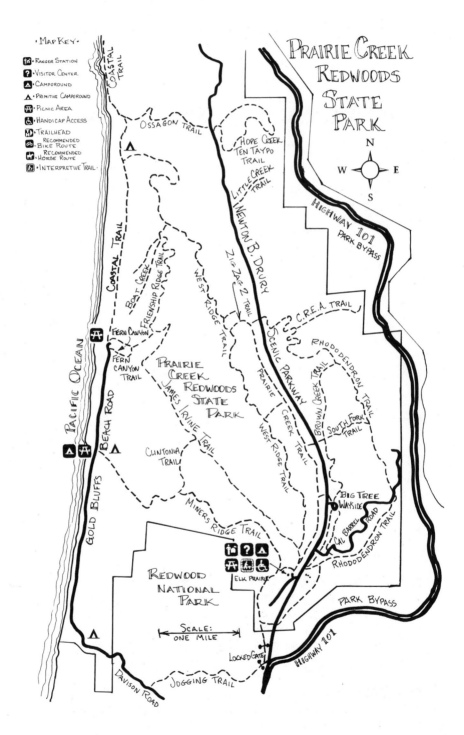

· Map Key ·

🏠 · Ranger Station
❓ · Visitor Center
🅰 · Campground
⛺ · Primitive Campground
🍴 · Picnic Area
♿ · Handicap Access
🅼 · Trailhead
🚲 · Recommended Bike Route
🐴 · Recommended Horse Route
🅰 · Interpretive Trail

PRAIRIE CREEK REDWOODS STATE PARK

N
W · E
S

Coastal Trail

Ossagon Trail

Hope Creek Ten Taypo Trail
Little Creek Trail

Newton B. Drury

Zig Zag 2 Trail

Highway 101 Park Bypass

Boat Creek
Friendship Ridge Trail

West Ridge Trail

Scenic Parkway

C.R.E.A. Trail

Rhododendron Trail

Brown Creek Trail

Fern Canyon

Pacific Ocean

Fern Canyon Trail

PRAIRIE CREEK REDWOODS STATE PARK

James Irvine Trail

Prairie Creek Trail

South Fork Trail

Beach Road

Clintonia Trail

West Ridge Trail

Gold Bluffs

Big Tree Wayside

Cal Barrel Road

Rhododendron Trail

Miners Ridge Trail

🏠❓🅰
🍴🅰♿
Elk Prairie

REDWOOD NATIONAL PARK

Park Bypass

Scale: One Mile

Highway 101

Locked Gate

Davison Road

Jogging Trail

meadow and then up the narrow, heavily forested canyon at the northern end of Prairie Creek. The parkway honors the first secretary of the Save-the-Redwoods League.

Newton Drury Does the Job

The individuals who met in 1919 to initiate the Save-the-Redwoods League were remarkable for their influence and success; they included such luminaries as Henry Fairfield Osborn, President of the American Museum of Natural History; Congressman William Kent; Robert G. Sproul, President of the University of California at Berkeley; and the Secretary of Interior, Franklin K. Lane. They were people used to making important decisions, and they now had to make one immediately: who would run the day-to-day operations of the League?

Their choice was a young Bay Area advertising executive, Newton Bishop Drury. It proved to be a wonderfully wise appointment; in a remarkable career that spanned parts of seven decades, Drury served the League not only as secretary, but later as its president and finally as chairman of the board. When he left the League in 1940 to become Director of the National Park Service, his brother, Aubrey, took his place. After Aubrey's death in 1959, Newton, then Chief of the California Division of Beaches and Parks, returned to his old redwood-saving job; for the first 52 years of the League's existence, no one but a Drury served as its secretary.

Affable and dapper, with a pencil-line mustache, Newton Drury looked not a little like character actor Claude Rains. On occasion, Drury could show his own sense of the dramatic, as he did during a stormy session of the Humboldt County Board of Supervisors in 1925.

The Board was holding a special hearing to consider an urgent proposal from the League: two choice tracts of southern Humboldt redwoods, owned by the Pacific Lumber Company, were slated for logging; only public acquisition of the property would protect the magnificent trees that grew there. In the middle of the heated meeting, Donald McDonald, the company's treasurer, almost came to blows with a local preservationist, attorney James Mahan. Drury hurriedly stepped between the men in an attempt to cool their tempers; within moments, he was handed a series of three telegrams, which he proceeded to read aloud. Each message pledged hundreds of thousands of dollars for purchasing the Pacific Lumber Company property, and all three were signed by prominent Bay Area bankers.

McDonald and Mahan went back to their seats; the duly impressed Board of Supervisors voted to accept the League's proposal; and Newton B. Drury, after an award-winning performance, returned to League's headquarters in San Francisco, where he resumed using more routine methods to save the redwoods.

The parkway begins at an interchange with the southern end of the Highway 101 Park Bypass. The route turns left at the bottom of the offramp, passes under the highway, and then bends north, crossing May Creek at 0.1 mile. On the left at mile 0.2 is an unmarked turnoff onto a dirt road; in a hundred feet this side route meets the **Jogging Trail**, which connects the campground at Elk Prairie with Davison Road and also serves as part of the **Prairie Creek Bicycle Loop Trail** (see p. 279). Locked gates bar motor vehicles from the path, whose course follows an old roadbed.

Prairie Creek Redwoods State Park

At mile 0.4 the Parkway crosses into **Prairie Creek Redwoods State Park**, passing the **Elk Prairie Trail**, left and right, while simultaneously entering the grassy expanse of **Elk Prairie**. In early days, miners from nearby Gold Bluffs used the redwood-fringed meadow to raise hay for their pack mules. Andrew Jackson Harris and Jane McIntosh Harris homesteaded the grassland in the 1890s but were besieged by the miners, who attempted to drive the couple off and retain the prairie for their own use. Two of the men burned the Harrises' barn, while others so harassed Jane Harris that she took to carrying a .45 Colt when she went to talk with them. The Harrises prevailed and had soon established a horse-powered sawmill and a small herd of beef cattle. In August 1902, it was reported that "Harris, who has a young elk in captivity, took it to Eureka for the Elks Celebration. He returned a few days ago, his elk apparently suffering no ill effects from its outing."

The following summer, Ethel Tracy, the schoolmarm at Stone Lagoon, travelled through the area with some friends. Soon after the trip Tracy wrote a luminous letter to her family, telling how she and her friends camped in a grove of tanoaks near the prairie, "paid our respects to the Elk," and took on a supply of Harris hay before heading north. The group then

> ...went through 12 miles of solid redwood! And they haven't been touched yet, either. Two or three times we passed homestead cabins, but they were deserted. It was a lonesome country, but grand...."

William Boyes bought the Harris property in the early 1900s. He set up a dairy farm and a hotel, appropriately naming the latter Elk Tavern. A visitor noted that "the estate is very beautiful and a delight to the eye as one emerges from the redwoods into the opening."

Early on, the Save-the-Redwoods League determined that the Prairie Creek area was among the choicest sites for a redwood park. Their hope became reality in 1923, when Zipporah Russ donated 160 acres in the heart of the creek canyon as the first land for the new Prairie Creek Redwoods State Park. Ironically, Zipporah's late husband, Joseph, had years earlier been implicated in the land fraud scheme that wrested away thousands of acres of nearby redwoods from the federal government.

Pacific giant salamander

Little additional acreage had been added by 1926, when the Redwood Highway replaced the wagon road through the canyon and rendered the park vastly more accessible to tourists. In 1931 much of the creekside corridor was at last protected when the Save-the-Redwoods League acquired nearly 5,000 acres from a large timber concern, the Sage Land and Improvement Company. During the Depression, a Civilian Conservation Corps camp was established on the prairie. Using cumbersome "drag" saws, the CCC workers cleared campsites and cut up tree remnants left from the highway work; some of the wood was split into the rails that fence the prairie. The crews also constructed a swinging bridge across the creek and built the park's charming visitor center, whose careful crafting features hand-hewn beams and a stone fireplace.

Elk Prairie Visitor Center

Over the years more land was acquired, filling in the main canyon and also extending the park westward over the ridge to Gold Bluffs and its adjacent beach. In 1965, Prairie Creek Redwoods acquired long-sought Fern Canyon, a 30-acre enclave of shadowy, foliage-covered cliffsides. Today, the park's seacoast, ridgetops, and creek canyons are linked by a network of some 75 miles of hiking trails. Notable among park events is an annual excitement known as the "Banana Slug Derby," whose concluding "Big Slime Off" race results in the winner being crowned "Top Banana."

Elk Prairie

A center of park activity is Elk Prairie, a golden sweep of grassland that provides prime viewing sites for its namesake species. Long pullouts along the parkway accommodate wildlife watchers who believe that the elk should be seen rather than "herd."

Several bands of elk now inhabit the park and surrounding areas, but 70 years ago the situation was far different.

A Very Exclusive Elks Club

It had become an extremely small group, the California elks' club; its membership was diminishing rapidly with little hope for recovery. Then a park was established near their "clubhouse," and the great hoofed beasts rallied, benefiting from the protection afforded by a stretch of fabulous forest.

The animal's impending demise had been part of a pattern established in the mid–19th century. Before then, elk had ranged over most of the United States, their stirring, buglelike calls resounding from the Berkshires of Massachusetts to southern New Mexico. Unfortunately the wapiti, as the Shawnee Indians called the great animal, proved commercially valuable, and the species had been nearly exterminated by hunters who coveted its meat, hide, and upper canine teeth.

By 1860 the eastern elk were completely eliminated; in the west hordes of hunters continued the slaughter. Only about 41,000 elk existed on the entire continent at the turn of the century, when Theodore Roosevelt led a movement to protect them—the western subspecies, *Cervus elaphus occidentalis*, was subsequently called the "Roosevelt" elk in his honor.

Even bearing the name of a president seemed to have little protective effect. By 1912 only an estimated 126 Roosevelt elk remained in Northern California; in the next decade, a rancher near Orick reported sighting a herd of about 100, but another account ominously claimed that only 15 elk were to be found in the entire state. It seemed that the species would go the way of the grizzly, which, despite appearing on the state flag, had been exterminated in California a few years earlier.

The elk made their last stand along a four-mile-wide strip of land, just inland from the ocean, that ran from the Klamath River down to Orick. Part of the area lay in the recently established Prairie Creek Redwoods State Park, and it was here, announced the Save-the-Redwoods League in a 1937 report, that the state's sole remaining herd had its only chance for protection.

The League's literature repeatedly stressed the importance of preserving additional Prairie Creek elk habitat, and through the organization's fundraising efforts, the Madison Grant Forest and Elk

Roosevelt elk, ensconced on the prairie

Refuge was established in 1948. Some 1,600 acres of woods and meadow, named in honor of one of the League's founders, was set aside at the Prairie Creek park. Bolstered by "the enthusiastic work" of Chief Ranger C. L. Milne and his assistants, a sizable herd developed along the creek. Two new bands had already appeared in nearby areas, one in Redwood Creek and another north of the Klamath, and by 1955 California's elk population had risen to over a thousand, securing the creature's future in the state.

Today Roosevelt elk are the animal celebrities of the North Coast, stopping more traffic than a movie star and lending a majestic presence to the redwood-rimmed prairies. Although they now flourish, the species survived here by the slimmest of margins, saved by the Save-the-Redwoods League while it was busy saving some redwoods.

The parkway continues through the prairie to mile 1.1, where it reaches an intersection with two paved roads. Right leads to several park residences and equipment buildings, including the old Boyes bungalow, that are centered among the hundred-year-old apple trees of the Harris homestead. The bungalow was built in 1919 as one of three houses made from a single redwood.

Park Visitor Center

Left from the intersection is the **Campground Entrance Station** and **Elk Prairie Visitor Center**. The 75-site campground, located in the woods between the prairie and the creeks, features fire rings, bear-proof food lockers, tables, piped water, and restrooms with showers and flush toilets; an amphitheater provides staging for ranger-led nighttime "campfire talks." Nearby are the **Redwood Access Trail** and the self-guided **Revelation Trail**, both wheelchair accessible, with the latter designed for both blind and sighted persons. The **Five-Minute Trail** starts at the rear of the Visitor Center and leads past such attractions as the "Church Tree," an enormous goosepen capable of holding a considerable congregation; the "Chimney Tree," whose hollow trunk offers a sky-scanning view through its open top; and the "Indian House Tree," the former seasonal home of a local Yurok family.

The Visitor Center features displays of plants, wildlife, and local history, along with a small but well-stocked natural history bookstore; restrooms are nearby. The **Nature Trail** (brochure available), crosses the bridge just northeast of the center's parking area, offering access to the **Prairie Creek Trail** (see p. 267), **James Irvine Trail** (see p. 262), **West Ridge Trail** (see p. 267), **Miner's Ridge Trail** (see p. 258) and **Elk Prairie Trail**. To the right of the bridge is the **Cathedral Trees Trail** (see p. 253); it runs under the parkway, via a culvert, to reach connections with three other routes: the **Foothill Trail**, which partly follows a remnant of the original roadway; the eastern end of the Elk Prairie Trail; and the **Rhododendron Trail**.

Resuming the parkway, the route immediately crosses Boyes Creek and leaves the prairie, plunging into the "Tunnel," where, for several miles, the redwood-dominated forest crowds the road corridor. Right at mile 1.5 is **Cal Barrel Road**, a sinuous gravel route that rises ridgeward, running through magnificent redwoods for two and a half miles before reaching a locked gate; motorhomes and trailers are not advised. The side road continues beyond the gate, arriving shortly at the Park Bypass; it then climbs east of the bypass to the ridgetop remains of an old Cal Barrel Company logging camp. *Note: in stormy weather Cal Barrel Road may be closed periodically; a gate near the start of the road is otherwise open 9 A.M. to 5 P.M.*

"It's getting late for #128"—
retired truck, Cal Barrel logging camp

Big Tree

The turnoff at 1.9 miles, right, is for **Big Tree**, a notably thick-trunked redwood specimen situated a hundred feet from the paved parking lot. Several hiking routes depart from the viewing area adjacent to Big Tree: to the northwest is a spur path that runs to the parkway and then connects with the Prairie Creek Trail on the far side of the road; north is a section of the Foothill Trail; eastward, the short **Circle Trail** loops past a junction with the Cathedral Trees Trail; to the south, another segment of the Foothill Trail runs towards Elk Prairie along the bed of the old county wagon road. Restrooms are located next to the Big Tree parking area amidst several aromatic California laurels.

Next the parkway passes the **Big Tree-Prairie Creek Trailhead**, 2.1 miles; to the left is access to the Prairie Creek Trail, while the route right leads back to Big Tree. The road then reaches a marked trail, mile 2.4, left, to the contorted **Corkscrew Tree**, whose multiple trunks twist around each other as they spiral skyward. The initial section of the trailbed follows the old county wagon road, and watchful hikers can continue northward on this long abandoned but still serviceable route if they steer straight ahead at the bottom of the downslope. The main path bends left, passes the Corkscrew Tree, and presently meets the Prairie Creek Trail; north from this junction is the ridge-climbing **Zig Zag Trail #1**.

Large redwoods shade the **South Fork-Prairie Creek Trailhead**, 2.9 miles. Left is an access spur for the Prairie Creek Trail, while the **South Fork Trail** (see p. 243), right, connects with the Foothill Trail and the **Brown Creek Trail** before climbing the ridgeside to end at the Rhododendron Trail.

Big Tree

Artfully angled bridge, Foothill Trail

Brown Creek crosses the parkway north of the trailhead; it was named for Jim Brown, an early-day homesteader whose cabin once sat at streamside. After acquiring title to the property, Brown journeyed to San Francisco, where he sold the land at a handsome profit. His trip was unexpectedly extended when he celebrated his sale with some newfound "friends" and then groggily awoke to find himself on board a ship bound for Australia. Only after an absence of many years did the shanghaied settler return to California.

The road continues through thick forest to reach, mile 4.5, the **Rhododendron–Zig Zag #2 Trailhead**. The way right commences the northern end of the rambling Rhododendron Trail; it connects with the **C.R.E.A. Trail**, a ridge-climbing route named for the California Real Estate Association. On the left, a short connecting path joins the Prairie Creek Trail just south of the **Zig Zag Trail #2**.

An unmarked trail leaves the parkway, mile 5.0, right, at the Moorman Grove; the pleasant path meanders up a surprisingly sunny canyon, crisscrossing a salmonberry-lined stream along the way. At mile 5.9 is a pullout for the **Little Creek Trail**, right, a suitably small route that briefly accompanies its namesake. Just north of the pullout, a gated park fire road, left, leads up to West Ridge. Near here in about 1890 an ambitious mining company, employing expert miners from Cornwall, England, constructed a tunnel through the ridge. The company hoped to thus supply their beachside placer mine with water from Prairie Creek, but Joe Stockel, who owned the property where the tunnel originated, did not take kindly to someone stealing his stream; he promptly divested the miners of their diversion — at gunpoint, according to some reports.

Many years after the tunneling incident, more diverted water made news at West Ridge.

When the Klamath River Came to Prairie Creek

Moistened by cool coastal fogs and protected by foot-thick bark, mature coast redwoods are considered relatively safe from fire. The worst that usually happens is a burning out of the lower trunk, resulting in the hollow "goosepen" trees often seen in the woods. Only when the flames rise into the limbs and crown to ignite the foliage is a redwood in true danger...and then so are all the trees around it.

One summer in the late 1980s, an illegal camper built a fire in a goosepen high on West Ridge, between the ocean and Prairie Creek. The camper left without fully extinguishing the fire, which subsequently burned along the duff-covered ground to reach several neighboring conifers. One of these was a hollow redwood with an open top. The fire entered the base of this "chimney" tree, creating an updraft that shot flames up the interior and out the opening. The limbs of the surrounding trees were soon ignited by this giant torch, and before long the crowns of seven large redwoods were ablaze.

Park personnel and fire fighters rushed to the scene. They trucked hoses and pumps to the end of the park road and then hand carried them to the site. The pumps pulsed their hardest, but the stream of water they produced fell far short of the flames.

The conflagration continued to burn throughout night as fire supervisors puzzled over their problem. Gale force winds were expected the next day, and pessimists predicted that the fire would dance across the treetops through the canyon of Prairie Creek, finally running all the way to the new bypass road on the far ridge. Thousands of old-growth redwoods were threatened.

Finally an idea formed in someone's mind: water wouldn't reach the trees from the ground up, but what about from the sky down? A call went out to Roseburg, Oregon, for a huge Sikorsky helicopter with a 3,000-gallon water bucket; another request was sent for a smaller chopper with a thousand gallon carrying capacity.

The next morning the helicopters went to work. The Sikorsky flew to the nearby Klamath River, filled its bucket with water, hurried down to the fire, and emptied its load above the flaming trees. The force of the falling water knocked burning limbs to the ground, where fire crews could at last use their hoses on them.

While the Sikorsky went back to the river, the smaller helicopter came in, loaded with fire-retardant foam. It sprayed the foam on limbs that were still attached and burning; the foam oozed down and around the entire limb surface, smothering the flames.

The helicopters made trip after trip, each time knocking back more of the fire. It was a race against the weather report, for the predicted gale could arrive at any time.

The winds never came. The weather instead consisted of an artificial rain composed of three parts Klamath River water and one part foam.

It proved to be a good formula. The flames were finally extinguished, and a new technique in fighting crown fires was born—all because the Klamath River (or at least a little of it) had come to Prairie Creek.

At mile 6.8 is the **Hope Creek-Ossagon Trailhead**. The **Hope Creek Trail**, right, forms part of a rousing, ridge-reaching loop that also utilizes a remnant of the **Ten Taypo Trail**. The **Ossagon Trail** (see p. 249), left, serves double duty as part of the **Prairie Creek**

Bike Loop Trail (see p. 279); the path crosses the hilltop to the northwest before descending through the canyon of Ossagon Creek to the beach. An elaborate dam and flume system once harnessed the creek's water for a mining operation at the beachside bluffs.

Rough-skinned newt

The parkway then climbs to the head of the Prairie Creek canyon. At the hillcrest, mile 7.7, dead-end **Ah Pah Road** branches right. *(Note: Ah Pah Road is scheduled for removal in 1995, when it will be replaced by a short trail and an interpretive display.)*

After dropping from the ridgecrest, the parkway comes to a junction with **Coastal Drive**, mile 8.3, left (see p. 154); this partly paved remnant of the Redwood Highway provides access to the **Coastal Trail**, the northernmost hiking route in Prairie Creek Redwoods State Park. Continuing downhill from the junction, the parkway ends, mile 9.3, at an interchange with Highway 101.

Side Trip:
Highway 101 "Park Bypass"

Starting at an interchange with the southern end of the Newton B. Drury Scenic Parkway, the side trip ends 11.4 miles later at an interchange with the parkway's northern end. The route is four-lanes throughout; it reaches a maximum elevation of nearly 1,500 feet. *Note: 1) except for infrequent logging truck use of dirt side roads, the Bypass functions as a freeway; stopping or parking at the edge of the Bypass or on the side roads is thus limited to emergencies, which prevents legal access to Cal Barrel Road, East Ridge Road, or any of the other park routes that depart the Bypass. For further information, contact the Cal-Trans district office in Eureka.*

Warning: beware of ice and snow during cold and wet weather.

(for map, see p. 138)

Completed in 1992, the Park Bypass was designed to alleviate traffic pressure in Prairie Creek Redwoods State Park, through which the old highway ran. It required eight years of work and an outlay of $115 million to cut the new route through the mountains east of the park. The project cost more than dollars, however, for the silt-filled runoff from several of its roadcuts has clogged Prairie Creek and several of its tributaries, damaging salmon habitat.

After crossing the overpass for the Newton B. Drury Scenic Parkway, mile 0.0, the Bypass rises up the broad valley of May Creek; the heavily logged watershed is now packed full of second-growth conifers. The Boyes Creek Viaduct, 3.0 miles, offers a view, left, far down the canyon to a grassy oval that is Elk Prairie. Beneath the viaduct once ran the Ah Pah Trail, used by Yuroks to connect their coastal villages with communities on the Klamath River.

At mile 3.9, sections of Cal Barrel Road depart from both sides of the Bypass: left descends into Prairie Creek Redwoods State Park;

the route right climbs to the hilltop ruins of an old Cal Barrel logging camp.

Massive earthflows have eroded the subsequent stretch of highway cutbank, right. The CalTrans remedy: extensive cutting and scraping—Bypass surgery done with bulldozers and dump trucks.

The roadway crests the route's summit, mile 4.4, and then winds along the eastern side of East Ridge; to the left, the towering old-growth redwoods of Prairie Creek Redwoods State Park stand in stark contrast to the regenerating treelets on the adjacent cutover lands. At mile 5.2, right, are vistas of the Klamath River drainage.

A side route, 6.3 miles, left, connects to part of East Ridge Road, which winds past several state park memorial groves. Following a view of the ruby-tinted ridgeline of Red Mountain, mile 7.1, right, is another route to East Ridge Road; this one lies behind a locked gate at mile 8.7, left. The Bypass ends at an overpass for the northern end of the Newton B. Drury Scenic Parkway, mile 11.4. Highway 101 continues northward as four-lane freeway.

The "Tall Tree Trippers" on square dance stump, May Creek

Side Trip: Coastal Drive

This scenic 9.9-mile route consists of three segments: 1) southern Coastal Drive, which follows the old Redwood Highway and is a mixture of two-lane pavement and one-to-two-lane gravel surfaces; 2) northern Coastal Drive, a one-lane, gravel route that runs along the even older county wagon road; and 3) Klamath Beach Road, whose two lanes of pavement run from the river's mouth to the 101 interchange just south of the Klamath Bridge. Trailers are not advised on Coastal Drive, which is dusty in dry weather.

(for map, see p. 168)

Features: (for key to symbols, see p. 89)

   ⚑🚛≋ Coastal Trail (mile 1.1)

   ᵒᵒ Gold Bluffs Beach Overlook (1.7)

   ᵒᵒ view of Split Rock (3.6)

   ⇌ junction with Alder Camp Road (4.4)

   ⇌⚑⊗🗋ᵒᵒ≋ side road to High Bluff Picnic Area (4.5)

   🚛 World War II radar station (5.3)

   ⚑🛆🚛 Flint Ridge Trail and access to Flint Ridge Primitive Camp (5.7)

   🚣🛆🐎🚛ᵒᵒ Klamath River Overlook; start of Klamath Beach Road (6.2)

   ⚑🚣🚛ᵒᵒ Douglas Memorial Bridge; Flint Ridge Trail (8.5)

   ⇌ interchange with Highway 101; end of route (9.9)

"Redwood Highway" Section

The southern end of Coastal Drive is at a junction with mile 8.3 of the Newton B. Drury Scenic Parkway. The route descends from

154

the parkway, soon winding through stately redwoods; a sweeping curve in the Ada Fenimore Bock Grove, mile 0.7, displays an especially striking arrangement of tall trees, left.

Carruthers (Crothers) Cove

Upon nearing the coast, the road appropriately passes the **Coastal Trail**, mile 1.1, left. This route follows an old roadbed for most of its descent to the beach at Carruthers Cove. Eureka newspaper publisher J. H. Crothers (not Carruthers) once owned the cliffside property above the cove, but the site would more appropriately have been named for its earlier residents, the Johnstons.

Johnstons'

From 1859 to 1899 there was only one place on the map between the mines at Gold Bluffs and the mouth of the Klamath River—Johnstons'—a sort of all-purpose homestead whose owners raised cattle, cared for travellers, and mined for gold. Today the name and location are largely forgotten, but a century ago, when it was a sanctuary from hard travel and killer tides, the spot was known to everyone who journeyed along the coast.

In 1851 Anthony Dale Johnston and Julia Sheridan Johnston settled on the first portion of what was to become a thousand-acre ranch. Anthony had earlier been a purser on a steamship, and the site they chose for their ranch house, a half-mile up the bluffs from the beach, allowed him to remain comfortably close to the sea.

The one-time purser also continued his interest in valuables, soon setting up the "Amony Placer Mine." A flume on the hillside carried water to the mine, which Johnston for a time worked with "great success." Sand subsequently covered the area and ended the operation.

The trail between Crescent City and Humboldt Bay passed along the beach below the Johnston Ranch, and the family's home soon became a "stopping place," where travellers could obtain a meal, overnight lodging, or both. The shoreline topography provided a unique set of trials for these early-day traversers, since the route past the ranch required not only hiking or riding along the beach, but also occasional forays up and over intervening bluffs. It was a problematic passage; when ascending an especially steep incline near the ranch, riders were known to dismount, grab their horses' tails, and let the animals pull them up the slope.

Danger compounded the difficulties. A Yurok woman walking below the ranch in 1872 was killed when a portion of the bluff gave way and fell on her.

Even more treacherous were the great waves that rolled across the beach to crash against the bluffs. Riders would have to time their trips to coincide with low tide or run the risk of being caught in the breakers. The Johnstons' sons, Joseph and Robert, knew this as well as anyone, but in December 1891 they gambled against the water—and lost. While riding along the beach near Lower Gold Bluffs, a huge wave caught the brothers, dashed them against the cliff, and then carried them out to sea. Robert saved himself by clinging to his horse's mane as the animal swam back to shore, but Joseph was never seen again.

A grieving Robert penned a letter to the Crescent City paper, asking locals to search for the body of his brother, but it proved to no avail. Less than two years later, a second tragedy struck when Julia Johnston died suddenly while travelling south of Eureka. Robert subsequently moved away, leaving his father Anthony alone on the ranch.

Not much later the county completed its long-awaited wagon road; the route passed along the ridge more than a half mile above the Johnstons'. No longer would beach travelers climb the cliff to gain a bed for the night or a bit of refreshment. But some people still recalled the ranch, and when newspaperman William Ayres came up the coast in 1897, he turned off the road at the Johnston mail box and hiked down the hillside towards the bluffs. The house was locked, since Anthony was off searching for his cattle, but about sundown the rancher

> ...came down off of the hill, [and] greeted me in a kindly, yet mournful way, as if the lonesome solitude of his situation and surroundings had cast a shadow over his spirits, which were ever wont to be lively and hopeful. He spoke more than once of his wife who died two or three years ago, and who had always been his sturdy companion...

> ...[Johnston] said to me, "It's very lonesome here now, and somehow I can't climb these hills like I used to; my legs are stiff, and I get tired and I have to sit down and rest quite often, where I used to run over the hills without thinking of getting tired. And the stock has to be taken care of. I can't go on much longer, and I don't suppose it matters much, for I am getting old."

Two years later, the solitary rancher was found dead, the victim of a heart attack. When his sister, Margaret Howe, heard the news in Detroit, her heart failed and she, too, died.

Anthony Johnston, it turned out, had still mattered to someone.

Not long after Johnston's death most of the ranch property was purchased by J. B. Hamilton and Frank Knight, who relocated the center of the operation a few miles north. *Humboldt Times* publisher J. H. Crothers bought a smaller parcel that contained the Johnston mine and ranch house and built a vacation home on the site. By World War II the building stood deserted, and the Coast Guard then used it to house personnel who were on beach patrol. Some scattered blufftop bricks still mark the Crothers house site, which lies directly astride the current park trail; across the canyon to the south is an earlier relic, the hillside flume of the Amony Placer Mine.

Immediately north of the Coastal Trail parking area, the road enters Redwood National Park. In this vicinity the route crosses a small stream called Smerkitur Wroi—"toothless"—by the Yuroks.

Split Rock, from
High Bluff Picnic Area

According to legend there were supernatural influences attached
to the creek that would cause anyone who drank its water to lose
their teeth.

Presently, the road approaches the cliffs above the ocean; at the
Gold Bluffs Beach Overlook, mile 1.7, left, a stone-walled pullout
offers a sweeping view southward along the coast. The roadbed
now occasionally narrows to one lane and intermittently turns to
gravel. At mile 2.3 is an access route, right, to Alder Camp, a state
prison honor facility. Coastal Drive proceeds along the rocky
mountainside, passing a pullout, mile 3.6, left, that provides a view
to the south of spectacular **Split Rock**. A second approach to the
prison camp is on the right, mile 4.4. Just ahead, another junction
offers a choice of historic routes: running to the right is more of the
original Redwood Highway; now designated **Alder Camp Road**,
its two lanes of pavement end in two miles at Klamath Beach Road.
Branching left is the continuation of the Coastal Drive side trip,
which follows the course of the 1894 county wagon road.

County Wagon Road Section

Bearing left, Coastal Drive departs from the junction as a one-lane, gravel roadway. The road to the **High Bluff Picnic Area**, 4.5 miles, left, descends one-third mile to a viewpoint, picnic tables, beach access trail, and restroom at the site of an old rock quarry.

Coastal Drive continues northward, its narrow, century-old roadbed running high upon the steep hillside. At mile 5.3 the route passes a pullout, left; here a short trail drops downhill, ending at what appears to be a pair of farm buildings.

Farm B-71

The "farmers" saluted, the "windmill" was a radar antenna, the ranch house a power plant, and the big piece of equipment inside the "barn" was not a milking machine but an oscilloscope. Built on the coastal hillside to look like a farm, it was actually Radar Station B-71, one of 65 early warning sites established along the coast during World War II.

The fictitious farm

The two buildings were constructed of cement blocks covered with wooden siding and false windows and dormers. Two 50-caliber machine guns guarded the facility, along with a mobile patrol of military police and guard dogs. No dairy products were ever sent from the "farm," but it transmitted a stream of secret messages that, in wartime, were even more valuable than cottage cheese and buttermilk.

At mile 5.7 is the parking area, left, for the western end of the **Flint Ridge Trail** (see p. 260), which climbs the hillside to the right. A quarter mile along the route is the **Flint Ridge Primitive Camp**.

The trailhead and camp occupy the site of the old Hamilton place, a combination ranch and resort. When Hamilton and Knight purchased 1,003 acres of the Johnston Ranch in 1902, they established their headquarters at this location, alongside the county wagon road and stage route. Soon the enterprise boasted a 19-room ranch house that served to accommodate travellers and family alike. Over the next few years the ranch doubled in size, while the "hotel" came to be a favorite of tourists and sportsmen, some of them perhaps enticed by the alluring 1915 announcement that Hamilton's featured not only a "grand ocean view with schools of whales in August," but also "[d]eer and bear hunting; good home table; fine home-made butter and cream; fresh vegetables and berries."

Later on, Ed Chapman, whose father had been superintendent at the Union Gold Bluff mine, purchased the ranch. Then known as the "Chapman Range," it became home to a most uncommon grazer. Startled drivers would discover this as they barreled around a corner and slammed on their brakes, having found their way blocked not by a steer or an elk, but by a buffalo that Chapman had somehow acquired as a sort of oversized, displaced pet.

The hotel was eventually taken over by the Crivelli family, who were the last to operate it. No buildings now remain at the site.

Mouth of Klamath

Coastal Drive then descends to the **Klamath River Overlook**, mile 6.2. A dirt road, left, leads to the remnants of Dad's Camp, a fishing resort that in recent years has been almost entirely washed away by the changing course of the river. Just below the overlook is the hillside cemetery of the Shortman-Williams family, the Yurok owners of the camp. Charlie and Annie Williams opened the resort in 1914; they also maintained a stop for travellers who were waiting for the Requa ferry, which crossed the Klamath near here. Their grandson, Timm, gained fame as "Prince Lightfoot," otherwise known as the Stanford Indian; in this role he danced for many years at the school's football games. Long active in Indian causes,

Mouth of Klamath,
from High Bluff Picnic Area

Harbor seals, mouth of Klamath

Timm used his connection with the university to help gain scholar-ships for Native American youths.

On the flat below the cemetery is a dance pit where contempo-rary stagings of the brush dance are held; in this vicinity was **Welkwau**, a small Yurok village. At one time Welkwau had three pairs of Yurok houses. One of the resident families held the spoken "formula" for the First Salmon Rite and also guarded the two soap-stone pipes that were used in the ceremony. The pipes were too sa-cred for viewing; when the ceremony master took them from their burial crypt, he did so with his face averted, and he then smoked the pipes without looking at them. In 1850 whites burned the house where the pipes were stored; one pipe was broken but later re-placed by a replica. Charlie Williams's father, Johnny Shortman, was the last curator of the pipes.

Another ceremony, the White Deerskin Dance, was also per-formed at Welkwau, but it had probably died out before the arrival of white settlers. On the last day of the ceremony, performers from two different villages would dance across the Klamath in their ca-noes and then finish on the hill above the Yurok community of Rek-Woi.

A toll ferry later crossed the Klamath near the old boat dance course; set up in 1876, the chancy conveyance ran intermittently for 50 years until the opening of the Douglas Memorial Bridge. For a time a Yurok named Captain Spott operated the ferry; sometimes passengers had to be carried by canoe when the ferry raft was hung up on shoals. One time Spott transported 1,800 head of sheep across the river; his price was 5¢ a head, but his profits diminished when three of the sheep were smothered at a cost of $2.00 each. On another occasion Spott was carrying a bull on its way to the Johnston Ranch. The bull suddenly jumped over the raft's railing into the river, compelling its owner to dive in after the animal and swim with it to shore.

Ferry use had increased dramatically by the 1920s, when over 9,000 entities crossed in a single year. Besides numerous buggies, wagons, trucks, autos, etc., the transportees included eight bicycles and their riders, 15 motorcycles, 22 caged animals, and 146 goats. But, unlike the days of Captain Spott, there were only 12 sheep.

Klamath Beach Road Section

Coastal Drive ends at mile 6.2 of the route, opposite the entrance to Dad's Camp. **Klamath Beach Road**, paved and two-lane, continues the side trip; it immediately descends to the flats near the river and proceeds upstream, running by several fishing and camping resorts along the way. At mile 8.5, the northern end of Alder Camp Road departs, right, promptly passing a paved parking area for the aerobic **Flint Ridge Trail**; picturesque **Marshall Pond** lies in the adjacent ravine. Opposite the junction is the southern end of the **Douglas Memorial Bridge**, all that remains from the 1964 flood. When the bridge opened in 1926, it closed the last gap in the coastal highway.

Northwestern
pond turtle

The Klamath Gets Its Bridge

The dedication of the Douglas Memorial Bridge was a spectacular event. Some 4,000 celebrants, including the club-wielding Oregon cavemen "in their striking picturesque costumes," and governors Friend W. Richardson of California and Walter M. Pierce of Oregon, attended. Contestants from Hoopa and Requa competed in an Indian stick game. A special highlight was "an exhibit of all the wild flowers in Del Norte county [that] was staged upon the bridge, and was beautiful."

There was ample reason to rejoice, for the Redwood Highway's greatest obstacle to through traffic had just been eliminated. For 50 years the only way to cross the Klamath River had been by ferry, a haphazard arrangement that at various times consisted of either a raft, a Yurok canoe, or nothing at all. Over the years the coastal trail that reached the river had grown first to a wagon road and then at last to a highway, but all traffic had come to a halt at the Klamath. Now there was a two-lane, 1,200-foot-long concrete bridge to span the river, the longest such structure in the state, so that tourists, truckers, and other travellers could ride for over 400 miles, from Sausalito to Crescent City, without interruption.

There was lots of traffic waiting to make the run. The previous October some 1,000 cars a day started south from Grants Pass on their way to redwood country, although their occupants had to endure some 70 miles of merely "magnificent" mountain roadway before they saw the first of the tall trees.

From the other direction the statistics were even more impressive—more than *50,000* scenery seekers would leave Sausalito on a single Sunday or holiday, heading north on the highway for San Rafael or Santa Rosa, Ukiah or Eureka, or some other dazzling destination. The auto had come into its own, and a host of delighted drivers now had a roadway worthy of their magical machines.

Turning a rutted wagon road into the Redwood Highway hadn't been easy. Although the improvement was authorized by a bond act in 1909, work at first proceeded slowly. The railroad moved quicker, claiming the prime route through much of Humboldt and Mendocino counties, the canyon of the Middle Eel. The highway was left to run along the river's more rugged tributary, the South

Fork, compelling the hard-pressed construction crews to sometimes pack in materials and equipment on muleback. Even where there was no competing rail route, the harried highway engineers often had trouble locating a convenient course; south of Crescent City, for example, the roadbed had to be carved from the crumbling coastal cliffs, while stretches through the redwoods required removing 200-ton trees and maneuvering through morasses of mud.

World War I interrupted work on the roadway, but the subsequent use of convict labor speeded construction. While construction continued on the Crescent City to Grants Pass portion of the highway, the coastal section neared completion. Only one spot was in question: the crossing of the Klamath River.

It fell to Gustave H. Douglas to do something about it. Known for many years as a dedicated doctor, he'd gained fame for having once pumped a railroad handcar 18 miles to a remote cabin, where he then saved a little girl's life. Now he took on a new challenge; after winning election to the state assembly, he made his sole cause the construction of the bridge. The effort killed him: Douglas died in office from overwork, but he'd done his job well—after his death the legislature approved his bridge bill unanimously.

Now the doctor's dream had become reality. At the dedication, his widow christened the structure and his son Donald unveiled a

The recently opened
Douglas Memorial Bridge

memorial tablet; the ceremony concluded, cars and trucks at last crossed the Klamath unaided.

For nearly forty years traffic rolled across the great bridge. The flood of 1955 battered it, but its long spans of concrete held fast. Then came the 1964 deluge; this time the raging water proved too much. Most of the bridge washed away, and for a while a new Klamath ferry, now operated by the military, again crossed the river.

Soon a replacement bridge was built a mile upstream, and the highway rerouted to reach it. But what of the old bridge? It held a special place in the hearts of the locals, for it had ended decades of uncertain dependence on the ferry and also honored the beloved Dr. Douglas. Would it now be forgotten?

The answer was to keep part of it. Some 50 feet of its southern section, along with its pair of eight-ton "California bears" remain where the highway once met the river. The far end of the fragment has been railed off, so that the bridge now leads nowhere ... except to the memory of a public-spirited physician and the first days of the "Redwood Highway."

Klamath Beach Road continues eastward, passing such cliff-clinging plants as licorice fern, alum root, goatsbeard and ocean spray. The route ends at mile 9.9, where it meets Highway 101 just south of the current Klamath River bridge.

Klamath Area

A route past ranches, resorts, and redwoods, this segment of Highway 101 crosses through the canyons of the lower Klamath watershed. The tour commences at the northern interchange with the Newton B. Drury Scenic Parkway and runs 11.6 miles to the bridge over Wilson Creek, in the southern part of Del Norte Coast Redwoods State Park. The road is initially four-lane freeway but becomes two-lane highway just south of the Klamath River.

Features: (for key to symbols, see p. 89)

- offramp for Klamath Beach Road; access to Coastal Drive (3.4 miles)
- Klamath River (3.9)
- town of Klamath; offramp for State Highway 169 — access to town of Klamath Glen (4.4)
- turnoff for Requa side trip (7.1)
- crossing for Hostel Trail-Hidden Beach Trail (9.8)
- Lagoon Creek Picnic Area; Hidden Beach Section of the Coastal Trail, Yurok Loop Trail (10.8)
- Wilson Creek Picnic Area; Wilson Creek Road — access to Redwood Hostel and Hostel Trail (11.5)
- end of route (11.6)

From its intersection with the Newton B. Drury Parkway, U. S. 101 continues northward as four-lane freeway. After cresting a long rise, mile 1.0, the route descends the canyon of Waukel Creek; the surrounding hillsides show the slowly healing scars of substantial clearcuts. At mile 3.4 is the offramp, right, for **Klamath Beach Road**. A left turn at the base of the offramp leads to the mouth of the Klamath and RNP's **Coastal Drive** (see p. 154). Just past this exit the highway narrows to two lanes.

167

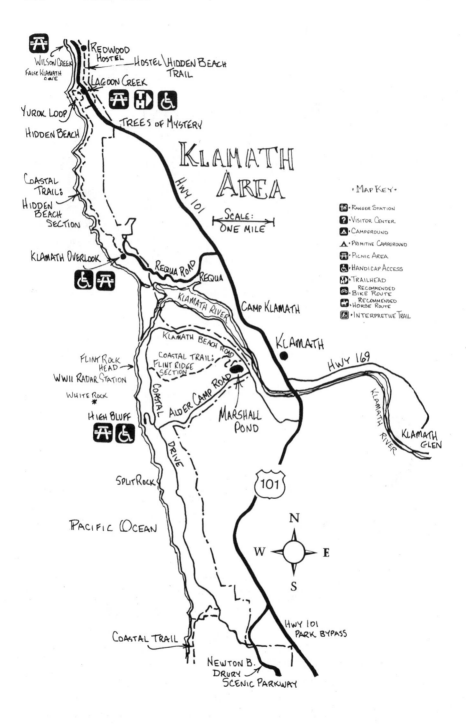

Klamath River

A pair of golden grizzly bears surmount the southern guardrails of the lengthy, two-lane bridge that spans the **Klamath River**, mile 3.9. Four similar bears had been placed atop the nearby Douglas Memorial Bridge for its 1926 opening, "perpetuating," it was said, "the indomitable spirit of Californians in their ceaseless efforts for progress and development...." Not mentioned was that one such effort had exterminated the grizzly from the state four years earlier.

The Klamath spreads widely beneath the bridge. By now the waterway has nearly reached the sea, having already run some 260 miles from its source in the Cascade mountains of southern Oregon, twisting past fertile farmlands, fir-clad mountainsides, and half-hidden hamlets along way. The history of the Klamath is one of legendary floods and like-size fish—freshets more than a hundred feet high and scale-breaking salmon. Yet one of the river's most exciting stories involved neither; instead it concerned a pair of brave but brash boatmen.

The White Water Daredevil Race

It was a publicist's dream—rampaging rapids, rocky gorges, a stirring contest between man and nature, so it was hardly surprising that someone finally suggested it—the Klamath River's "White Water Daredevil Race."

White water there was aplenty, so much of it that the full 176-mile course from Yreka to the coast had never before been run. As for finding the daredevils, $1,000 in prizes and the chance for a little fun took care of that.

The first race was held in the summer of 1949. Dawn was just breaking over Yreka on Friday, July 8, when several pairs of contestants readied their boats below the Highway 99 bridge. Perhaps it was the look of the river or some sudden lapse into common sense, but at the last minute all but two sets of daredevils proved not so daring and withdrew. The remaining teams waited until starter Henry Clineschmidt dropped his flag, and then they were off.

For a time it looked like the race would end almost at its start. The Klamath was at its summer low, studded with hull-ripping rocks; after 12 miles Loren and Vernon Myers hauled up to shore with seven holes in their boat. Their run at the river was finished.

It wasn't going much better for Oscar Taylor and Merton "Slim" Coates. Taylor had injured his leg while practicing for the race, and now, while lowering the boat over a set of rapids, he slipped on some rocks and gashed his side. Later, as the men were shooting a less daunting stretch near Happy Camp, the frame on their Evinrude motor snapped. The damage was impossible to repair, and from then on, according to Coates, the motor shook "like an old maid's proposal." If that weren't enough, the pair suddenly found themselves dumped into the water, their boat overturned by the Klamath's treacherous turbulence. Washed away were all the necessities for survival—food, clothing, blankets, and cigarettes.

A procession of some 500 cars had started after the boatmen, snaking along the narrow road that ran above the river. Some observers dropped out along the way, but more than half continued, perhaps hoping to confirm the report that the men really had lost everything, even their duds. Maybe someone among the onlookers would catch a glimpse of "Trouserless" Taylor or "Coatless" Coates.

On Sunday the race was front page news. The headline in the *Humboldt Times* announced:

Intrepid Boaters
Reach Perilous
Ishi Pishi Falls

Late last night Merton Coates and Oscar Taylor had inched over some of the roughest spots in the treacherous Klamath River and tied up at Ishi Pishi Falls to repair their badly battered boat and return to the undaunted assault on the unconquered river early in the morning.

Although the race rules allowed a portage around the falls themselves, the men were required to shoot the nearby rapids, a run reported to be "15 full miles of somersaulting waters, swift and unrelenting." To make matters worse, the Klamath remained extremely low, and the rocky riverbed sometimes left the men only inches to spare when running the course. As they did for most of

The Daredevils,
daring the Ishi Pishi Rapids

the race, Taylor, a Yurok who was known as an "insuperable boat-man," handled the motor, while the powerful Coates served as guide. At times the men rowed through rough stretches; on other occasions they again lowered their boat by ropes. Often they were swept past huge outcroppings—"boulders," as the pre-race publicity put it, "as big as cottages." Once, near Thompson Creek, their boat leapt from the rapids and soared six feet in the air. Their gear already gone, all Coates and Taylor had left to lose were their lives.

Sunday evening arrived. The crowd near the mouth of the Klamath grew as dozens, and then hundreds, of motorists drove up. It had been two and a half days since Coates and Taylor left Yreka. Leaning out of car windows, the people talked among themselves as they waited. Then, upriver to the east, there came a faint buzzing sound. Suddenly all grew quiet. A few moments later a small boat came into view, and the celebration began. Car horns tooted, bells rang, sirens screamed, and fire whistles echoed as Coates and Taylor made their way under the Douglas Memorial Bridge, the race's finish line. It was more of a sight than some spectators had anticipated, for trouserless Taylor and coatless Coates "were sunburned badly from their shoetops up."

The reddened river runners received a hero's welcome as they debarked. A dance was staged in their honor by the local Yuroks. Both men were interviewed.

Coates allowed that he "...wouldn't want to go back up there just now."

Taylor, more sunburned than his partner, announced that "All I need is a good and big steak."

An ambulance rushed the men to the local hospital for a quick examination. Then, after showering, Coates and Taylor lit into a pair of two-pound T-bones. There was nothing like a weekend on the river to give a man an appetite.

The Klamath has long been a favorite of fishermen. King salmon is the most important anadromous species on the river—in the 1930s, fishing guide Ed Hughes witnessed the catch of a 78-pounder—but these days most of the king and silver salmon found on the Klamath are from hatcheries. Other fishes include steelhead, coastal cutthroat trout, green and white sturgeon, eulachon (candle fish), and Pacific lamprey, often called eel. In bygone days commercial canneries operated at nearby Requa, and today several shops on Highway 101 sell jerky and canned fish.

Lewis Oscar steering his niece, Lillian Ames Salazar,
and three of her seventeen children up the Klamath, c. 1926

Over the years a number of guides gained fame for their work along the lower Klamath. Jack "the Swede" Husberg was one of the best known; he rowed his wooden boat at the river mouth until he was 88. Ed Hughes began fishing the same area in 1924 and was still active in the 1990s. Notable among the Indian guides have been Sandy Sanderson, who wore a hard hat to protect himself from other fishermen's lead weights and made a whooping cry when he had a catch; Sonny Smith Williams, from the family that runs famous Dad's Camp; Ron Genshaw, with his cocked black derby hat; and two guides who drowned in the river, Eddie Spott and James "Jimmy" Brooks.

Death Waited on the Klamath

The Klamath has always been a river to be reckoned with, and during the summer of 1927 it was at its most dangerous. First, on August 28, it tried to take two 13-year-old boys, Wesley Brooks and Mervin Woods, when their boat capsized at the river's mouth. Only the rescue efforts of their friend Raymond Figueva, himself only 15, saved the pair from drowning.

Barely a week later, on September 7, the Klamath struck again. This time three people were washed from their boat, again at the river mouth. Bystanders watched from shore, fearful of going to the victims' aid, and it fell to two teenage boys, Jimmy Brooks and Carl Seidner, to risk their lives trying to rescue the trio. They brought Kirby and Floyd Peters in alive but were unable to save Maud Peters.

Three years later both Brooks and Seidner were awarded the Carnegie Medal for their bravery. Brooks, who became one of the best local fishing guides, continued to defy the dark side of the river, "many times saving the unwary from a watery grave." The Klamath, however, finally exacted its price.

On August 18, 1949, Brooks was on the water about a mile above Klamath Glen with Beverly Ricalde in his boat. He then put the woman ashore and returned to the boat to work on its motor.

No one saw what happened next, but several people on shore heard the motor suddenly roar to life. A few moments later they observed the boat circling in the river. There was no one in it.

When investigators boarded the boat, they found that one of the motor's sparkplug wires had been disconnected; it appeared that Brooks, while working on the engine, had accidentally touched the wire to the plug, causing the motor to surge and throw him into the river. Three days later searchers found Jimmy Brooks's body.

Some people were surprised to learn that a riverman of such experience had drowned in the Klamath. Others, however, already knew what the river had just discovered—Jimmy Brooks never learned how to swim.

Hydraulic "monitor" on the Klamath

In times past, much more than water came down the Klamath. Early-day gold miners in the interior were quick to use huge "monitor" nozzles for hydraulic mining, washing away thousands of tons of topsoil in their quest to expose gold-bearing deposits. As a result, upstream salmon spawning beds lost valuable gravel while rearing areas along the lower river were damaged by the disrupted sediment.

Starting in the 1930s, timber companies transported logs down the Klamath from inland cutting sites. The logs were bound together to form rafts, which either floated downstream on their own or were pulled by tugboats. Between 1952 and 1964 over four million board feet of timber cruised down the Klamath; the operation ceased only when the nearby forests had been depleted.

Noted locations on the lower river include the two Blue Creek fishing lodges, both washed out by floods, and the Ah Pah Ranch. Luther Burbank visited the latter location in the early 1900s; an orchard of Gravenstein, Pippin, and Winter Banana apple trees was still growing at Ah Pah seventy years after the famed horticulturist planted them.

Beyond the Klamath bridge is the offramp for **State Highway 169**, mile 4.4, right. The two-lane, paved route runs upriver two miles to **Terwer Valley** and an additional mile to the fishing resort of **Klamath Glen**.

Town of Klamath

Highway 101 now enters the southern precincts of **Klamath**, pop. 150, elev. 26, a flood-ravaged community currently in its fifth incarnation. "Klamath City" was established in 1851 by settlers who envisioned it as a seaport for supplying the inland mines. The bar at the river mouth proved too treacherous for large ships to cross, and within a year the town was abandoned and its 30–odd buildings — including an iron "fort" — removed. By then, some 29 of the town's residents had died, the victims either of drowning or disagreements with the local Yuroks; Klamath City, it was said, "lasted quick." Next came the Klamath Indian Reservation in 1855, reinforced by Fort Ter-Wah two years later. The fort was established by then-Lieutenant George Crook, who later gained fame for his pursuit of Geronimo. Many Indians had already left the reservation before the winter of 1861-2, when a great flood washed away most of the arable land and left the nearby fort in shambles; a few months later both sites were abandoned. Squatters subsequently took over portions of the property, but they were evicted by the government in 1877 during a bitter dispute.

Activity then shifted downstream to Requa, where the recently established ferry crossed the river. After a lapse of nearly 50 years, Klamath again came to life in 1926, when the brand-new Douglas Memorial Bridge brought the Redwood Highway past the old townsite; soon a sizable string of stores lined the roadsides.

Pre-flood Klamath

The 1955 flood removed "entire rows" of buildings from the town, but the resilient residents rebuilt. A bigger flood hit in 1964, and this time only one shop was left standing; when federal disaster assistance was slow in coming, many of the town's inhabitants left. The washed-out bridge was replaced upstream by a new structure and the town relocated on higher ground east of the rerouted highway. Some 90 lots were subdivided, but this time Klamath found it harder to bounce back; today much of the business district remains undeveloped.

Other nearby locations have also been challenged by the Klamath, and so far, the river has always won. Safford's Island, a pretty homestead and longtime local gathering place, was eventually washed away by the channel's changing currents. A few miles upstream, Klamath Glen has also felt the water's wrath. One bankside fishing resort was first destroyed by the flood of 1927 and has been under water many times since. The entire operation is now mobilized—the office, washrooms, and other facilities are housed in trailers that can be hauled to high ground before the rainy season.

Contemporary Klamath offers restaurants, tent and RV parks, burl shops, gas station, motel, grocery store, post office, and tackle shop. Additional businesses are located north of High Prairie, some four miles ahead.

Ranching had long been a major activity in the area around the lower river, but for a few years during Prohibition, a less reputable enterprise also flourished. On February 12, 1926, Del Norte County Sheriff Jack Breen and two deputies were kept busy raiding a pair of "moonshine" operations concealed on local ranches. One site featured both a brewery and a distillery, but it could not compare with the second location, which was equipped with an 80-gallon still, cleverly hidden underground and "ingeniously camouflaged so that it could not be seen by anyone even a few yards distant." The "cavern" that housed it was lined with cement; water was piped in from a nearby spring. All in all, it was an admirably modern and sanitary operation, but the sheriffs were not impressed. The 2,000 gallons of mash on hand were summarily destroyed; the still was confiscated, and its operator, obviously a man of vision, was fined $500.

North of Klamath is **Requa Road** (see p. 181), mile 7.1, left; the paved, two-lane route leads to the historic town of **Requa** and to the **Hidden Beach Section, Coastal Trail**. The route also reaches a stunning overlook of the mouth of the Klamath River.

Immediately beyond Requa Road, the highway crosses Hunter Creek. In the 1890s both the creek area and nearby High Prairie were known as "good dairying districts." A report from a few years later noted that "tourists enjoy basking in the sun on Hunter's Creek and landing on the banks some of the lusty beauties of young salmon and trout with which the stream abounds."

Highway 101 continues northward to High Prairie, reaching a northern extension of the Klamath business district at mile 8.7. Ahead on the right is a marked turnoff for the **Yurok Tribal Office**, a weathered wooden structure that dates from the early 1940s. The building displays the skill of master craftworkers; notable among their creations are such finely-wrought features as a matched pair of three-tiered stone chimneys; numerous casement windows; and various interior panelings of redwood, Douglas-fir, Port Orford cedar, and spruce.

The privately owned **Trees of Mystery** appears on the right at mile 9.8, where a pair of brightly painted folklore figures make the spot difficult to miss. Nearly as big as a grain elevator, plaid-shirted Paul Bunyan greets visitors with a barrage of breezy chit-chat (provided by an amplified hidden observer) that astounds the unwary with its astuteness and is all the more remarkable given the bearded giant's glazed-eyed gaze. Close examination of his companion, a barn-sized Babe the Blue Ox, will reveal that an overzealous sculptor has restored the once-blighted bovine to bullhood.

A museum (no admittance charge) inside the Trees of Mystery gift shop houses an extensive collection of Indian artifacts, including basketry and other items from both local and out-of-area tribes. At the west end of the Trees' parking lot is the **Hostel Trail**, which follows a hillside logging road to the Redwood Hostel, two miles to the north; across the highway from the parking area is the **Hidden Beach Trail**, a rambling route that runs west to the ocean.

Coastal Area

Left at mile 10.8, the **Lagoon Creek Picnic Area** fronts a lovely expanse of yellow pond-lilies; non-motorized boating is allowed on **O'kwego Oke'to**, as the lagoon was called by the Yuroks. The **Hidden Beach Section, Coastal Trail** (see p. 254) leads around the water to meet the **Yurok Loop Trail**. Along the latter route lay the Yurok village of **O'men**, while nearby stood **O'kwego**, an "arrow tree." Passing Indians would shoot arrows into the trunk of such a tree, possibly to acknowledge its power. The lagoon witnessed a different awareness of trees in the 1940s, when the now-vanished Crescent Plywood mill began operating there.

The highway then reaches the ocean at rock-strewn **False Klamath Cove**, where, according to Yurok legend, the Klamath River once emptied into the ocean. Ahead on the left is the **Wilson Creek Picnic Area**, mile 11.5; opposite it on the right is a junction with **Wilson Creek Road**, which offers access to the **Hostel Trail** and to the **Redwood Hostel**, a well-restored ranchhouse that for decades was the hillside home of the DeMartin family.

DeMartins'
Del Norte Domain

It was a considerable proposition for Agnes and Louis DeMartin to set up their ranch on Wilson Creek in 1877. The sole land route connecting them with "civilization" in Crescent City was a primitive trail over difficult Damnation Ridge, while the surrounding steep canyonsides rendered the ranch site as rugged as it was remote. Compounding their problems, the DeMartins first chose to raise sheep—3,000 in all—but wild dogs and bears beat the butchers to most of them and the project had to be discontinued.

Still, the family managed to survive. They grew potatoes. Hogs and milk cows replaced the sheep. The DeMartins churned the cream into butter and fed the milk to the hogs; soon they were shipping not only the butter and potatoes but also lard, hams, and bacon to Crescent City. Transporting the goods via the overland route proved too difficult, so Yurok Jim Isles, aided by seven oarsmen, carried the cargo in his ocean-going dugout canoe. On occasion Agnes DeMartin also made the trip, bringing with her a child who needed to be baptized; it would be their only outing for the year. One son, Milton, was four years old before he first visited the city.

The DeMartins raised ten children, so meals were necessarily hearty; "an omelet wasn't worth making unless it had 50 eggs in it."

The DeMartin House, now the Redwood Hostel

Often the family ate wild game—deer, elk, bear, and panther, the latter a favorite that tasted something like turkey and was at its most flavorful if the predator had recently been eating sheep.

As with many of the early-day ranches, DeMartins' became a stopping place for travellers; a meal cost 25¢ and a bed for the night was usually the same. One visitor in 1880 wrote that he "lunched at Mr. DeMartin's and was pleasantly entertained by his good lady, who by the way, is an excellent cook and an agreeable hostess. Mr. DeMartin's place [is]...an evidence of thrift and enterprise."

Mail at first came only once a week, then thrice weekly. Delivering it was sometimes a risky proposition. One of the mail carriers, John Waggle, was swept from his horse and drowned while trying to cross Wilson Creek in a flood. His body washed out to sea, but it was later recovered and buried near the scene of his demise.

Mindful of his ranch's isolation, Louis DeMartin strongly advocated creation of a coastal wagon road. The project was finally approved and DeMartin constructed the section that crossed his property, including a bridge over Wilson Creek for which he charged the county $75. When a four-lane highway bridge was built across the creek in 1957, the span was named in Louis's honor. It was a fitting tribute for someone who, 80 years earlier, had known only horse trails and dugout canoes.

At mile 11.6 the highway crosses the Louis P. DeMartin Sr. Bridge.

Side Trip: Requa

A rustic, riverside village and an ocean overlook are attractions on this short side trip. The 2.5-mile, paved, two-lane road runs from Highway 101 to the hilltop above Requa.

(for map, see p. 168)

Features: (for key to symbols, see p. 89)

⚓🏄🏕️🐦✕🍴⛵🚗 town of Requa (0.9 miles)

🅿️⊗🚻💬 Klamath Overlook; Hidden Beach Section, Coastal Trail: (2.3)

🚗 end of route (2.6)

Town of Requa

After leaving Highway 101 north of Klamath, Requa Road winds westward through damp pastureland, turns southwest, and at mile 0.9 reaches the historic hamlet of **Requa**. A gleaming white inn, several aged houses, and a sunny hillside cemetery mark the sites of two earlier, larger communities: the substantial Yurok village of **Rek-woi** and the clamoring cannery town into which it was transformed. Although its current name would seem to be a transliteration from the Yurok, some people argue that it actually honors either the schooner *Requa*, which entered the river in 1887, or a man variously known as John B. or Issac Lawrence Requa, who may have either built a sawmill on the site or traded salmon there.

Modern Requa got its start in 1876 when Martin Jones and George Richardson began catching and salting fish near the old Yurok village; Jones added a sawmill five years later. Next came R. D. Hume of Gold Beach, Oregon, who sailed a scow down to the townsite, built a structure on it, and opened a waterborne general

181

merchandise store and salmon saltery. Soon dairy farms dotted the fertile bottomland east of town. Dairying there was an all-consuming occupation; when Lottie von Albensleben milked the cows she couldn't be distracted, so her baby daughter Helen was kept out of harm's way—tied inside a wooden box nailed to the barn wall.

Requa recreationists

By 1909 booming Requa boasted a post office, store, hotel and feed stable, blacksmith, a few dwellings, and "two places for satisfying the unnatural thirst." Prospects seemed bright for the town, but one illumination proved to be a problem instead.

"Roll out the Barrel": The Great Requa Fire of 1914

Early August, 1914. In Europe troops were mobilizing for the start of the "Great War." Half a world away, the residents of Requa still peacefully slept their nights away.

They would have done better to have been more alert. One evening a dull glow began to grow in the basement of the Pioneer Hotel. It went unnoticed until daybreak, and by then it had grown into a full-blown fire. A bucket brigade was organized but had little effect. Soon a good portion of the town was ablaze—Brizard's and

Paul's stores, the livery stable, the dance hall, several homes, and, worst of all, both saloons.

The buildings were beyond saving, but several quick-witted Requians managed to stave off total disaster. The saloons were heroically entered and their contents carried out. Given the state of emergency, bottled goods were consumed immediately, while casks of hard liquor were rolled down the hill into the protective waters of Klamath Slough. They would be sorely needed during the cleanup work.

The flagging fire-fighting efforts were further hampered by some of the more intemperate imbibers, who became incapable of standing and were in danger of tumbling sloughward down the slope. An ingenious remedy was devised: the men were tied to nearby trees until the sheriff arrived.

As the hotel continued to conflagrate it was discovered that its dishwasher, an extremely sound sleeper, was still inside. Two burly fishermen burst into the flaming building to attempt a rescue. They soon emerged with the dishwasher, who'd been pulled from his bed in a state of near nudity. The man had to be restrained from reentering the hotel to retrieve his pants; his motivation, it turned out, was not modesty but money, his trousers having contained all the wealth he possessed.

As soon as the ashes cooled, Requa rebuilt. The saloon keepers, the disheveled dishwasher, and the other inhabitants totaled up their substantial losses, but the disaster was not without its brighter side. For years, it is said, those who were present would gaze fondly at the slough below town and recall the day they "rolled out the barrels" in Requa.

Salmon canneries were the big business in town. A whistle announced the start of each day's fishing, and supervisors watched closely as derby-hatted fishermen boated their catch; when the observers calculated that there were enough fish to keep the cannery running for the rest of the day, the whistle blew again and the fishermen quit. The daily quota often ran to as many as 7,000 to 10,000 fish, a figure sometimes reached in only one or two hours. During salmon season, entire Yurok families left their upriver homes to come fish the lower Klamath or to work in the canneries.

Packing 'em in at the salmon cannery

One cannery worker had a remarkable job: making all the cans by hand. Jimmie Genshaw would cut sheet metal with tin shears, enamel the insides, and then solder the pieces together. Jimmie and his wife Kitty, both Yuroks, were childless, but they raised six generations of orphans and their "hospitality home" offered free lodging and meals to Indians and whites alike. Their generous way of life had its rewards, for Kitty lived to be 98 and her husband 106.

Among other local notables were several sailors.

Captains Courageous

Navigating the bar at the mouth of the Klamath had early on proved dangerous. In 1850 the brig *Tarquin* lodged on the northern spit and was soon pounded into fragments. Within a year the residents of nearby Klamath City tired of the river's treachery and abandoned their fledgling community.

Other settlers soon arrived in the area, however, and other boats came to serve them. The results were often unfortunate: the schooners *Charlotte* and *Gold Beach,* both wrecked in 1856; the *Centennial,* lost in 1877; the *Mayflower,* 1893; the *Dauntless,* 1894. Despite these disasters, various captains continued to attempt the bar, meeting with mixed results.

William Crone arrived in Requa the summer of 1902 as a crewman on a gold mining dredge from Sacramento. The dredge's skipper succumbed to a heart attack and the vessel never made it to the gold fields, so Crone stayed on in Requa. He took work first at the cannery, then as a gill netter, and in 1908 was crewing on the *Dawn* when she sank near Trinidad after hitting a submerged rock. Undeterred by the mishap, Crone secured financial backing, purchased the *Coaster,* and sailed her out of Requa for many years.

Crone was deemed a skillful and competent skipper but, like many of his ilk, was extremely superstitious. He refused to sail on Fridays, which he'd determined to be his personal bad luck day. Perhaps it had been a Friday when Crone had endured his most perilous experience, a dry-land episode that had him cutting the branches off a big spruce as he climbed its trunk, only to find himself caught part way up with no limbs left to get him back down. The crisis was resolved when the spruce's owner attached a rope to an arrow and shot it up to the stranded seaman. Later in life, having survived innumerable Fridays, Crone and his wife ran the local inn for over 20 years. Always public spirited, the Captain was especially active during the great influenza epidemic, ministering "to the needy with his personal whisky bottle."

Captain Gus Smith also navigated the perilous mouth of the Klamath. His gas-powered schooner *Katata* initially lacked carrying capacity for the Requa-Eureka run, so Smith sawed the ship in two, added 13 feet to the center of its hull, and then happily transported many extra tons of wood products and salmon. The *Katata* plied the briny waters until the fall of 1914, when a crosswave hit her broadside and sent her onto the rocks north of the Klamath's entrance. The ship was a total loss, but most of the cargo washed up onto shore undamaged—case after case of canned salmon, making an unexpected last migration landward.

A third skipper was even less fortunate. In April 1915 Captain Walter Johnson and the *Magnolia* were headed for the Klamath

Wreck of the *Katata*

shortly before daylight. In the darkness Johnson overshot the river entrance by 200 yards and had to turn seaward to reattempt the entrance. In the middle of this maneuver a breaker hit the *Magnolia* sideways; all of her cargo was on deck, and the top-heavy ship "rolled over like a log." Johnson and one crewman were washed overboard and claimed by the ocean, while the engineer never escaped the engine room. Word reached Requa, however, that sailors were seen clinging to the ship's hull, so Captain Crone rounded up a crew of volunteers and took the *Coaster* over the treacherous bar; finding no one to rescue, they then towed the *Magnolia*, hull up, to Eureka for repairs.

In the end, despite the courageous captains, it was the Klamath that triumphed. During the 1920s Crone skippered a new boat, the *Golden West*, as it transported hundreds of tons of cement and steel for the construction of the Douglas Memorial Bridge. The river failed to sink his ship, but, in a sense, the bridge finally did—once the structure was completed, freight trucks easily serviced Klamath and Requa, leaving the *Golden West* without work and Captain Crone nearly as high and dry as he'd once been in his spruce tree.

Commercial salmon fishing was banned on the Klamath in 1934. Once the canneries closed, the lower river became dominated by sport fishermen. In 1939, *National Geographic* noted that "from far and near, the angling brotherhood flocks here to the Klamath River during the early fall salmon run. The silvery giants are caught by trolling from rowboats." Not many years earlier, one well-known fisherman caught a giant indeed.

Zane Grey's Fish Story

The settings for Zane Grey's novels were usually the land of slickrock and sagebrush, but when the author chose a locale to relax in, it was often the forested, fish-filled Pacific Northwest. His favorite haunt was Oregon's Rogue River, but once, on the way south from there, Grey and two companions stopped to test the waters at Requa. The first afternoon the trio had nary a strike, but the prime time for fishing was morning, and Grey persuaded his cohorts to stay over and try again then.

Come daybreak, the men set out in two boats for the mouth of the river. When they reached their destination, Grey took in the surroundings, and

...[t]he charm of the place suddenly dawned on me. Looking out toward the sea I saw the breakers curl green and sunlit and fall with a heavy boom. Along the rocky point of the channel there was a line of white water, turbulent and changing, the restless chafing of the waves. And that river of dark ocean water, rushing in, swelling in the center, swirling along the rocks, and running over the sandy bar, assuredly looked as dangerous as it was beautiful.

"Angling brotherhood,"
at the mouth of the Klamath

Not as exciting, perhaps, as the exploits of Grey's *Hash Knife Outfit* or his *Riders of the Purple Sage*, but there was more to come.

After plying the lower river for a while, Grey at last had a strike. It was a big fish, and it was full of energy. Grey fought with it as his oarsman rowed to keep up. The struggle seemed endless: "My arms ached, my right hand had become almost numb. I grew breathless, hot and wet with sweat, and...my eyes began to dim from the strain of nerve and muscle...."

But the fish was tiring too, and it finally gave up before Grey did. The angling author at last hauled aboard a huge King salmon that weighed in at 57 pounds. The episode not only put food on the table, it gave Grey grist for his writing mill; he subsequently produced a lengthy magazine article about landing his catch. Although no rival to *The Old Man and the Sea*, the account at least was popular on the Klamath, since the salmon-satiated Grey concluded that Requa was "the most thrilling and fascinating place to fish I had ever seen."

Even though white settlers had encroached on Rek-woi, built their own buildings, and changed the town's name, the Yuroks continued to maintain their own dwindling community. In 1917 this consisted of one old-style family house, several collapsed sweat houses, a caved-in ceremonial house, some graves, and a few pits where other houses had earlier stood. Only four families, all living in weathered, white-style frame houses, were left. Lye-eck, the last remaining redwood slab house in Rek-woi, was eventually restored by its owners and the Del Norte County Historical Society. Recent years have seen a resurgence in Requa's Yurok population as members of the tribe continue to share the area with white residents.

Klamath Overlook

Requa Road's name changes to **Patrick J. Murphy Memorial Drive** near the inn. The route then climbs through the town, passing a lovely hillside cemetery and residential district before finally emerging from the forest onto open slopes. Ahead at mile 2.3 is Redwood National Park's **Klamath Overlook** and the southern

Mouth of river,
from Klamath Overlook

end of the **Hidden Beach Section, Coastal Trail** (see p. 254); a short
side trail descends the hillslope to an awe-inspiring overlook of the
mouth of the Klamath. The site also provides picnic tables and
restrooms. At road's end, mile 2.6, is a former air force surveillance
installation that now houses both a California Conservation Corps
center and maintenance facilities for Redwood National Park.

Del Norte Coast Redwoods State Park

Stretching from Wilson Creek to the outskirts of Crescent City, this 11.3 mile section of Highway 101 runs almost the entire length of Del Norte Coast Redwoods State Park. The route is mostly two-lane pavement, with a short section of four-lane road in the south and several passing lanes to the north. *Warning: use caution along the narrow section of roadway near mile 2.0 and also on the sharp turns north of the Mill Creek Campground turnoff.*

Features: (for key to symbols, see p. 89)

🏕 DeMartin Section, Coastal Trail (0.0)

🏕⛺🌊 Footsteps Rocks Trail (0.7 mile)

🏕 access to DeMartin Section, Coastal Trail (1.5)

🏕🚲🚂 Last Chance Section, Coastal Trail (2.9)

🏕🚲🚂 Last Chance and DeMartin sections, Coastal Trail (3.0)

🏕⛺🌊 Damnation Creek Trail (3.3)

🚗🏕🏠🏕🚂 side road to Mill Creek Campground; trail access (7.6)

🚗🏕🚂 junction with Hamilton Road; access to Rellim Ridge Trail (10.1)

🚗 intersection with Enderts Beach Road and Humboldt Road; end of route (11.3)

Wilson Creek was once the approximate boundary between the Yurok and Tolowa Indian tribes. Just to the south lay a border village, **Tages Lsatun;** it was a large gathering place, with "sometimes a hundred canoes there." Upon crossing the creek, Highway 101 passes the **DeMartin Section, Coastal Trail,** mile 0.0, right.

190

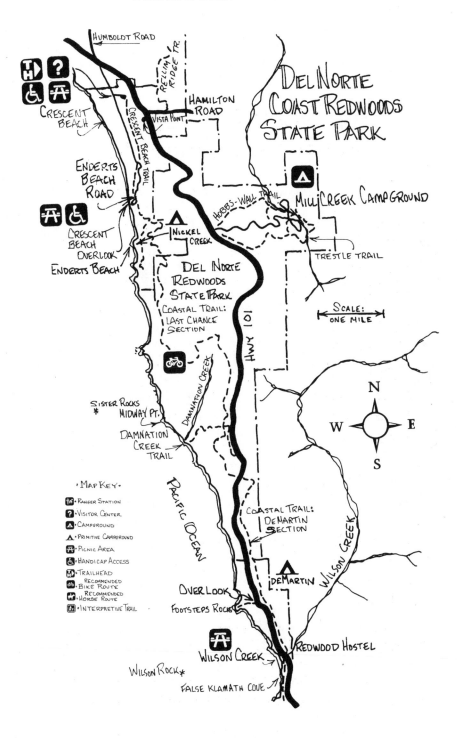

A short stretch of four-lane roadway takes the route up a steep incline. The earlier county road, which ran to the east, used a series of switchbacks to ascend the grade; the big Pierce Arrow motor stages would have to back up three or four times to negotiate some of the tighter turns.

Nowadays, the interest is all to the west, where the shimmering sea splashes against a spectacular, rock-strewn shore. Just north of a vista point, mile 0.7, left, Highway 101 passes the unmarked start of the **Footsteps Rocks Trail**, left. This picturesque route drops a half mile to a stunningly scenic jumble of coastal rock.

At mile 1.5 an unmarked dirt road, right, leads past a locked gate to the middle portion of the **DeMartin Section, Coastal Trail**. Highway 101 continues up the mountain slope, soon reaching a narrow passage along an often unstable cliffside. *Drive with caution along this stretch.*

As the highway crests the grade, it passes a dirt road, mile 2.9, left, that was once a part of the Redwood Highway and now forms a segment of the **Last Chance Section, Coastal Trail**; the route is open to bicyclists (see p. 279). Highway 101 then enters old-growth redwood forest, and at mile 3.0 the **Coastal Trail** crosses the road. Leftward the trail drops over the ridge to reach the Last Chance Section, while to the right the path descends southward on the DeMartin Section. *Watch for hikers.*

Del Norte Coast Redwoods State Park

Although it stretches from False Klamath Cove to the Foothills southeast of Crescent City, the heart of **Del Norte Coast Redwoods State Park** is the magnificent forest through which the highway now passes. When the site was established in 1925, it consisted solely of a 157–acre grove dedicated to Henry Solon Graves, former Chief Forester of the U. S. Forest Service. Within six years the park had grown to 2,360 acres, and traffic through it on the Redwood Highway often exceeded 1,500 cars a day. The attractions of the area had been noted by an observer in 1898, who found "redwoods which are full of beautiful rhotodendrons (sic) and numerous wild flowers, and which makes the scenery most delightful as one rides along." About this time, an advertising-minded merchant added his contribution to the local landscape.

Xerxes Alexander Phillips: Modern-Day Conqueror

The signs were neatly posted, one per mile, along the road from the Klamath to Crescent City:

— Miles to X. A. Phillips
Good Goods at Honest Prices
Crescent City, California

Phillips had come to the North Coast at the turn of the century "with a wagon loaded with merchandise and a personality loaded with charm." He set up shop in Crescent City but wandered along all the roads between Requa and Gold Beach, Oregon, lodging with families throughout the area, bringing gifts to the local children, and staying away weeks at a time.

X. A. Phillips and his "Travelling Emporium"

But X. A. soon found a reason to remain closer to home. She was Anna Mischler, who had arrived in 1906 to teach at the Crescent City high school. Anna was attractive and well educated, and she was available. Phillips fell for her like a box of goods dropping from the back of his wagon.

It was a new kind of product that X. A. was now peddling—himself. He got his first chance at the Odd Fellows auction, where he donated a beautiful doll, bid a fantastic price for it, and then presented it to the beautiful teacher.

The days passed, and although Anna Mischler may not have known it, her new suitor was beginning to have an effect. During her ancient history class, Anna unwittingly asked a portentous question: "Who," she inquired of the students, "can tell me about Xerxes and Alexander?" The scholars knew their history, both ancient and local, and the room resounded with their laughter.

Anna looked puzzled. The class continued to titter. She remonstrated: "What! No one can tell me about the two greatest names in ancient history?"

"Not so ancient!" one of the students finally blurted out.

The uncomprehending teacher struggled to restore order. Only after class had been dismissed did a lone female student remain to enlighten her.

"Miss Mischler," the young woman inquired, "didn't you know that X. A. Phillips's name is Xerxes Alexander?"

This time the teacher joined in the laughter.

Phillips had yet to pop the question, but had he been outside the classroom that afternoon, he would have known the answer—he and Anna Mischler were married in September 1908. It had been a great challenge for a humble peddler to attempt such a conquest, but anyone named Xerxes Alexander was bound to succeed.

A parking area at mile 3.3, left, serves users of the **Damnation Creek Trail** (see p. 244). The route was laid out during the park's early days by landscape architect Emerson Knight and Deputy State Forester W. B. Rider. It lessened the grade of an older Tolowa trail that had descended the mountainside to the ocean.

The highway now runs along the top of Damnation Ridge, passing through stands of immense redwoods. In late spring the rosy bloom of countless rhododendrons brightens the forest; they are followed by a roadside profusion of leopard lilies. Then, during late summer, come displays of two colorful berries, the gleaming red of fat false Solomon's seal and the shining blue of clintonia.

In 1828, Jedediah Smith's party struggled through the difficult terrain that later became the park, encountering much brush and fallen timber. Things were little better in 1890, although by then a mail route wound through the woods; one traveller who followed it concluded that the trail was "about the very worst in the country." The county wagon road that mercifully replaced it a few years later is still sometimes visible next to the highway. To ease travel on the often muddy wagon route, former ox driver Andy Hamilton created a sort of "redwood pavement" by laying eight-foot-long puncheons across the roadbed; Hamilton also operated a ridgetop stage station called Skunk Camp. Andy had a reputation as a mild-mannered sort, for he had been the only Del Norte "bullwhacker" who didn't cuss his oxen as they moved logs through the woods.

Mouth of
Damnation Creek

Mill Creek Campground

At mile 7.6, right, is the turnoff for the **Mill Creek Campground**. A two-lane, paved road descends two miles into the scenic canyon of Mill Creek, where vestiges of an old logging operation are still visible; the workers lived just north of the current park boundary.

Camp 12–2

It was the thirteenth camp that Hobbs, Wall & Company set up, but the loggers were a superstitious lot and so Camp 12–2 became its name. The site lay deep in the canyon of Mill Creek, surrounded by soaring redwoods that clung to the steep hillslopes. The remote location could be reached only by the timber company's private railroad, the Del Norte Southern, whose tracks ended a short distance south of the camp.

A system of railed "inclines" linked the surrounding ridges with the canyon below; logs cut high on the hillsides were loaded onto railroad flatcars, hauled by train engine to one of the inclines, and then lowered crosswise by steam donkey down the 65° slopes. Sometimes the flatcars carried an additional cargo—Dorothy Smith, the teacher at the camp's little school. Keeping company with a load of logs was only one of Dorothy's adventures; she spent her evenings in her quarters—a rude cabin on stilts—staring at the stars through a broken shake roof.

The camp's few families each had houses of their own, but the unmarried men lived in small cabins arranged in rows next to the railroad. Every morning and evening 165 hungry workers would troop to the cookhouse to be fed, as two cooks and three waitresses struggled to keep the dishes filled. Each man had his regular spot at one of the tables, and woe to the newcomer who sat in someone else's place.

The loggers took their lunch with them into the woods—steaks, potatoes, canned vegetables, bread, butter, and dessert, all stuffed into a five-gallon coal oil can and carried on an ax handle across one of the men's shoulders. The grub was cooked, during the hour and a half lunch break, in the loggers' lunchroom—a temporary shanty made of peeled bark. After working nine and a half hours each weekday, the men knocked off early on Saturdays for a shower and a meal before catching the logging train into Crescent City. There the bars and red light district kept them busy until about five on Monday morning, when they would ride the Del Norte Southern's version of the red-eye special and return to their jobs.

Some of the men operated on a different schedule, staying in camp for two or three months at a time and carefully saving their

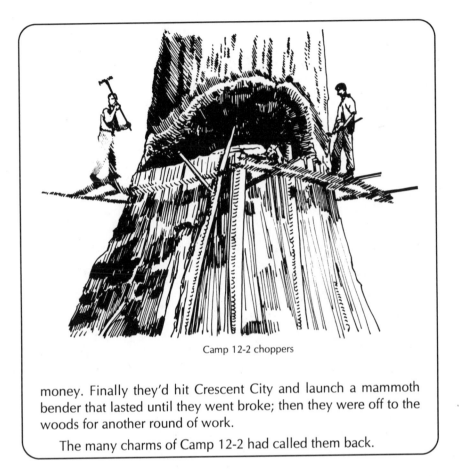

Camp 12-2 choppers

money. Finally they'd hit Crescent City and launch a mammoth bender that lasted until they went broke; then they were off to the woods for another round of work.

The many charms of Camp 12-2 had called them back.

Mill Creek Campground's 145 sites are situated amid the leafy beauty of the shaded stream canyon. Several hiking routes leave the camping area: the **Trestle Trail** (see p. 241), which passes the remains of the old logging railroad; the **Saddler Skyline Trail**, a hillslope traverse that for a time follows one of the inclined rail routes; the **Nature Loop Trail**, whose course crosses through thick forest; the streamside **Mill Creek Trail**; and the **Hobbs, Wall Trail**, a circling route up to the ridgetop. Numerous stumps, overgrown with the vegetation of six decades, rise from among the campsites.

North of the campground turnoff, Highway 101 begins its long, twisting descent towards Crescent City. The sharper curves are marked with warnings to reduce speed, but many motorists still have mishaps. *Drive with caution.*

When the current, ridgetop roadway was constructed in the early 1930s, it replaced a rapidly deteriorating section of the original Redwood Highway that ran across the crumbling, ocean-fronting cliffs far below. Throughout the few years of its troubled existence, the cliffside route was beset by numerous road-closing landslides, an inconvenience for which its spectacular scenery could not compensate.

Highway cliff cut
south of Crescent City

During its descent, Highway 101 crosses the ridgeline of **Ragged Ass Hill**, mile 8.5, which formerly served as the route for the county wagon road. The hill's name does not derive from the escapades of any donkey.

Motorists who glance skyward, mile 9.6, are liable to sight a large tree limb surmounted by a circular mass of sticks. The striking structure is an osprey, or fish hawk, nest.

Mile 10.0 offers a vista point, left, whose access is made dangerous by two lanes of oncoming traffic. Just ahead, **Hamilton Road** branches right, mile 10.1; it passes the aging timbers of a Del Norte Southern trestle before arriving at a parking area for the Miller-Rellim Lodge. A short trail through the timber company's "demonstration" forest crosses steep inclines down which logs were skidded. North of the parking area is the **Rellim Ridge Trail**, an RNP route through mostly cutover land that runs northward to the Mill Creek Horse Trail.

Hobbs, Wall & Company Camp 12 was situated near the Miller-Rellim Lodge. In the early 1920s workers east of the camp felled an enormous redwood close to Mill Creek that measured 23 feet across its butt and stood almost 300 feet tall. Two choppers took seven days to drop the tree, which contained enough wood to build 50 "cottages."

The highway continues its descent, leaving Del Norte Coast Redwoods State Park just before reaching the coastal plain. The tour route then concludes, mile 11.3, at an intersection with Enderts Beach Road and Humboldt Road.

Vista Point—
Crescent City in distance

Crescent City Area

Beginning a short distance north of Del Norte Coast Redwoods State Park, this 6.8-mile section of Highway 101 passes a stretch of seacoast, crosses through Crescent City, and ends at the turnoff to Jedediah Smith Redwoods State Park. The road is mostly two-lane highway, with short stretches of parallel, one-way, multiple-lane traffic in Crescent City and four-lane freeway north of town.

(for map, see p. 213)

Features: (for key to symbols, see p. 89)

➥ 🅿 🚲 ⚓ ♿ 🚻 ‼ ≋ turnoff for Enderts Beach Road — access to Crescent Beach, Crescent Beach Overlook, Enderts Beach, and various trails (0.0 miles)

➥ ✈ ⚓ ⓘ ♿ 🚻 ⛺ ⛽ 🍴 🛏 ☕ 🚐 ‼ ≋ Crescent City center; turnoff to Redwood National Park headquarters (2.4)

➥ Highway 199 interchange; end of route (6.8)

Crescent Beach Area

The route starts on Highway 101 at the first intersection north of Del Norte Coast Redwoods State Park. Right is **Humboldt Road**, a two-lane paved route; it runs north one mile to reach Howland Hill Road, an alternate approach to Jedediah Smith Redwoods State Park. To the left is **Enderts Beach Road**, two lanes, paved; it leads through Redwood National Park land that was once part of the Alexander/Pozzi Ranch. Started by Henry Alexander in 1869, the operation featured sheep, cattle, and dairy cows; in 1879 the dairy produced a whopping two tons of butter. After purchasing the property in 1914, the Pozzi family ran the ranch until the 1980s, when it was taken over by the park. Enderts Beach Road passes the Pozzi house, left, and the turnoff to the **Crescent Beach Picnic Area** and **Crescent Beach Trail**, right, on its way to **Crescent Beach Overlook** some two miles ahead. The road ends at a turnaround and parking area just beyond the overlook; here the **Last Chance Section, Coastal Trail** (open to bikes) departs southward, leading to the **Enderts Beach Trail**, the **Nickel Creek Primitive Camp**, and the **Nature Trail**. The Last Chance route begins along an abandoned, cliff-hugging section of the original Redwood Highway, later departing from the relict roadway in the lush canyon confines of Nickel Creek.

Crescent City

Straight ahead through the intersection are the southern environs of **Crescent City**, pop. 8,513, elev. 44, the Del Norte (the "e" is silent) county seat. As with other early North Coast communities, the town owed its start to gold strikes in the inland mountains. Initial contact with the townsite was inauspicious; when three vessels

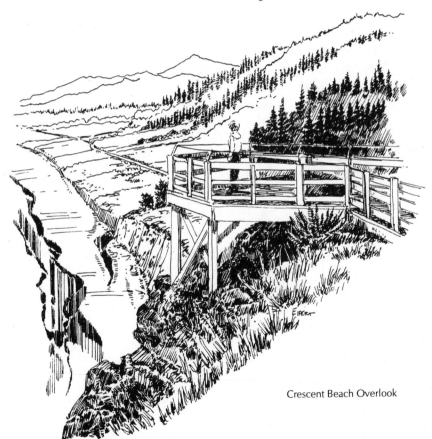

Crescent Beach Overlook

anchored in the bay in 1850, one of them, the schooner *Paragon*, wrecked on the beach. The following winter a party of prospectors viewed the wide-curving shoreline from the far hilltops, but did not venture down to it. That was left to an expedition from the mining camp of Althouse, Oregon; in September 1852, the group sent one game soul south to charter a boat in San Francisco while the others cut their way through the mountains to the coast. The men camped on the beach and waited; in due time the schooner *Pomona* arrived and soon afterward the town was laid out. Although one observer found the resultant collection of tents and split board houses to be "more crescent than city," by the spring of 1856 the local paper could claim:

> Here is a town with 500 inhabitants, 160 houses...an annual trade amounting to 4000 tons of merchandise...two express offices, a Fire Company, a Theatre, a Church and sometimes a School...."

If the community was weak on education, it was strong on business enterprise. During an active week as many as 1,000 pack mules were loaded with goods and dispatched for locations like the mining metropolis of Jacksonville, in Oregon Territory, or for the gold diggings on the Klamath River. The steamers *America* and *Columbia* brought the supplies into port, often landing merchandise of special importance to the miners: when the *Columbia* carried her first shipment of mail to Crescent City in 1857, the remainder of her cargo consisted of 40 barrels of whiskey and a lone barrel of sugar—the sugar, it turned out, had been overlooked on the ship's previous trip.

By then, the *America* was no longer in operation. The ship's charred hulk had been beached two years earlier after a mysterious fire. Her demise, however, was not the worst maritime disaster the community would encounter.

The Sinking of the
Brother Jonathan

In early August, 1865, the bodies of a horse and camel washed up on the beach several miles north of Trinidad. The event was unusual but not unexpected, for the animals were but two of the numerous victims of a recent shipwreck. Along with some 213 humans aboard the *Brother Jonathan*, they had drowned in the most deadly sinking ever recorded on the Pacific Coast.

The ill-fated steamer had left San Francisco on July 28, bound for Portland and Victoria. Besides her passengers, who included General George T. Wright, commander of the Columbia military district, there was a varied cargo on board: several horses, including one belonging to the general; a strong box containing some $300,000 in pay for the soldiers at Fort Vancouver; two camels that were reportedly bound for the Portland zoo; a good deal of mining and milling machinery; and, according to some accounts, a load of iron railroad rails.

The *Brother Jonathan*

At the dock in San Francisco, Captain Samuel J. DeWolf had protested to his superiors that his ship was overloaded. They responded that the *Brother Jonathan* would sail as she was, with or without DeWolf on board; reluctantly, the captain returned to the vessel.

On the morning of July 30 the heavily laden *Brother Jonathan* passed the harbor of Crescent City, fired the usual one-gun salute, and by noon was about four miles north of Point St. George. A gale had come up, a true Nor'wester, and, according to the ship's quartermaster, "the sea was running mountain high and the ship was not making headway." Captain DeWolf decided to return to Crescent City and lay over until the storm abated.

The *Brother Jonathan* came about and headed for the harbor, passing Seal Rock at 12:45 PM. About an hour later, a terrific jolt shivered the ship's timbers, slamming the passengers to the deck.

The vessel had struck a submerged rock with devastating force. Immediately the *Brother Jonathan's* foremast plunged through her hull, crashing the yardarm onto the deck; worse yet, part of her keel broke off and came alongside the remainder of the battered boat. Three cannon shots—the distress signal—boomed out as the crew attempted to launch the lifeboats. One boat was immediately swamped and another capsized by the churning seas, but a third managed to make it away from the doomed ship; its 19 occupants were to be the only survivors.

General Wright's wife had been put aboard the last lifeboat, but she insisted on returning to her husband on the deck. There the couple stood, side by side, as the *Brother Jonathan* sank.

Late that afternoon the lone lifeboat came around Lighthouse Point and entered the harbor at Crescent City. A crowd quickly assembled to meet the vessel at the shore, where the survivors brought first word of the catastrophe. Soon several rescue boats started for the site of the wreck, but they were all turned back by the heavy wind and high seas.

A few days later the bodies and wreckage began to wash ashore. Some of the victims were recovered as far south as the Mad River in central Humboldt County. The dead were mourned and buried, and the inevitable treasure seekers came to look for the submerged military strong box and other valuables. The searchers were all unsuccessful. Spurred by the wreck, the federal government eventually built a badly needed lighthouse at Point St. George. That seemed to be the end of the story, but then, years later, there came a report from Victoria regarding the *Brother Jonathan's* sister ship, the *Pacific*: she had sunk offshore, with the loss of 200 lives.

> *Brother* and sister both at the bottom of the sea; more than 400 persons drowned. It was quite a record for a fatal family.

By the 1880s Crescent City claimed a population of about 1,000, along with the usual collection of hotels, stores, churches, fraternal halls, and drinking establishments. The community had two newspapers, one run by "a stalwart Republican," the other by "a strong Democrat...[who] is afraid to say so and supports no politics in particular."

Although most of the town changed little during the decade, there was some progress—the number of saloons more than doubled. Among those vying for patrons were the "XX," the "Crystal," the "Belvedere," and the languor-inducing "Laboring Men's Resort." One saloonkeeper stood (or sat) out from the rest: Wolf Morris had started his establishment back in the early mining days and, like his business, had expanded with age. Old and heavy, Morris often had customers wait on themselves so that he didn't have to rise from his chair.

After the mining boom subsided, logging became the lifeblood of Crescent City. Starting in 1871, Hobbs, Wall & Company (first called Hobbs, Pomeroy Company) employed most of the men in the community, and the company's store provided residents with all the "necessities of life." During nearly 70 years of operation Hobbs, Wall logged much of the nearby forest, built miles of railroad to transport the timber, milled the logs, and sent its lumber products on its own steamers to San Francisco. When the company closed in 1939 the shattered county almost went bust, scraping by until the post-World War II housing boom revived the local timber industry. By 1954, more than 60 percent of the county's work force was employed in lumbering and related activities. Decades later, Del Norte again came on hard times as the timber supply dried up, but the region's economy was recently rejuvenated when Crescent City became the site for California's premier penitentiary. With Pelican Bay State Prison providing a new source of employment, felons have replaced forests as the county's cash crop.

It is not the first time that criminals have been big news in Crescent City.

His Honor, the Bandit

The wire service story was too good to be true. Editors had a field day with it, for the account yielded headlines like the following:

Former Bandit Is
Elected As Mayor
Of Crescent City

The story that followed was even better:

Al Jennings, former outlaw, one time nominee for governor of Oklahoma and at present mayor-elect of Crescent City, today pledged himself to preserve law and order.

Jennings told the United Press that his trigger finger and eyesight are as good as ever but expressed the desire that the community support him in his efforts toward a peaceful administration.

It had been a busy time for the new mayor, who had arrived in Del Norte only that week, accompanied by Frank Mormon, "L. A. capitalist," and actress Hazel Bedford. Jennings purchased some property near town and promptly found himself elected honorary mayor by the city council. He telephoned news of his triumph to

Bantam bandit Al Jennings receiving the gavel of office as mayor

his Oklahoma friend, the "roping and lecturing comedian," Will Rogers.

The new mayor's first week in office was an active one, as he gave not one, but two eagerly awaited lectures. The first was for his new constituents, held at Enderts Theater in Crescent City. The other took him to the Smith River highway labor camp, where he spoke to an appreciative audience of the workers, who were all convicts.

When the local paper displayed a photograph of the mayor the following week, there was reason for some confusion. It seemed impossible that the short, bespectacled man in the dapper dark suit and hat could be the ex-desperado, yet it was indeed he who was receiving the gavel of office. The explanation for Mayor Jennings' amazingly innocent appearance was not, however, hard to find: until recently he had merely been a bandit and was only now becoming a politician.

City Center

At mile 2.0, Highway 101 reaches an intersection with **Elk Valley Road**; a right turn connects with Howland Hill Road, a partly-paved, partly-gravel route that traverses the southern section of Jedediah Smith Redwoods State Park (see p. 223). The highway bends left, dividing as it enters downtown Crescent City; for a short distance, north- and southbound motorists are now separately routed on one-way streets a block apart. The first subsequent intersection is **Front Street**, mile 2.4, where a left turn leads to the **City Center** and its large adjacent park. Farther west, at the corner of Front and H streets, the hollow shell of the Surf Hotel stands sentinel over land inundated by the 1964 tsunami. North on H Street at 6th Street is the Del Norte County Historical Society's **Main Museum**, whose compact but remarkably complete collection of local memorabilia is incarcerated in the former county jail. A second society museum, the **Battery Point Lighthouse**, lies two blocks south of the intersection of Front and B streets. A short footpath allows low-tide access to the scenic structure, which looks out upon the city harbor and several offshore rocks. Two of the latter, Steamboat and Fauntleroy, were temporary resting places for a World War II casualty.

Battery Point Lighthouse, Crescent City

The Emigrating *Emidio*

Following the Japanese bombing of Pearl Harbor, a wave of fear washed over the West Coast; no one had thought it possible that the Japanese would attack Hawaii, but now that they had done so, it seemed that no location was safe. Such concerns were to prove unfounded for most Californians, but, as it turned out, coastal sailors had good reason to be afraid.

On December 19, 1941, less than two weeks after the Pearl Harbor attack, Japanese submarines found their first stateside target. It was Richfield Oil's *S. S. Agwiworld*, sailing near Cyprus Point, about 100 miles south of San Francisco. The sub fired eight shells at the tanker but scored no hits; the *Agwiworld* eluded its pursuer and reached safety in the Santa Cruz harbor. Four other attacks followed before Christmas, including one off the Humboldt coast.

The *S. S. Emidio*, a General Petroleum tanker, was steaming south late in the morning of December 20 when it sighted the

Blunt's Reef Lightship off Cape Mendocino. At 1:10 P.M. another vessel appeared. Unlike the stationary lightship, this one was moving towards the *Emidio*—it was a submarine, and it was only a quarter mile away.

Captain C. A. Farrow, the *Emidio's* skipper, attempted evasive action by zigzagging at full speed. The sub, however, closed the gap, and about half an hour later a gun crew appeared on its deck and commenced firing at the ship's radio antenna. Wireless operator W. S. Foote managed to send out an SOS, but the sub's second shot hit its target and the radio went dead. The submarine then began to shell the *Emidio's* lifeboats.

At 2:10 P.M. Captain Farrow gave two orders: stop engines and prepare to abandon ship. As the crew lowered away one of the lifeboats, a Japanese shell shattered the davits that held the boat in place, plunging three crewmen into the sea. While Farrow and most of his men conducted a vain search for the lost sailors, two American bombers appeared overhead. Just as the submarine ceased firing, one of the planes dropped a depth charge. The charge apparently missed its target, and a moment later a swirling line appeared in the water—the sub had fired a torpedo at the *Emidio*.

In the ship's boiler room, Third Assistant Benjamin Winters and Fireman Kenneth Kimes were waiting for steam to build up. Suddenly the torpedo burst through the side of the room, sailed through the air to the far wall, and exploded.

Kimes and Winters were killed instantly. As the stricken *Emidio* sat dead in the sea, the remainder of her crew finished piling into a pair of lifeboats. The bombers then passed over again and dropped a second depth charge; there was a spray of water, followed by a cloud of black smoke, and, as far as the men in the lifeboats could tell, their ship was avenged.

Although the tanker was still afloat, the *Emidio's* survivors gave her up for lost and turned to their oars, heading back towards the Blunt's Reef Lightship. They reached it 13 hours later and were taken to Eureka by a rescue vessel the next day.

The *Emidio* had been badly wounded, but she wasn't dead yet. Crewless, with a gaping hole in her side, she now charted her own course up the coast, a determined derelict in search of safe harbor. She nearly reached it four days later, when on Christmas Eve she

The *Emidio* on the rocks

came to rest on Steamboat Rock, just outside the anchorage at Crescent City.

Almost safe, but not quite. For three weeks the immobilized *Emidio* remained lodged on the rock, her stern submerged, her bow bobbing on the waves as townspeople came to the Battery Point Lighthouse to watch. Then, on January 14, the persistent ship made another try for safety, drifting off her perch and coming to the harbor entrance. There she stopped, however, and began to wallow in the rolling water. After two futile attempts to salvage her, she was at last allowed to drift again. This time the *Emidio* reversed her course and lodged on nearby Fauntleroy Rock. There she remained for almost nine years until her bow was finally salvaged and her stern sunk. The following year a piece of the bow was included in a monument to the ship's lost crewmen that was constructed in Crescent City's Beachfront Park. No one had thought to honor the *Emidio* herself, although she had sailed a hundred miles of ocean on her own and nearly navigated the entrance to the town's harbor. Some sea captains had done no better.

The next intersection after Front Street is **Second Street**; two blocks left is **Redwood National Park Headquarters**. A combination bookstore-information center is a major attraction.

In an earlier time, Second Street was the scene of a most unusual type of commuter traffic. Dr. Ernest M. Fine had come to Crescent City in 1899 and bought a red Ford roadster six years later, but for the short trip between his home and office he preferred using the Harley-Davidson motorcycle that he subsequently acquired. Fine's cycling style was unique; eschewing the rutted city streets, he would maneuver his machine along the sidewalk as the compliant citizenry parted before him to allow the good doctor an uninterrupted ride. Consensus in the community was that it constituted a "Fine" way to travel.

Various shopping centers line the highway as it continues north; the route leaves the city limits, mile 3.4, heading northeast, and soon turns to four-lane freeway. At 6.8 miles is the offramp, right, for **Highway 199**, which leads to **Jedediah Smith Redwoods State Park** (see p. 212), the Smith River National Recreation Area, and Grants Pass. Highway 101 continues north on its way to the Oregon coast.

Second Street in Dr. Fine's day

Jedediah Smith Redwoods State Park

Paved, two-lane Highway 199 begins at an intersection with Highway 101, approximately three miles north of Crescent City. The tour follows 199 eastward for 7.2 miles to its junction with South Fork Road, passing through the northern section of Jedediah Smith Redwoods State Park. *Warning: the section of highway just east of Walker Road is often congested; watch for sightseers and merging vehicles.*

Features: (for symbols, see p. 89)

    🚗🚂 junction with King's Valley Road; access to view of Camp Lincoln (0.6 mile)

    🚗 entrance to Jedediah Smith Redwoods State Park (1.0)

    🚗🌳🎣🛶🚂 junction with Walker Road; access to Leiffer and Ellsworth Loop Trails (2.8)

    🌳 Simpson-Reed Trail, Peterson Trail, Hatton Loop, and Hatton Trail (2.9)

    🌳📷 Phillips Point Trail (3.1)

    🚗🌳🎣🛶 access road to Smith River; Hiouchi Trail (4.1)

    📷 Smith River (4.2)

    🚗 junction with North Bank Road [Highway 197] (4.2)

    🌳 Wellman Trail (4.6)

    🌳🎣🛶ⓘ♿🚻⛺🏕🌳 turnoff to Jedediah Smith Redwoods State Park Campground and Visitor Center; trail access (4.9)

    ⓘ♿🚻 entrance to Hiouchi Ranger Station (5.0)

    ⛺🏕🍴🛏️🏪 town of Hiouchi (5.6)

    🚗 turnoff for Howland Hill Road side trip; end of route (7.2)

212

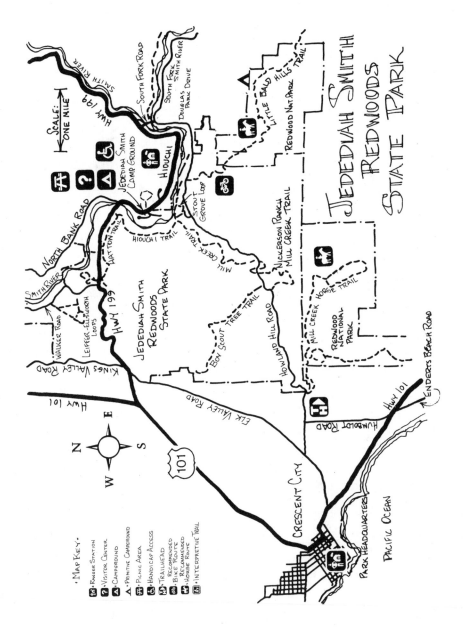

Officers' barracks, Camp Lincoln

Soon after leaving the 101 interchange, Highway 199 crosses Elk Valley Road, an alternate approach to Crescent City, mile 0.4, and then reaches another intersection, 0.6 mile. Right is Parkway Drive, while left is Kings Valley Road, a two-lane, paved route that in approximately one mile passes **Camp Lincoln**, a military installation in the 1860s. During its heyday the camp's buildings, which were painted the government's standard "yellowish hue," formed a hollow square around the parade ground. Here "a solitary sentinel paced his lonely round, his well polished musket flashing in the sunlight at every turn...." Today only an officer's cottage, now a ranger's residence, remains.

Jedediah Smith Redwoods State Park

Highway 199 rises up the hillside beyond the intersection, entering, at mile 1.0, **Jedediah Smith Redwoods State Park**. Known by various names during its history, the park got its start in 1928 when it acquired the 20–acre Webber Tract on the hillside near here. Only a few small groves had been added by 1939, when the state obtained nearly 7,000 acres from the Del Norte Lumber Company. The cost was a seemingly paltry $80,000, but much of the land should not have left government ownership in the first place; during the 1880s it had been fraudulently acquired by Herbert Kraft, a

Red Bluff banker, who arranged land patents for numerous "home-steaders," few of whom ever set foot in Del Norte County. Eventually the park took the name of explorer Jedediah Smith, who had crossed through the area during an epic trek in 1828.

Jed Smith, Sitragitum, and Tcunsultum

For nine years, Jedediah Strong Smith, fur trapper and legendary traveller, blazed like a comet across the wide lands of the West; from 1822 to 1831 he ranged through what would later become the Dakotas, Montana, Wyoming, Utah, Nevada, California, Oregon, Washington, and Idaho, part of the great wave of pathfinders that presaged the westward migration of a generation later. Much of his journeying was in the beaver bastions of the Rockies, but twice he made his way to the shores of the Pacific, and on one of those occasions led the first traverse by whites across the mountains of the North Coast.

In the spring of 1828 Smith and his band were in central California, bound for the summer trappers' rendezvous in the Rockies. Worried about encountering snow in the Sierra Nevada, Smith instead chose to make a wide detour, exploring new country as he went. So it was that he headed *northwest* out of the Sacramento River Valley, towards the coast. With him were 19 other trappers, along with some 300 horses and pack mules. It took the party an entire month to reach the valley inhabited by the Hupa tribe; another grueling month and they arrived at the ocean, a few miles north of the Klamath River. Along the way the expedition had endured encounters with Indians, trail-clotting tangles of timber, and mule-killing mountainsides. The trappers then cut through what later became Del Norte Coast Redwoods State Park, and after a few days on the coastal plain, entered another great forest and crossed the sparkling river that would later bear Smith's name.

Within a few weeks the expedition was nearly exterminated by Indians on the Umpqua River; only Smith and two others escaped, struggling northward until they reached Fort Vancouver. It was the third massacre that Smith had survived, but his luck with Indian attacks was nearing its end. Three years later he was killed by Comanches while searching for a water hole near the Arkansas River.

More than a century after Smith's death, California's northern-most redwood park was named in his honor. When he passed through the vicinity during his 1828 trip, Smith had spent some-what less than a day on what was later to become park land.

Others have had a more permanent connection with the place. The Tolowas had a pair of villages within what are now the park's boundaries, but today the names of these spots are seldom spoken. It is Smith's name we hear when we visit the area, not Sitragitum and Tcunsultum, for these Tolowa words have travelled like the wind and water, fading to faintness as they pass beyond our time. Yet try their sounds on your tongue and something strange may happen, for perhaps you will hear more than what you spoke—the call of the thrush in the deep forest...the splash of the canoeman's oar in the bright river...the whisper of all that once was here, softly returning again.

Highway 199 twists through tight turns in thick redwood forest, finally straightening just before it passes the turnoff for **Walker Road**, mile 2.8, left. This one-lane gravel park route extends north-ward for nearly two miles, ending at the riverside site of the Walker Ranch. Along the way are the lovely **Leiffer-Ellsworth Loop Trails**

Hobbs, Wall & Company's Camp 6, just north of present park boundary (see p. 246), and, on a side road, right, access to the Smith River at **Peacock Hole**. Here a long mound of river rock supports a profusion of plantlife: California Indian pink, black cottonwood, Pacific ninebark, ocean spray, and bouncing bet are among the most prominent. Nearby, the first road between Crescent City and the southern Oregon mines once crossed the Smith River.

Planks and Peacocks

Crescent City got its start as a supply center for the inland gold diggings, and it was not long before some of the town's boosters realized that their community would do much better if the mine-bound merchandise was transported by road rather than on a narrow pathway. The reasoning was simple: a pair of horse-drawn wagons, pulled in tandem with a single driver aboard, could carry more goods than a packtrain of 30 mules that were tended by two or three men. So it was that the Crescent City Plank Road was created—the "planks" being puncheons of split redwood that were laid across muddy stretches in the lowlands.

Building the road took several years, for the work was hampered by lack of funds. A ferry was set up at the crossing of the Smith River, and the revenue from an adjacent toll station was used to repay the road's investors. The ferryman was George Peacock, who had a ranch on the north side of the river.

Once beyond the Smith, the road climbed into the Siskiyou Mountains, passing several Del Norte mining camps on its way into Oregon. One of these was Low Divide, a place not known for its amenities. "We had rainy weather part of the time," wrote William Brewer in 1863,

> ...which increased my discomforts—standing at night in a crowded bar room, with seats for half a dozen, while twenty or thirty wet, dirty men from the mines steamed around the hot stove. To go to bed was no relief. We slept on the floor upstairs, some 20 or 25 of us—they kept running in and out all night. The noise from below prevented sleep until late, and the last of the card players would be getting to bed in the morning after the first risers were up.

In 1881 a flood washed out Peacock's ferry; the next year a new route, farther to the north, replaced the Crescent City Plank Road.

Time has since taken its toll on the old toll road, and today few traces of it can be found. If the planks have vanished, the Peacocks have not; the ranch still remains in the family, watched over in the 1990s by Thomas Peacock and his wife, Mary. Thomas, a noted local historian, has often written about the area, keeping alive many memories of the traveller's crossing. Mary knows a bit about travelling herself; her father was X. A. Phillips, Del Norte County's most famous itinerant peddler.

East of the Walker Road turnoff, the highway offers pullouts for several short hiking routes. On the left are the **Simpson-Reed Trail** and the **Peterson Trail**, a pair of connected loops that wander across a creek-cut flat. To the right are the **Hatton Loop**, a short but somewhat steep circuit, and the hillside climbing **Hatton Trail**, which parallels the highway eastward to the Smith River. *Warning: both motorists and pedestrians should use caution in the congested highway area near the trailheads.*

The obscure **Phillip's Point Trail** departs into the forest at mile 3.1, left. The route rambles almost a half mile to a rocky promontory above the Smith.

On the left, mile 4.1, a short dirt road drops to a large gravel bar beside the Smith, while across the highway is the northern end of the **Hiouchi Trail** (see p. 245). Highway 199 then crosses the **Smith River**, mile 4.2, on a recently constructed bridge. In 1929 the original span, which seemed to have sprung from a giant erector set, was christened "Hiouchi," a Tolowa reference to the Smith meaning "what a river!"

Smith River

The undammed **Smith River** drains the northwest corner of the state as the last free-flowing major stream in California. Fed by an annual rainfall that averages 99 inches within its watershed, the Smith drops some 5,800 feet during its 45-mile journey to the sea, its often-white waters churning through spectacular rocky gorges before reaching the calming coastal floodplain. The Smith enjoys federal protection as a wild and scenic river, while its drainage upstream from the park constitutes the 305,000-acre **Smith River National Recreation Area**. The NRA's headquarters and information center are located at the Gasquet Ranger Station, some nine miles east on the highway.

Once across the bridge, Highway 199 curves right to follow the river upstream, while **North Bank Road** (State Highway 197) forks left, mile 4.2. This paved, two-lane route passes through undeveloped parkland on its way north to meet Highway 101.

Original Hiouchi Bridge

Highway 199 then runs through more large redwoods; at mile 4.6, left, the steeply inclined **Wellman Trail** ascends the nearby hillslope. The entrance to the **Jedediah Smith Redwoods State Park Campground and Visitor Center** is on the right, mile 4.9. Spread out along a forested bend in the Smith River, the site provides picnicking, hiking, campfire programs, fishing, boating, and swimming, along with 106 shaded campsites. Running between the picnic area and campground are the **River Beach Trail** and the **Nature Trail**; a summer bridge connects with trails south of the river. The park's compact bookstore–information center operates in summer, while a boat launch is open during the winter.

Redwood National Park's **Hiouchi Ranger Station**, mile 5.0, left, occupies the site of an early-day motor court. In addition to its **Visitor Center** there are restrooms and a picnic area.

Hiouchi

The highway continues eastward along a broad flat, entering the hamlet of **Hiouchi** at mile 5.6. The roadside community offers a cafe, motel, gas station, market/general store, and RV/tent camp. In early days the Catching family ranched on part of the flat; their produce, including praiseworthy peaches, was shipped to Hobbs, Wall & Company in Crescent City. Bill Hawkins then took over the operation, but he proved to be a poor farmer. After giving the flat his name, he subsequently sold his portion of it for summer home lots. The area also failed as an agricultural site for John Hartman, who told David and Mary Zopfi, "You can't raise anything on that place but kids. If you want it, you can have it!" and promptly sold them *his* ranch for only the title transfer fee. The property proved more congenial to the Zopfis, who not only produced a bumper

A pair of Hiouchi humdingers

The Forks
of the Smith

crop of children but kept the ranch in the family until it was taken over by Redwood National Park in the early 1990s.

East of Hiouchi the highway enters the Smith River National Recreation Area, mile 6.4. The road then winds around a craggy cliff, passing a dramatic view, right, of the confluence of the South and Main forks of the Smith in its red-hued, rocky gorge. The section of canyon just downstream served as a setting for the 1936 version of *The Last of the Mohicans,* a United Artists extravaganza that starred Randolph Scott, Bruce Cabot, and Binnie Barnes, and also featured a score of so-called "Klamath" Indians.

After crossing the Myrtle Creek Bridge at mile 7.1, the highway reaches a junction with **South Fork Road**, mile 7.2, right. This route starts the Howland Hill Road side trip, a leisurely drive through the Mill Creek section of Jedediah Smith Redwoods State Park (see p. 223). Highway 199 continues on to the small community of **Gasquet** and the boulder-strewn Main Fork Smith River; the route, which still serves as the northern section of the "Redwood Highway," eventually ends in Grants Pass, Oregon, some 73 miles ahead.

Side Trip: Howland Hill Road

The southern section of Jedediah Smith Redwoods State Park is traversed by this rambling route, which follows the course of an old wagon road. Running 9.9 miles, the side trip begins on South Fork Road at its junction with Highway 199, and then travels on Douglas Park Road, Howland Hill Road, and Elk Valley Road before ending at a junction with Highway 101 in Crescent City. The surface varies from one- and two-lane pavement to one-lane gravel. *Note: motorists should watch for bicyclists and hikers on Howland Hill Road and should be prepared to back up when encountering oncoming traffic.*

(for map, see p. 213)

Features: (for key to symbols, see p. 89)

⚉ Main Fork Smith River (0.0 mile)

⤙⤸🔲 Smith River Launching Facility; river access (0.2)

⮕⚉ South Fork Smith River; begin Douglas Park Drive (0.4)

⮕ Jedediah Smith Redwoods State Park; begin Howland Hill Road (1.7)

🅿🚲🅰🚂 Stout Grove Loop Trail; access road to Little Bald Hills Trail (2.1)

⮕🅿🔲 turnoff to Stout Grove (2.9)

🚂⚉ Jack Breen Bridge across Mill Creek (4.2)

🅿 Mill Creek Trail (4.3)

🅿🚂 Nickerson Ranch/Mill Creek Trail (4.8)

🅿 Boy Scout Tree Trail (5.1)

🅿🚂 Nickerson Ranch/Mill Creek Trail (5.3)

⚉ Howland Hill Giant (5.4)

⮌🐾🚗 junction with Bertsch Road; access to Mill Creek
Horse Trail (7.9)

🚗 begin Elk Valley Road (8.8)

🚗 junction with Highway 101; end of route (9.9)

Paved, two-lane **South Fork Road** departs Highway 199 and
immediately crosses the **Main Fork Smith** on the Neils Christensen
Memorial Bridge. Christensen was an energetic local who constructed the first road south of the river, built and operated a hotel
near the road's end, and only retired from active work at age 86.

At mile 0.2, right, is the **Smith River Launching Facility**, a For-
est Service site for boaters. The main road then crosses the **South
Fork Smith**, mile 0.4, and reaches an intersection. Left leads up-
stream, offering access to the **Smith River National Recreation
Area** and the **Siskiyou Wilderness**. Right takes the side trip onto
Douglas Park Drive, two lanes, paved; the route will soon narrow
to a single lane of gravel — *trailers are not advised ahead*. Christensen
Way forks right, mile 0.5, at the start of a small residential area.

Great blue herons

Howland Hill Road

The road soon picks up the Smith River, following its south bank downstream. A modern but strangely gothic-looking covered bridge spans Sheep Pen Creek, 1.1 miles; presently the roadway passes through **Douglas Park**, a riverside home tract, and narrows to one lane. At mile 1.7 the route enters **Jedediah Smith Redwoods State Park,** turns to gravel, and becomes **Howland Hill Road;** the speed limit here is 15 miles per hour, and dry weather motorists who wish to avoid creating large clouds of dust will drive no faster.

Now the road travels through mature forest, the right-of-way often constricting considerably when it passes between a pair of roadside redwoods. The **Stout Grove Loop Trail** (see p. 240) exits to the right, mile 2.1. Here also a road spur branches left, leading 50 yards to a parking area for the **Little Bald Hills Trail** (see p. 264). This route was once a roadway onto the ridgeline between the Mill Creek and South Fork Smith drainages; even earlier, the rocky hills were home to various mining operations, while a patch of prairie contained the Murphy Ranch and its "St. Charles Hotel."

Too Many Bullets in the Little Bald Hills

Towards the end of July 1890, readers of the *Del Norte Record* received a bucolic report from the Murphy Ranch:

> I am rusticating at present at the St. Charles Hotel, owned and run by that prince of caterers, Edward Murphy, Esq. This hotel is located near the summit of the Bald Hills, about twelve miles from Crescent City. A delightful, cool spring of water bubbles from the ground about twenty yards from the hotel.

The correspondent noted, however, that the pastoral peace had recently been disturbed by the exploits of John McLaughlin, a well-known Crescent City bartender, who went hunting a short distance from the hotel. Seeing a band of deer on the distant hillside, McLaughlin raised his rifle, closed his eyes, and fired. After hurrying to the spot where the deer had stood, the abashed bartender discovered he had shot a black ram from Murphy's flock of sheep, thus ensuring that the "prince of caterers" would feature mutton on the St. Charles's menu that night.

The free shooting spirit was still strong some 40 years later, this time along the lower section of the Little Bald Hills Road. In June 1930 Earl Weavil, a disgruntled logger, waited in ambush near the road's start for his co-worker, Merle Reimer. When Reimer and a companion, Ken Cunningham, started their truck up the road, Weavil fired at the vehicle, sending two shots through the windshield. Reimer slumped over the truck door, struck in the head by a bullet that entered above the right eye and came out in back of his ear. Cunningham immediately turned the truck around and rushed Reimer to the Crescent City hospital, where, amazingly, the victim was found "to be in no great danger." Weavil fled to the hills, having shown Reimer that he should fear his fellow timber fallers as much as falling trees.

Murphy's Ranch has by now virtually vanished; only a bit of fencing, an apple tree, and the spring-fed stream remain. The St. Charles Hotel has been replaced by less formal accommodations— prairieside campsites for backpackers and horseback riders. The one-time road is now receding to a trail, and the earlier excitement offered by bleary-eyed bartenders and out-of-whack woodsmen has long been absent. As far as the peace-loving park officials are concerned, it's all for the best—there were just too many bullets in the Little Bald Hills.

A somewhat-stout Herbert Hoover, center, and others encircle the Stout Tree

Howland Hill Road then reaches an spur road, mile 2.9, right, that offers access to the **Stout Grove**, a stand of brawny bottomland redwoods centered around the startling **Stout Tree**, whose great girth amply justifies its designation. A paved walkway descends from the parking lot to meet the Stout Grove Loop Trail; left at this junction leads past the fenced-off tree, which was in fact named not for its substantial circumference but for a Chicagoan of substance, Frank Deming Stout. No sign identifies the tree; its base has been damaged by the foot traffic of overeager admirers, and the long-suffering sempervirens is now afforded the protection of growing incognito. Astute observers are nonetheless likely to soon locate it. The grove's loop trail is linked to the park campground and the Hiouchi and Mill Creek trails by summer bridges.

Mill Creek

After following Mill Creek upstream, the road crosses the creek at mile 4.2 on the **Jack Breen Bridge**. A pair of dedication plaques inform the deceased Breen, who was a longtime local scout leader and sheriff, that "Your Boys of Scout Troop #10 Miss You." It was Breen who first noted the so-called "Boy Scout Tree," a mammoth, double-trunked redwood at the western edge of the park.

The road continues up the creek canyon, passing, at mile 4.3, right, the unmarked but remarkably lovely **Mill Creek Trail** (see p. 257); across the way, a short track leads down an old roadbed to a one-time creek ford. Howland Hill Road then passes several path fragments before reaching the **Nickerson Ranch-Mill Creek Trail**, mile 4.8, left (see p. 248). In this vicinity once ran the old Kelsey Trail, a mountain-crossing pack train route that connected Crescent City with mining areas on the Klamath River. Built in 1855, the pre-cipitous pathway served extensively for some 25 years, during which time "tens of thousands of tons of supplies were freighted by mule train into the interior." Since it took a dozen mules to transport a ton of goods, the route may have witnessed as many as a million mule trips. The Kelsey Trail, like many others of the time, offered its share of excitement: one winter a severe storm caught a party of 80 miners between Crescent City and Happy Camp; to make their way out, the group dug for 36 hours to cross through 16 miles of snow, all of it four to five feet deep. As it was, a third of the men were reported "badly frozen."

The Jack Breen Bridge

Kelsey built his route upon paths long used by the local Indians; after more than a century of logging, mining, and weathering, little of his handiwork now remains. Portions of the trail are still preserved in the Siskiyou High Country and in the Little Bald Hills, but the Mill Creek section, which crossed the stream canyon near the Nickerson Ranch, is no longer traceable. Gone too is Nickerson's place, a one-time gold mining site that even in 1969 consisted of only "a few boards lying in the woods just beyond an overgrown orchard."

Also mining along Mill Creek was Hiram Rice, who panned the stream's gravel and tunneled into the canyon's cliffs. Rice claimed to have "made a comfortable living by these means," although his take was only 3¢ to 25¢ a pan.

At mile 5.1 is the parking area for the **Boy Scout Tree Trail**, right (see p. 252). Additional pullouts at mile 5.3 are for the western end of the **Nickerson Ranch-Mill Creek Trail**, left. On the right side of the road is an unmarked path formerly known as the Stage Coach Trail; it runs west a short distance before being obstructed by brush and fallen timber. Several still-visible puncheons recall the route's days as the Crescent City to Grants Pass road.

Rough Ride through the Redwoods

The county road that Neils Christensen constructed over Howland Hill and down into the Mill Creek bottom followed much of the Cold Spring Mountain Trail, which had been the original route to the Oregon mines. Wide enough to accommodate wagons and fortified with a plank covering through its muddy sections, the road was a great improvement over the trail, but it still offered its share of trials to the unwary traveller. One early excursionist, trying to put the best face on it, concluded that "the road is not half as bad as people imagine, though a little muddy and rough...."

It became more than a "little" rough, however, when one of the planks wore out, an occurrence that left a gaping hole in the road-bed. Billy Briggs discovered this while driving his 1904 Orient one-cylinder car along the route; although only going about six miles an hour, Briggs struck one of the gaps with such force that his frail auto broke in two. The floorboard and chassis came to an abrupt stop, while, as Briggs watched in amazement, the rest of the car—front wheels, dashboard, and steering handle—continued, driverless, down the road. Soon a lumber wagon arrived at the scene of the Orient's accident; the driver conveniently provided some 2x4s and baling wire for the bemused motorist, allowing Briggs to reunite the two sections of his divided vehicle and continue his trip.

To avoid such difficulties, the operators of Crescent City–Grants Pass stage line purchased several sturdy International Harvester Company autowagons. Boasting three rows of leather covered seats, the little IHCs had high, wooden-spoked wheels with hard

IHC autowagon

rubber tires; thus equipped, the motor stages could plow through mud two feet deep, but the bumpy ride they provided always "made an indelible impression" on the passengers.

The Christensen-built county road ended at the South Fork of the Smith; the thoroughfare then continued on to Oregon via a bridge and toll road constructed by Horace Gasquet, who operated a store several miles up the Smith's main fork. Stretches of the route that ran through the river's rocky gorge, while scenic, were even more daunting than the Howland Hill section:

> The road skirts along the faces of cliffs high above the canyons yawning at the edge of the narrow road and considerable skill is needed to make the route....[A]ny person inclined to be nervous should not attempt to drive the road.[1]

Today, more than 60 years after it was replaced by the Redwood Highway, much of the older, nerve-wracking road is no longer usable. The Howland Hill segment of the route can of course still be driven, but it is now graded gravel, so motorists should no longer worry that, like Billy Briggs, they will meet a puncheonless pothole and suddenly become "dis-Oriented."

At mile 5.4 the route passes the **Howland Hill Giant**, an enormous redwood that stands some 15 feet to the left of the roadway.

A victim of the vicissitudes of forest life, the tree bears a hundred-foot-plus scar on its lower trunk, no doubt the result of a long-fallen canyon companion that once scraped against it. According to local experts, the tree qualifies as the world's third largest "champion" coast redwood, a designation determined by combining the tree's height, circumference, and crown spread.[2] The two higher-ranking champions are found in Prairie Creek Redwoods State Park, but neither of them can be clearly seen by motorists.

Soon Howland Hill Road begins its climb to the top of the ridge, reaching the summit at mile 7.0. The hill was named for Robert Howland, an early rancher in the Elk Valley area that lies just downslope to the west. A story is told about a visit paid to the Howlands by their minister, who requested the family Bible. Turning to her young son, Mrs. Howland bade him to "fetch us the large book that we read from every day." The boy hastened to obey, returning promptly with a well-worn Montgomery Ward catalogue.

Branching left at the hillcrest is a gravel-surfaced park road with a locked gate; the route connects with the Mill Creek Horse Trail. Descending the ridgetop, Howland Hill Road runs through a stand of alders and then turns to pavement, mile 7.3, near a vista of the ocean. The road exits the park at 7.6 miles, widens to two lanes, and soon straightens. **Bertsch Road**, mile 7.9, left, leads a short distance to RNP's **Mill Creek Horse Trail**, which climbs back over the ridge to reach the logged-over but regenerating middle section of Mill Creek; the horse trail connects with another RNP route, the **Rellim Ridge Trail**. The course of Bertsch Road follows the old Del Norte Southern logging rail line, which came east across Elk Valley from the Hobbs, Wall & Company mill in Crescent City, ran along what is now Howland Hill Road, curved south at the Bertsch junction, and gradually climbed the ridgeside on its way into the timber-rich Mill Creek watershed.

Howland Hill Road then passes the **Elk Valley Rancheria**, right; the property belongs to a branch of the Tolowa tribe. **Humboldt Road**, 8.2 miles, left, offers a shortcut to southbound motorists seeking Highway 101.

At mile 8.8 Howland Hill Road deadends at **Elk Valley Road**, two lanes, paved, which once served as the highway course between Crescent City and the newly-established redwood park. A left turn onto Elk Valley Road leads to end of the side trip, mile 9.9, at an intersection with U. S. 101 in the southern part of the city. Appropriately, the final segment of the Redwood Highway auto tour thus concludes on a long-bypassed section of the roadway's early route.

Section III

* * *

Hiking Trails

Twenty-Five Favorite Hikes

Dozens of delightful trails traverse the northern redwood parks, offering a wide range of excursion opportunities. Hikers can perambulate the perimeter of prairies, skirt the slopes above the seacoast, trek through tall timber, or otherwise experience many a pleasing park pathway. The trails are as numerous as they are varied; altogether there are over 70 of them to explore, and many once-hiked routes seem even richer when re-experienced.

The following four chapters describe the authors' most highly esteemed hikes; some consist of but a single path, while others combine two or more trails to form a longer route. Important historical, botanical, and scenic features are highlighted for each hike, along with summary information about location, length, and degree of difficulty.

*Notes: 1) With the exception of the access route to Endert's Beach, pets are **not** permitted ✇ on park trails. 2) Most paths are open to foot traffic only; the exceptions are: a) the Mill Creek Horse Trail and the Redwood Creek Horse Trails, also open to horses ⊡; b) the Holter Ridge-Lost Man Creek Bike Trail, the Prairie Creek Bike Loop, and the Last Chance Section of the Coastal Trail, also open to bicycles ⊛; and c) the Little Bald Hills Trail, also open to horses ⊡ and bicycles ⊛. 3) Several hiking routes (the Redwood Creek Trail, Trestle Trail, Stout Grove Loop Trail, and the access path from the Jed Smith Campground to the south side of the Smith River) cross streams on "summer" bridges — temporary structures that are removed during the rainy season; check with park officials to determine if these bridges are in place. 4) Some trails near the coast may be seasonally congested with heavy vegetation; check with park staff to determine which have been cleared recently.*

(A locator map on the reverse of this page shows each of the featured routes.)

Twenty-Five Favorite Hikes

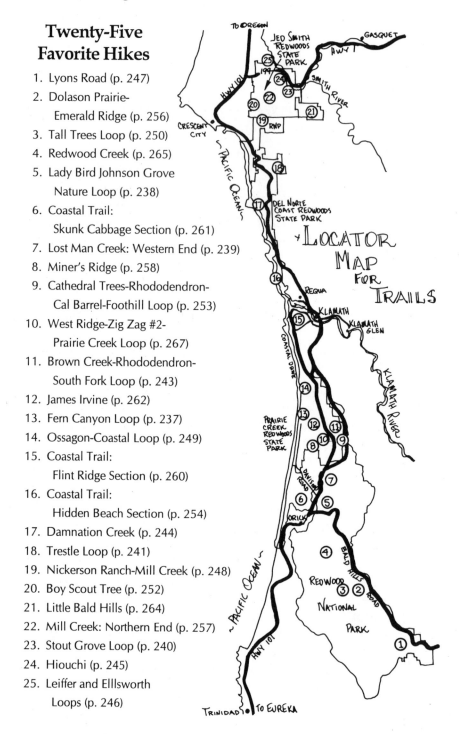

Short Strolls: Less than 2 Miles

Fern Canyon Loop

Summary: A winding, steep-walled canyon corridor, cliffsides covered with delicate five-finger ferns and other exquisite foliage, two small waterfalls, and a blufftop prairie are all found along this charming circuit.

Distance: 0.8 mile, round trip

Elevation Change: 200 feet

Location: just north of the end of Gold Bluffs Beach Road, 7.1 miles northwest of Highway 101

Note: Home Creek must be forded at several points in Fern Canyon.

Description: A pair of paths head north from the parking area, both of them immediately crossing Home Creek: the way left is the Coastal Trail; the route right promptly leads to another junction at the mouth of Fern Canyon. Here the James Irvine Trail, left, climbs the bluffs, while Fern Canyon Trail, right, commences the loop route by entering the narrow stream gorge. Ferns are nearly everywhere, forming a dark green fabric that clothes the pebble-imbedded cliffs; most noticeable is the delicate five-fingered fern, which hangs in lacy festoons from the shadowy canyonsides. In early summer, clasping twisted stalk decorates the darkness with a profusion of dangling red and white berries.

At mile 0.3 a short spur path, right, climbs 30 feet to a small, recessed waterfall; a second fall lies on a track to the left, 0.4 mile. The trail then ascends from the canyon floor via a long series of steps. At the top of the bluff, mile 0.5, the Fern Canyon Trail ends at a junction with the James Irvine Trail; here the loop takes the route to the left and begins its return. A side path subsequently branches left to cross Alexander Lincoln

237

Prairie, a pleasant patch of grassland that, at its far side, provides an unfenced overlook of the fern-filled canyon far below. ***Warning: use caution when approaching the edge of the cliff.*** Years ago, the prairie was occupied by the numerous structures of the Upper Gold Bluffs mining operation, but no trace of the buildings now remains. After passing several skunk cabbages on a short boardwalk, the James Irvine Trail descends the bluffs through a stand of alders, completing the loop at mile 0.8.

Lady Bird Johnson Grove Nature Loop Trail

Summary: Regal ridgetop redwoods are the main attraction on this easygoing loop route; along the way is the dedication site for Redwood National Park.

Distance: 1.3 miles, round trip

Elevation Change: negligible

Location: the trail starts at the grove parking lot, mile 2.7 of Bald Hills Road

Dedication plaque,
Lady Bird Johnson Grove

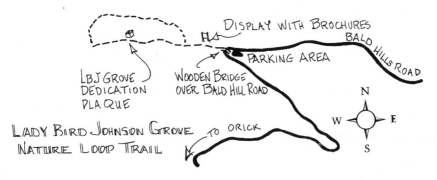

Description: The route immediately crosses Bald Hills Road on a handsome wooden bridge, soon passing a display where trail guide brochures are available. The path heads west along a broad ridgeline, following the course of the original Bald Hills Road.

Large redwoods rise from the surrounding shrubbery; black huckleberry, salal, and rhododendron provide most of the foliage. The trail passes a cascade of honeysuckle at 0.4 mile, right, and then drops slightly downhill, cutting between the mossy earthen berms of the old roadbed before reaching the grove's commemorative plaque; here, in August 1969, President Richard M. Nixon dedicated the site to Lady Bird Johnson, who the previous year had herself officiated here at the dedication of the park.

Soon the trail turns sharply to the right, mile 0.6, and leaves the roadbed, reversing course to return along the northern side of the ridge. Douglas-fir, western hemlock, and redwood cover the hillslope. At mile 1.1 the trail completes its loop; a left turn leads back to the parking area.

Lost Man Creek Trail: Western End

Summary: Lovely Lost Man Creek is the companion along this charming section of canyon-bottom trail. A plethora of plants enhances the pathside.

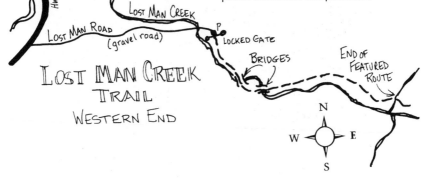

Distance: 2.0 miles, round trip

Elevation Change: negligible

Location: the trailhead is at the Lost Man Creek Picnic Area, off a park access road that exits Highway 101 some four miles north of Orick

Description: The "lost man" in question was an early-day timber locator who never found his way back from the creek's remote upper drainage; hikers of today will experience no such difficulty if they merely follow the old logging road up the stream canyon. The road, which now serves as the park trail, immediately passes a series of picnic sites shaded by statuesque redwoods; nearby are elderberry and crimson columbine. A marker at mile 0.1 commemorates Redwood National Park's 1982 dedication as a UNESCO World Heritage Site.

As the trail leaves the picnic area, views to the right reveal the alder-choked channel of the creek. At mile 0.2 an old logging bridge offers sights of the stone-studded streambed and the foliage-covered banks. Ahead on the right is a profusion of piggyback plant, coast

boykinia, and five-fingered fern. At a second bridge, 0.3 mile, is a cliffside collection of California hazel and thimbleberry, left.

A border of inside-out flower, fringe cups, and trail plant grows by the roadside, mile 0.4; large redwoods and small tanoaks rise overhead. Bolander's phacelia provides summertime color along the next stretch of the route. A large cluster of alum root covers the roadbank, 0.9 mile, while coast boykinia and redwood sorrel grow nearby. After crossing a side creek, mile 1.0, the road begins to climb uphill, marking the turnaround point for this undemanding but spectacularly scenic hike. Walkers who want a longer workout can continue up the road through hillside redwoods, eventually reaching the cutover lands of Holter Ridge.

Stout Grove Loop Trail

Summary: This short route surveys the south side of the Smith River and also loops through a stand of superb bottomland redwoods.

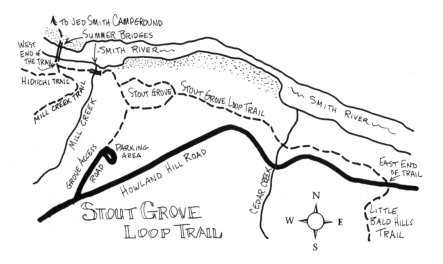

Distance: 1.8 miles, round trip

Elevation Change: negligible

Location: the east end is at mile 2.1 of the Howland Hill Road side trip, while the west end is at a junction with the Hiouchi Trail next to the campground summer bridge; a third approach is via a spur trail from the grove parking lot, which is off mile 2.9 of the Howland Hill Road side trip

Note: the west end of the trail crosses Mill Creek on a summer bridge

Description: Leaving Howland Hill Road, the trail follows the nearby Smith River downstream, dropping on stairs past alum root, five-fingered fern and thimbleberry. A curving bridge, mile 0.3, is enhanced by nearby rhododendrons. Soon the route reaches a narrow benchland populated by alder and tanoak. The flat widens, and at mile 0.5, the trail forks amid towering redwoods; bearing right, the route twists past several large downed redwoods, reuniting with the other end of the loop, mile 0.8. Continuing to the right, the path drops to cross Mill Creek on a summer bridge and then ends at the bridge to the Jed Smith park campground, 0.9 mile. The return trip completes the loop through the grove before reaching the trailhead; hikers will enjoy determining which of the corralled redwood colossi is the undesignated Stout Tree.

Trestle Trail Loop

Summary: Part of this circling path follows the bed of the old Hobbs, Wall & Company logging railroad that ran beside Mill Creek; the rotting timbers of a remnant trestle highlight the route.

Distance: 1.3 miles, round trip

Elevation Change: 100 feet

Location: the trailhead is just northeast of the bridge in the middle of the Mill Creek Campground, Del Norte Coast Redwoods State Park

Description: Big stumps and bigleaf maples initially embellish the trail, which runs close to the creek before rising, mile 0.1, onto the hillside via a set of steps. The bank above the path is adorned with Bolander's phacelia, California harebell, and western bleeding heart. A short descent leads to a leafy collection of alder, California hazel, and vine maple, which is followed at 0.2 mile by a wooden bridge that crosses a side creek.

Now the route runs along the old railbed, passing through clusters of second-growth redwoods that form "cathedrals" around the stumps of trees cut by Hobbs, Wall & Company more than 50 years ago; a rusty residue of old logging cables protrudes from the forest floor like large roots. Next to a bigger bridge, mile 0.4, the decaying posts of the trail's

Trestle remnant, Trestle Trail

namesake trestle poke above the foliage to the left. Just beyond the bridge, the trail winds past a large patch of inside-out flower and then regains the railbed; several ties still lie in place.

At mile 0.5 the trail leaves the railbed, turning right and entering a stand of second-growth Douglas-fir and redwood. A summer bridge spans Mill Creek, 0.6 mile; at high water, hikers will probably elect to turn back here.

The path climbs the hillside on the far side of the creek, passing moss-covered alders and piggyback plant before levelling at mile 0.8. After dropping to cross a side stream on another bridge, the route ascends to a junction with the Saddler Skyline Trail, 1.0 mile. Bearing right, the Trestle Trail then heads north, descending the slope to reach a campground road at mile 1.2; a left turn takes the route to an intersection by the campfire circle, where another left leads north through a second intersection and on to the Mill Creek bridge and the trailhead.

Moderate Meanders: 2 to 5 Miles

Brown Creek-Rhododendron-South Fork Trail Loop

Summary: Two lovely stream canyons, a haunting hillside memorial, and lots of June-blooming rhododendrons combine to make this route a compelling circuit.

Distance: 3.6 miles, round trip

Elevation Change: 600 feet

Location: the route begins and ends at the South Fork–Prairie Creek Trailhead, mile 2.9 of the Newton B. Drury Scenic Parkway

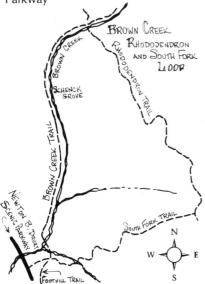

Description: Sword ferns gather darkly beneath robust redwoods as the trail winds across the benchland south of Brown Creek. Just before mile 0.2 the Foothill Trail branches right; bearing left, the main route follows the South Fork of Brown Creek. After passing both coast boykinia and inside-out flower, the path crosses a bridge over the burbling brook, mile 0.2, and immediately comes to another junction. The South Fork Trail continues to the right, while the loop route turns left onto the Brown Creek Trail.

The path crosses Brown Creek at 0.5 mile. Vine maples congregate in the shaded canyon; to the right, numerous dry, brown sword fern fronds hang from the bank, as if part of a huge hula skirt. The route now twists up the canyon, first passing mock azaleas and then a large western burning bush, mile 0.7, right, that spreads over the stream.

At mile 0.8, right, a bridge offers access to the Carl Alwin Schenck Grove, which lies in a shadowy stand of redwoods across the creek. Schenck, who founded the first school of forestry in the United States, helped create a unique monument: he selected 20 giant trees and named each for a personage famed in the field of forestry; a final tree, the largest of the lot, was dedicated collectively to his "old boys" at the Biltmore

243

School. Cement columns bearing the names of the dedicatees were placed in front of the trees. Most of the obelisk-like markers still line the grove's short, hillside-climbing loop trail, but several have been obliterated by large redwoods that over time have crashed to the forest floor. Seen on a foggy day, the remaining pillars rise eerily in front of the trees' huge trunks, their aging gray concrete recalling the headstones in some long-forgotten graveyard.

At mile 1.0 the main trail reaches a marker for the Frederick Law Olmsted Grove, left; in 1928 Olmsted, an internationally known landscape architect, conducted a survey that served as the basis for California's state park system. The route then rises along the hillside, drops to cross a lovely side stream, and passes a sediment monitoring station, mile 1.3, right.

Presently the Brown Creek Trail intersects the Rhododendron Trail; a right turn here continues the loop. Mock azalea and vine maple shade the subsequent crossing of Brown Creek, after which the route climbs past a scattering of trilliums and leopard lilies, mile 1.6. The trail now undulates along the hillside, providing striking views down the redwood-filled slopes. Rhododendrons line the way, while Pacific starflower, fairybell, and Indian pipe diversify the plantlife.

At 2.6 miles the South Fork Trail departs to the right. The loop route follows it along a spur ridge, encountering fat false Solomon's seal and more lilies, before descending on switchbacks, mile 2.8; windflower, deer fern, and vanilla leaf are among the plants found near the bottom of the grade. Immediately ahead is the Brown Creek Trail junction, 3.4 miles, where a left turn retraces the initial section of the loop back to the trailhead.

Damnation Creek Trail

Summary: A strenuous but scenic route, the trail passes scores of fairybells on its way to a plant-packed beachside bluff and a wide-ranging view of the rocky coast.

Distance: 4.2 miles, round trip

Elevation Change: 1,000 feet

Location: in Del Norte Coast Redwoods State Park, 3.3 miles north of the Wilson Creek bridge on the west side of Highway 101

Description: The trail climbs though lush forest, briefly joining the bed of the old county wagon road before cresting

Mouth of Damnation Creek

the ridge, mile 0.2, and beginning a long drop to the ocean. Redwoods and rhododendrons are prominent, but most noteworthy is the profusion of Smith's and Hooker's fairybells that line the trail during much of its course.

At mile 0.6 the path crosses the worn pavement of what was once the Redwood Highway; this long-abandoned remnant now serves as the Last Chance Section of the Coastal Trail. After running out onto a ridgespur, the Damnation Creek Trail begins to drop quickly via switchbacks, passing a plenitude of cliffside flowers and ferns; most dramatic are some huge, bushlike Hooker's fairybells at 1.3 miles. Sitka spruce and Douglas-fir then gradually replace the once-prevalent redwoods as the route nears the coast. The canyonside above Damnation Creek is brightened by both bigleaf maple and alder.

The route levels, mile 2.0, and crosses two handsome kingpost[1] bridges before rising onto a small headland. A miniature forest of vegetation covers the area: iris, cow parsnip, and mission bells are among the most prominent. Steep cliffs make for a difficult descent to the rocky beach, but the blufftop offers dramatic views of the ocean and coastline.

Hiouchi Trail

Summary: Running from the Hiouchi Bridge to Mill Creek, this redwood-filled route rambles along the hillside above the shimmering Smith River.

Distance: 4.0 miles, round trip

Elevation Change: negligible

Location: the northern trailhead is at the west end of the Hiouchi Bridge, mile 4.1 of Highway 199; the southern trailhead is at a junction with the Stout Grove Trail and the summer bridge connection with the Jed Smith campground

Note: the Hiouchi Trail reaches both the Stout Grove and the campground by summer bridges that are removed during the rainy season

Description: Departing a cleared area next to the Hiouchi Bridge, the route switchbacks uphill to meet the Hatton Trail, mile 0.1, right. Here the main path drops to the left, arrives above the river at 0.3 mile, and then enters a mixed forest of tanoak, madrone, California laurel, rhododendron, and redwood.

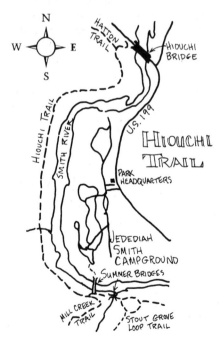

A railed overlook, mile 0.8, allows observation of the Smith and the opposite riverside. The route then winds its way through thick forest, crossing several small creeks; boulders occasionally bulge from the shadowy hillside. At mile 1.9 is another overlook, followed by a lovely benchland filled with vine maple, alder, California laurel, and a succession of statuesque redwoods. The Mill Creek Trail branches right, 2.0 miles, just before the main route descends a set of stairs and ends at the beach.

Leiffer-Ellsworth Loop Trails

Summary: Both of these connected loops climb heavily-forested hillslopes; some remarkable redwoods, a historic wagon road, and leaf-shaded lowlands lie along the way.

Distance: 2.6 miles, round trip

Elevation Change: 300 feet

Location: the south end is on Walker Road, 0.4 mile from Highway 199; the north end is also on Walker Road, 1.2 miles from the highway

Description: The northern end of the route begins on an old roadbed; presently it passes around a large redwood log, whereupon the trail is nearly engulfed by plants: California spikenard, vanilla leaf, and trillium are some of more than a score of species. Redwoods rise overhead, including four old-timers that form a row along the pathside, right.

Near the Don J. Leiffer bench several burned snags mingle with assorted stumps and goosepen trees; they are joined by inside-out flower, bigleaf maple, and wild ginger. At mile 0.2 the

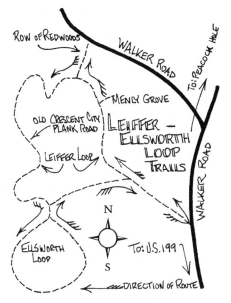

Leiffer Loop divides; the main route, right, zigzags up the hillside. After encountering some western hemlock, the loop meets a section of the old Crescent City Plank Road, 0.5 mile, which it follows briefly downhill. The trail returns to the lowlands and passes a second Leiffer bench before arriving at a junction, mile 0.8. Here the Ellsworth Loop branches right to make its own hillside foray, passing through a stand of magnificent redwoods on its descent. This second loop returns to the junction at 1.4 miles; a right turn then continues the route, passing along a corridor of vine maples lined with clusters of coast boykinia. The Leiffer Loop reaches another fork; mile 1.6; continuing right, the path crosses a small stream, passes numerous clintonia, and then arrives at the southern trailhead, 1.8 miles.

The return to the northern trailhead retraces the route to the previous junction and then bears right. The trail crosses through a lovely, leafy stand of California hazel and vine maple before passing

beneath more mammoth redwoods. A spur route, mile 2.3, right, leads 200 feet to the secluded Meuly Grove. The trail then reaches the original Leiffer Loop junction at 2.4 miles; to the right is the northern trailhead, mile 2.6.

Lyons Road

Summary: This scenic dirt road leads to the remnants of the "Home Place," center of the original Lyons Ranch. A weathered barn and bunkhouse still perch on the hillside high above Redwood Creek.

Distance: 4.0 miles, round trip

Elevation Change: 400 feet

Location: at the Lyons Ranch Historic Site parking area, mile 17.0 of Bald Hills Road

Description: Leaving the small parking lot, the route crosses Schoolhouse Pasture, a grassy ridge saddle named for the first Bald Hills School, which was located nearby. The road runs south, passing Schoolhouse Pasture Rock, mile 0.1, right, and then swings east at 0.4 mile to angle down the ridgeside. To the left is the Coyote Creek drainage, with Coyote Peak at its head. The metal roofs of two Lyons barns glint from the distant slopes.

Home Place Barn

The road enters a hillside grove of Oregon white oak, mile 0.9, and presently crosses two small creeks. Giant trillium, Smith's fairybell, and Siberian candyflower cover the banks of the second stream; bigleaf maples spread overhead. Some fifty feet above the road, a sparkling waterfall mists a group of giant chain ferns. At mile 1.3 a side route, left, leads east to the hillside barns; the main road reenters the prairie and swings west. Southward across the canyon of Redwood Creek is a view of the rectangular clearcuts of Simpson Timber Company, which decorate the Devils Creek drainage.

In springtime the sloping prairie is speckled with western blue flax, blue dicks, and bright yellow California poppies. Just beyond a bend is the oak-shaded Lyons Ranch Barn, 1.9 miles. On the flat below is a remnant orchard, and to its left, the site of at least one of the four Lyons ranch houses that succeeded one another on the Home Place

property; fires destroyed each of the first three dwellings. A small family cemetery lies in the woods downslope from the orchard.

After crossing a small, shady stream, the hiking route ends next to the corrugated tin walls of the ranch's one-time bunkhouse, mile 2.0; on the flat to the right was the last Lyons ranchhouse. An overgrown section of the road continues northwestward to a small grassy area. The nearby woods contain western hound's tongue, vanilla leaf, and, just west of the bunkhouse, the home of a current ranch resident—the stickpile nest of a resourceful woodrat.

Nickerson Ranch-Mill Creek Trail

Summary: After first following magnificent Mill Creek, this varied route concludes by crossing a redwood-filled flat.

Distance: 3.2 miles, round trip

Elevation Change: negligible

Location: the north end is at mile 4.8 of the Howland Hill Road side trip; the south end is at mile 5.2 of the same route

Description: Leaving the northern trailhead, the route passes through a stand of mature redwoods; western hemlock, vine maple, and several fern species are also present. Mile 0.5 brings a series of magnificent, mossy bigleaf maples whose leaves glow golden in the fall. After crossing through a stand of scouring rush, the trail passes a rocky creek pool and then turns sharply, mile 1.1, to climb past a large, hollow log. At the base of the incline a faint track branches left, cuts through a thicket of salmonberry, and finally emerges at a low-water ford of Mill Creek. This route once led across the creek to the site of the Nickerson "Ranch," an early-day mining operation.

The Mill Creek Trail concludes at this unmarked junction and the Nickerson

NICKERSON RANCH/MILL CREEK TRAIL

Ranch Trail commences uphill to the right. After levelling, the path winds beneath thick-trunked redwoods, crosses a couple of creeks, and then ends, mile 1.6, at Howland Hill Road. The recommended return goes back along the same route; an alternative is to follow the road northeast a half mile to the original trailhead.

Ossagon–Coastal Trail

Summary: This short but steep route traverses the Ossagon Creek drainage, finishing on the beach at the awesome Ossagon Rocks.

Distance: 4.2 miles, round trip

Elevation Change: 600 feet

Location: the east end is at the Hope Creek–Ossagon Trailhead on the Newton B. Drury Scenic Parkway; the west end is at Ossagon Rocks

Notes: 1) during wet weather Ossagon Creek may flow high enough to discourage crossing it near the Ossagon Trail's junction with the Coastal Trail; 2) hikers should be prepared for cyclists as the Ossagon Trail forms part of a bicycle loop route

Description: Upon leaving the parkway, the trail crosses Prairie Creek and then climbs the canyonside, soon reaching an old roadbed; for many years autos could travel below the Gold Bluffs north of Fern Canyon and then turn inland on this route to reach the highway. A stand of small Sitka spruce, mile 0.3, is followed by a prolonged descent through alder and additional spruce. The route levels at 1.1 miles and then crosses Ossagon Creek on a wooden bridge; a dam upstream once impounded the creek's water for use at a hydraulic mine near the beach. On the

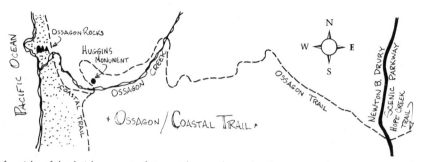

far side of the bridge, a set of steps takes the trail up the canyonside. More alders cover the hillslope, mile 1.4, surrounding a small prairie, right, that still bears a remnant fencepost from its days as a pasture. Elk now graze the grassland.

Soon the trail begins descending; it makes a switchback, encounters several western wax myrtles, and then passes a large rock, left, that bears a marker for Fred and Mary Huggins. Here, for 50 years, the couple "preserved the beauty of the forest and the seacoast," finally conveying their homestead to the park in 1963. Just below the marker, the trail reaches the mouth of Ossagon Creek, 1.6 miles. The route then runs south across the grassy, alder-bordered flat to an unbridged creek crossing at mile 1.7. Fifty feet farther, the Ossagon Trail ends at a junction with the Coastal Trail.

When creek conditions permit, hikers may turn right on the Coastal Trail, proceed to another crossing of Ossagon Creek, and then continue north, eventually cutting across the dunes to the striking Ossagon Rocks, mile 2.1. A small lagoon east of the rocks holds water from Ossagon Creek.

Tall Trees Loop Trail

Summary: The main route to the Tall Trees Grove, this steep trail descends through dense hillside forest; the loop through the grove features not only skyscraping redwoods but also a beautiful stand of bigleaf maple and California laurel.

Distance: 3.4 miles, round trip

Elevation change: 600 feet

Location: the east end is at the parking area for the Tall Trees Access Road; the west end is at a junction with the Redwood Creek Trail

Description: The path drops from the parking area through a rampage of rhododendrons, passing the turnoff for the Emerald Ridge Trail at mile 0.1, left. In springtime, the thick forest is brightened by a patch of toothed monkey flowers, 0.4 mile.

Trailside markers are keyed to a brochure available at the trailhead; marker #5, mile 1.0, indicates the route of the long-abandoned Trinidad Trail, a thoroughfare to the inland gold mines during the mid-19th Century. Behind the marker, a series of orange flags mark the still-visible track as it heads up the hillside. Leafless wintergreen grows close by, on the main trail.

After passing a restroom, the trail levels and reaches the grove loop at mile 1.3. The route described in the brochure proceeds clockwise, immediately passing a spur path, left, that drops to Redwood Creek; in summer a bridge here connects to the Redwood Creek

Trail on the south bank (see p. 265). Near the Redwood Creek crossing was once an enormous hollow redwood, reported by *Hutching's Magazine* in 1856 to be 33 feet across. According to the article:

> Men have frequently camped in that tree, not from choice, however, but because they were caught by night, whose dark mantle falls upon the wayfarer in those sombre old woods much sooner than in the open country.

Nowadays, gigantic girth has been preempted by heroic height—ahead on the loop is the reputed "World's Tallest Tree," an estimated 367 feet high. Some researchers, however, believe there may be taller trees within the park.

The trail then enters an enchanting, grassy glade where a grove of thick-trunked, large-limbed bigleaf maples and California laurels enshadow the level benchland. California spikenard and Siberian candyflower brighten the lower greenery, while alder and cottonwood stand closer to streamside. At mile 1.7 the trail reenters the redwoods; here marker #13 indicates a brine vat, made out a hollow redwood log, that settler Bert Robinson used for curing salmon he'd caught in the nearby creek. Soon the path passes the "Sixth Tallest Tree," followed by the "Third Tallest," mile 1.9. The loop concludes at 2.1 miles, where a left turn starts the return to the parking area.

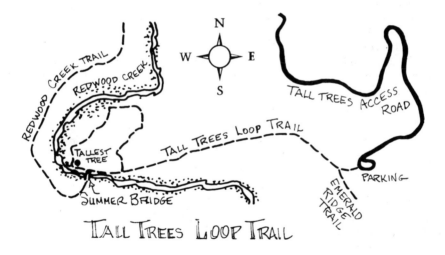

TALL TREES LOOP TRAIL

Exhilarating Excursions: 5 to 9 Miles

Boy Scout Tree Trail

Summary: Hikers will find a huge, double-trunked redwood and a sparkling waterfall at the far end of this rewarding route.

Distance: 5.6 miles, round trip

Elevation Change: 400 feet

Location: the trailhead is at mile 5.1 of the Howland Hill Road side trip

Description: Starting at a small roadside parking area, the trail travels through mature mixed forest, encountering large redwoods as it climbs at mile 0.2. The route undulates past rhododendron, 0.4 mile, milkmaids and clintonia, mile 0.6, and then yerba de selva, iris, and false lily-of-the-valley. Crossing a hillslope at 0.8 mile, the path passes Pacific starflower, trail plant, and yerba de selva; a subsequent stand of stately redwoods is supported by sword fern and both coastal and spreading wood fern. The trail drops to a creek crossing, 1.4 miles, where vine maple and salmonberry embellish the banks; another set of impressive redwoods appears at mile 1.9. A second stream canyon, mile 2.2, brings red huckleberry, mock azalea, and California hazel.

The route reaches a junction at mile 2.4; a short spur path, right, climbs the hillside to the Boy Scout Tree, a spectacular specimen whose huge base splits into a pair of trunks, one of which is girdled by a circle of burls. The tree

was "discovered" by Sheriff Jack Breen, who founded the local scout troop. The main trail bears left, reaching the hillside above scenic Fern Falls at mile 2.8.

Cathedral Trees-Rhododendron-Cal Barrel-Foothill Trail Loop

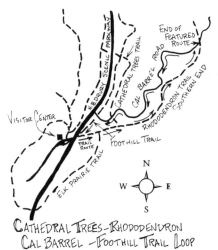

CATHEDRAL TREES-RHODODENDRON CAL BARREL -FOOTHILL TRAIL LOOP

Summary: Redwoods in several guises are the highlight of this high climbing hillside route: a row of towering prairie-side giants, "cathedrals" that rise around their dead ancestors, a pair of walk-through goosepen snags, and a roadside "window" tree are among the striking sempervirens found along the way.

Distance: 5.3 miles, round trip

Elevation Change: 700 feet

Location: the start and finish is at the Elk Prairie Visitor Center

Description: Beginning at the trailhead east of the Visitor Center, the route follows the Cathedral Trees Trail eastward, briefly running beside the campground entrance road before bending left and passing under the Newton B. Drury Scenic Parkway, mile 0.1; here the trail shares a culvert with Boyes Creek. After entering a stand of alders, the path crosses the creek on a wooden bridge and then arrives at a junction with the Foothill Trail, which forks left at 0.2 mile.

Bearing right, the route runs beside a small patch of picturesque prairie; a magnificent row of redwoods lines the way, left. After crossing through a cluster of California laurel, the path meets the Elk Prairie Trail, mile 0.4, right. Here the course continues to the left, coming close to Boyes Creek, mile 0.5, amid

bigleaf maple, alder, and more laurels; salmonberry and elderberry fill many of the openings. At a junction, mile 0.8, the route turns onto the Rhododendron Trail, right, immediately passing between a pair of immense "cathedrals"—circular clusters of redwoods that have sprouted from a vanished parent tree.

Soon the trail begins to climb, passing leopard lily at mile 1.0 and then offering an overlook of several mock azaleas as it winds around a small side canyon. After encountering a thicket of California hazel, 1.4 miles, the route levels amid rhododendron and redwood. A spur path, mile 1.6, left, leads 75 feet up the bank to Cal Barrel Road.

Presently the main trail starts downhill, twisting between and beneath a gigantic jumble of fallen redwoods. The path then fords a skunk-cabbage-clotted creek and levels, meandering across the forest floor until it begins to rise at mile 2.0. After ascending a set of steep switchbacks, the route crosses through a hillside stand of awesome, ancient redwoods. The trail climbs more switchbacks, passes through a burned-out, double-trunked redwood, mile 2.7, and then encounters clintonia, leopard lily, and windflower. Soon the route runs through another great goosepen, rises past milkmaids and wild ginger, and finally descends through more windflower before reaching Cal Barrel Road at mile 3.2. From there the Rhododendron Trail continues uphill, leaving the opposite side of the road some 250 feet ahead; the hike loop, however, turns left and drops down the Cal Barrel route.

A mature hillside redwood forest encloses the road; thousands of sword ferns cover the slopes. At mile 4.1 is the unmarked spur connection, left, to the Rhododendron Trail. After passing the Remembrance Grove marker, 4.3 miles, the route descends past California hazel

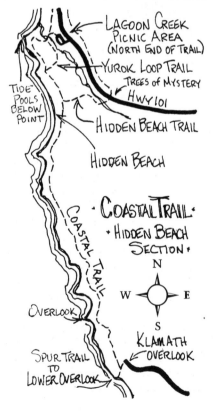

before reaching a large redwood, mile 4.6, left, with a strangely flared, burned-out base. An accommodating aperture provides an entryway into the hollow lower interior; another opening, opposite the road, serves as a window for the redwood-enclosed room.

Cal Barrel Road intersects the Cathedral Trees Trail, mile 4.7, conveniently close to a pair of benches for the Declaration of Independence Grove. Now the route drops sharply downhill, levelling at mile 4.9 and then reaching the Foothill Trail, 5.0 miles. A left turn here continues the loop route, travelling along the paved course of the original county road; the pathside marker for the Rotary Grove stands in sylvan solitude, mile 5.1, left. The spires of an enormous, three-trunked redwood mark the imminent junction with the Cathedral Trees Trail, 5.3 miles; a right turn retraces the initial stage of the loop, arriving at the Visitor Center at mile 5.5.

Coastal Trail: Hidden Beach Section

Summary: One of the North Coast's most photogenic pathways, this route runs above the ocean bluffs north of the Klamath River. Rocky headlands, alder groves, and secluded Hidden Beach offer striking scenery.

Distance: 8.0 miles, round trip

Elevation Change: 400 feet

Location: the southern end is at the Klamath Overlook parking lot, mile 2.3 of Requa Road/Patrick J. Murphy Memorial Drive; the northern end is at the Lagoon Creek picnic area, on Highway 101 a mile north of Trees of Mystery

Description: Upon leaving the overlook parking lot, the trail immediately drops

Hidden Beach   EIFERT

down grassy bluffs; to the west and south are exciting views of the seacoast, the mouth of the Klamath, and, across the river, conifer-crowned Flint Ridge. At 0.1 mile a spur trail, left, descends to a vantage point nearer the ocean. The main route then levels and turns north, crossing open hillslopes colored with cow parsnip, lupine, and wild cucumber in spring. Come summer, a celebration of firecracker flowers bursts near the trailside at 0.4 mile.

A fenced overlook, mile 0.7, marks the trail's entrance into an alder thicket; the trees shade the path as it first passes a small pond, 1.0 mile, right, and then a lovely, flower-filled flat. An opening at mile 1.1 offers iris and crimson columbine. The path then reenters forest, and soon twists downhill through a throng of ferns—leather, lady, sword, deer, and spreading wood species. Picking up an old roadbed, the route rambles past a huge alder, mile 1.6, right, and soon reaches a foliage-framed vista of Crescent City and the adjacent coast. Elderberry, thimbleberry, and salmonberry then mass with the greenery of alder, spruce, and flowering currant. After dropping downhill, the trail levels at mile 2.9 and meets the Hidden Beach Trail, right, which approaches from Trees of Mystery. Just ahead, a spur route, left, descends to the boulder-strewn beach and its beautiful cove.

The main trail proceeds north, soon reaches open grassland, and then passes through intermittent bowers of windswept alders. At 3.4 miles the Yurok Loop Trail branches right. The Coastal Trail continues northward to mile 3.8, where it turns inland at a vista of False

Klamath Cove; tidepools repose in the rocks below. The route meets the other end of the Yurok loop at mile 3.9, right, and then crosses Lagoon Creek on a wooden bridge. Just beyond the bridge the trail forks: left leads to the beach below Highway 101, whence hikers can continue north to the Redwood Hostel and the DeMartin Section, Coastal Trail; right enters a thicket of willows and soon reaches the route's end at the Lagoon Creek picnic area.

Dolason Prairie- Emerald Ridge Trail

Summary: Descending the eastern slope of the Redwood Creek drainage, Dolason Prairie Trail passes through cascading meadows, oak woodlands, and mature mixed forests; a picturesque barn punctuates the main prairie. The Emerald Ridge Trail completes the hike, ending at the Tall Trees parking lot.

Length: 5.9 miles, one way (9.8 miles, round trip, for the Dolason Prairie Trail)

Elevation Change: 2,200 feet

Location: the northeastern trailhead is at a parking area, mile 11.4 of Bald Hills

Road; the southwestern end of the route is at the parking lot for the Tall Trees

Note: *The described route requires taking the park's shuttle bus from the Tall Trees parking area to the Dolason Prairie Trailhead on Bald Hills Road; check at the Redwood Information Center for details. Hearty hikers may prefer a round trip on just the Dolason Prairie Trail, which offers a substantial upgrade on its return.*

Description: The trail begins in the small second growth of an old mill site and immediately drops downhill, soon passing numerous foxgloves and several "wolf" Douglas-firs; these large trees have a distinctive set of huge limbs extending from their lower trunks, an indication that the area around them was once kept clear by either Indians or ranchers. At mile 0.4 the route turns right onto the old K and K logging road, following it below a sloping meadow to mile 0.7. Turning left off the road, the trail descends through a mixed woodland that includes bigleaf maple; the path then emerges onto the main section of Dolason Prairie, where an aging barn reposes on the grassy hillside, mile 1.3. The once-larger structure (it has lost

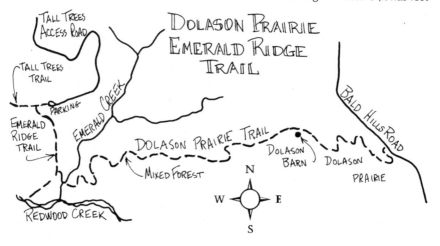

part of its east and south ends) served as a "sheep shed" for the Sherman Lyons Ranch; probably built in the 1890s, it features hand-hewn timbers, along with rafters made from peeled logs. The surrounding prairie provides a panorama of the Redwood Creek drainage, with clearcut-scarred Rodgers Peak dominating the ridgeline to the west.

At the prairie's far edge, the path passes a patch of Oregon white oak; beneath the trees is a springtime sprinkling of western dog violet, while blue dicks, California poppy, and miniature lupine grow nearby in sunnier spots. The trail drops into deep forest, mile 1.5; grand fir and Douglas-fir shade calypso orchid, western trillium, and other woodland plants. A subsequent stretch of grassland is notable for the purple blossoms of broadleaf lupine. Redwoods then rise above fetid adders tongue, vanilla leaf, and redwood sorrel, mile 2.5.

Several other tree species fill out the forest during the trail's continuing descent—California laurel, madrone, western hemlock, several large tanoaks, and, at mile 3.3, a few golden chinquapins. Three bright bloomers—rhododendron, milkmaids, and clintonia, provide seasonal color.

After a long descent, the trail crosses the deep gorge of Emerald Creek on a long wooden bridge, mile 4.7; far below, five-finger fern and deer fern border a series of small pools and rocky riffles, while western burning bush, dogwood, and California hazel spread their leafy limbs over the stream. The route then climbs the canyonside to end, mile 4.9, at a junction with the Emerald Ridge Trail. The path left drops down to the bed of Redwood Creek; the way right rises to reach the Tall Trees parking area and hike's end at 5.9 miles.

Mill Creek Trail: Northern End

Summary: A lovely trail for viewing fall colors, the path passes through striking stands of streamside maples and climbs high onto a redwood covered hillside.

Distance: 6.0 miles, round trip

Elevation Change: 200 feet

Location: the trail's south end is at mile 4.3 of the Howland Hill Road side trip, a short distance upstream from the Jack Breen Bridge; the north end is at the Hiouchi Trail, near the summer bridge to the Jed Smith campground

Description: Departing from the west side of Howland Hill Road, the unmarked trail enters a shrubby thicket that includes California hazel, western burning bush, and osoberry. After crossing a redwood filled flat, the path climbs the hillside, levels, and then follows a contour across the sword-fern-covered slopes. The route continues along the hillside until it switchbacks down to the wide mouth of a side stream, 0.7 mile.

After winding around a gigantic fallen redwood, the trail passes a succession of statuesque bigleaf maples, mile 0.8; long tendrils of moss trail from the trees' twisted limbs. Soon several very large redwoods also claim attention. At mile 0.9 the trail rises to a higher benchland; here are first clintonia, mile 1.0, and then rattlesnake orchid, 1.3 miles.

A short spur trail, mile 1.6, right, leads streamward to a small gravel bar; in fall, wine-tinted vine maples color the creekside. The main path now runs past such pleasing plants as vanilla leaf, western wild ginger, inside-out flower, and false lily-of-the-valley. At 1.9 miles a compact kingpost bridge spans a side stream that then splashes down a picturesque minigorge, right.

The route continues through redwood forest, passing patches of rhododendron and several large hemlocks. At mile 2.8 a short spur, left, soon reaches the Jensen Grove. The main trail turns right and drops to a riverside flat, ending at the Hiouchi Trail, mile 3.0.

Miner's Ridge Trail

Summary: This historic trail traverses varied terrain on its way from Elk Prairie to Gold Bluffs Beach, running along a redwood-covered ridgeline on a one-time mine route and passing through a soggy, spruce-filled canyon via a logging company's plank road.

Distance: 8.6 miles, round trip, including the approach trail

Elevation Change: 400 feet

Location: the route's eastern end is at the Elk Prairie Visitor Center; the western end is at Gold Bluffs Beach Road

Description: The hike leaves the Visitor Center on the Nature Trail, bearing left at junctions with the Prairie Creek Trail and the James Irvine Trail. After passing over Godwood Creek, the Nature Trail arrives at the Miner's Ridge Trail, which forks right, mile 0.2.

Turning right, the route runs across a benchland, crosses a tributary of Godwood Creek, and then ascends the end of Miner's Ridge, levelling somewhat at 0.5 mile amid Douglas-fir and redwood.

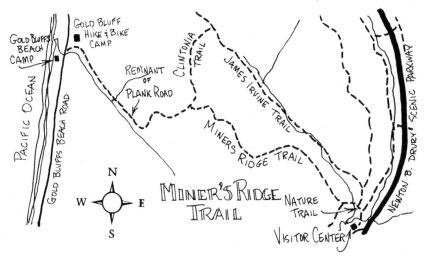

The route reaches the ridgetop at mile 1.2, and picks up an old roadbed; in bygone days this was a thoroughfare to both the beach mine at Fern Canyon and to a hillside mining operation near the western end of the ridge.

After undulating along the ridgeline through old-growth redwoods, the path drops to a junction, mile 2.3, with the Clintonia Trail, right. Here the route turns left onto an old logging road, moving gradually downhill through partially cut forest. A bend left at mile 3.1 takes the trail southeast; it then crosses Squashan Creek on a wooden bridge, 3.3 miles, and turns west, heading down the canyon. Mature redwoods mix with alder and second-growth spruce in a moss-filled rain forest setting. The path soon passes over a second bridge and then follows another roadbed; this one is lined with a series of parallel wooden planks—tracks that Cal Barrel loggers once drove their trucks on.

Black bear

The trail presently climbs up a hillside above the creek, again following the road; at mile 4.3 it reaches a spur trail, right, to the Gold Bluffs Beach Hike and Bike Camp and then crosses the creek. Gold Bluffs Beach Road and the end of the route lie just ahead.

As an alternative on their return trip, hikers may elect to turn onto the Clintonia Trail, take it to the James Irvine Trail and then follow the latter route back to Prairie Creek.

Terrific Treks:
More than 9 Miles

Coastal Trail:
Flint Ridge Section

Summary: Birds, beavers, ridgetop redwoods, and an ocean overlook lie along this likable but little-known park route.

Length: 9.4 miles, round trip

Elevation Change: 700 feet

Location: the eastern trailhead is at the junction of Klamath Beach Road and Alder Camp Road, south of the Klamath River; the western trailhead is at mile 5.7 of the Coastal Drive side trip

Description: Departing a shaded parking lot opposite the remains of the Douglas Memorial Bridge, the east end of the trail promptly drops down into the canyon of Richardson Creek. At mile 0.1 the path winds between Marshall Pond and an abandoned mill site. The pond was created in the late 1940s for the mill; nowadays a crew of beavers busily continues with the wood-cutting work. The placid waters accommodate many birds, including short-eared owls, kingfishers, and wood ducks.

After bending around the mill clearing, the trail briefly follows an access road before turning left, 0.3 mile, and heading south. A short stretch of grassland leads to a stand of alders; the path now runs between the pond and the base of Flint Ridge. To the left of the trail, mile 0.5, several gnawed trees await removal by the beavers. The route then climbs uphill on an old roadbed, passing piggyback plant, western wild ginger, and various ferns; a switchback, 0.7 mile, signals the start of the climb up the ridge.

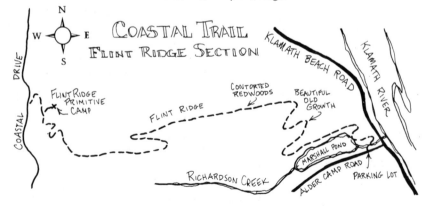

Presently the trail leaves the roadbed, moving into old growth redwoods. By mile 1.0 numerous other plants fill the forest: tanoak and Douglas-fir provide background greenery, rhododendron and mock azalea offer spring blooms, and both vine maple and California hazel create color in fall. The vegetation intensifies at mile 1.4, where fringe cups and gooseberry are also present.

The route comes out on the end of the ridgeline, mile 2.1, and bends left, soon climbing on switchbacks past redwood violet and baneberry. At 2.5 miles the trail is in mixed conifer forest; here the redwoods display the branching trunks, ropy bark, and numerous low limbs that indicate close proximity to the coast's stultifying salt air. Harebell and honeysuckle, mile 2.8, are followed by leopard lily, starflower, and bedstraw.

At mile 3.0 the trail drops down part of the ridgeslope, zigzagging on switchbacks. After then following a contour westward, the way is along another old logging road, 3.7 miles; a fork of Richardson Creek lies in the alder-filled canyon to the left.

Leaving the road remnant, the shaded path proceeds downhill, switchbacking at mile 4.3 and then levelling. A spur trail, 4.5 miles, right, climbs to the hillside prairie where the Flint Ridge Primitive Camp is located. Continuing on the main route, a final descent through the site of the old Hamilton Ranch leads to Coastal Drive, mile 4.7; a barn site across the road provides parking and a wide-angle view of the coast.

Coastal Trail: Skunk Cabbage Section

Summary: Spruce forest, slews of skunk cabbage, and a loop route to the beach

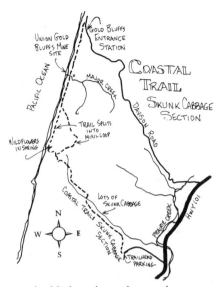

are highlights along the southern section of this trail. The northern half offers haunting clifftop stands of alder and the site of an early-day gold mine.

Distance: 10.6 miles, round trip

Elevation Change: 400 feet

Location: the southern trailhead is at the end of a marked park road that leaves Highway 101 about two miles north of Orick; the northern end is at Gold Bluffs Beach Road just north of Espa Lagoon

Description: The route from the southern trailhead first follows an old logging road through mixed forest; Sitka spruce were cut here decades ago, but some large specimens remain. At mile 0.5 is a view across the canyon of a sharply demarcated clearcut done by Arcata Redwood in the 1970s; the incident spurred on protectionists during their drive to expand Redwood National Park.

A vast flow of skunk cabbage follows the creek drainage, the plant's large leaves often form a continuous coverage of the boggy ground. At mile 1.4 the path crosses the main creek and moves through second-growth forest. Near a bridge on the creek's north fork, mile 2.1, are clasping twisted stalk and Smith's fairybell. The route then climbs out of the canyon and crests at an ocean overlook, 2.7 miles.

Here the trail splits; its two branches will reconnect later on the beach. The recommended course is to turn left at the junction, dropping via switchbacks to the beach below. At first the descent is through a thicket of thin-trunked alders; a concluding zigzag runs down an open hillside that is bedecked with lupine in spring and an attractive alien, white nightshade, during summer and fall. The trail reaches the beach, mile 3.1, where a right turn continues the route. At mile 3.7 is a marked junction, right, with the other branch of the loop, which has just descended its own section of the bluffs.

The way along the beach is brightened by matlike clusters of sea rocket and sand verbena. An opening in the bluffs, 4.1 miles, is for the debouchure of Major Creek; on the grassy hillside to the north is the site of the Union Gold Bluff Mine, whose heyday was more than a century ago.

After another stretch along the strand, the trail crosses the outlet for Espa Lagoon, climbs a low bluff, and reaches a beach access road. Right 50 yards on this route is the trail's end at Gold Bluffs Beach Road, 5.0 miles. Unless hikers have arranged a car shuttle, they will need to retrace their beach route to the trail junction, mile 6.3, where they can ascend the alternate section of the path. Switchbacks climb up the cliff, crossing through wind-sculpted salal bushes and a corridor of truncated Sitka spruce; soon the trail turns inland, following the side of a sword-fern-filled canyon before

reaching the alder-shaded blufftop, 6.6 miles.

The route continues to climb, passing bedstraw, foxglove and additional thickets of alder; the trees' thin, nearly limbless trunks twist tortuously towards the canopy, reaching their reward in a culminating crown of leaves. After cresting at a small clearing, mile 7.5, the trail bends right and picks up an old logging road, descending as second-growth redwoods shade the way. The loop section of the hike concludes, 7.9 miles, at the original blufftop junction. Bearing left, the route then returns along Skunk Cabbage Creek; ending at mile 10.6.

James Irvine Trail

Summary: Canyons are a constant companion along this low-elevation route, which runs through mature mixed forest and beside deeply cleft creekbeds, connecting, as it does so, the Prairie Creek area with the ocean beach.

Distance: 9.4 miles, round trip, including the approach trail

Elevation Change: 200 feet

Location: the east end is at the Elk Prairie Visitor Center; the west end is at the mouth of Fern Canyon next to the northern end of Gold Bluffs Beach Road

Description: From the Visitor Center, the route follows the Nature Trail north, crossing Prairie Creek and then following the stream southwest. After passing the turnoff for the Prairie Creek Trail, mile 0.1, right, the path reaches the start of the James Irvine Trail, 0.2 mile, right.

The trail initially follows a wide track, moving northwest up the wide canyon of Godwood Creek. John Godwood, an Englishman, homesteaded land along the creek in 1878; the remains of his

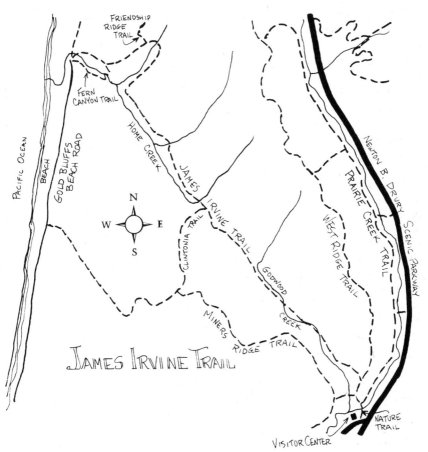

JAMES IRVINE TRAIL

cabin were reportedly still visible in the 1950s. The West Ridge Trail branches right, mile 0.3, while the main route enters a collection of California hazel, thimbleberry, and cascara. At mile 1.0 the path passes close to Godwood Creek, left; a large burl juts from a redwood, right.

Soon after crossing Godwood Creek, mile 1.4, the trail rises along the southern side of the canyon. The forest here displays all four of the primary coastal conifers: coast redwood, western hemlock, Douglas-fir, and Sitka spruce. After dropping off the hillslope, mile 2.0 , the path crosses through a large cut log, 2.5

miles, and immediately bends around an especially enormous redwood. The route regains the hillside and meets the Clintonia Trail, 2.8 miles, left. Continuing to the right, the main trail descends into the Home Creek drainage, crossing the stream at 3.0 miles.

A scattering of small rocks on the trailbed indicates the canyon's conglomerate composition; at mile 3.3 and mile 3.5 side streams have cut deep defiles in the gravelly ground. Among the plants in the second ravine are mock azalea, red huckleberry, and four varieties of ferns. The composer Ernest Bloch and his wife Marguerite are honored by a trailside bench, 3.7 miles, that is located appropriately close to the musical gurgle of the creek.

After crossing though a small clearing, the route bends north to follow a side canyon, finally crossing a tributary stream, mile 4.0, on a charming wooden bridge; in the middle of the structure a pair of chairs offer an upstream view of a small waterfall. Proceeding back down the side canyon, the path meets the Friendship Ridge Trail, mile 4.1, right. The main route continues through spruce forest, passing wood nymph and gnome plant, and then meets the Fern Canyon Trail, 4.4 miles, left. The James Irvine Trail continues

west, soon skirting Alexander Lincoln Prairie, left, and then descending on stairs to the mouth of Fern Canyon; just ahead is the parking area at the end of Gold Bluffs Beach Road, mile 4.7.

Little Bald Hills Trail

Summary: This intriguing trail follows an old mining route up to and along a scenic ridgeline, passing the site of the historic Murphy Ranch. The area's serpentine rock base supports a distinctive plant community not found elsewhere within the parks.

Distance: 10.0 miles, round trip, to the park boundary and back

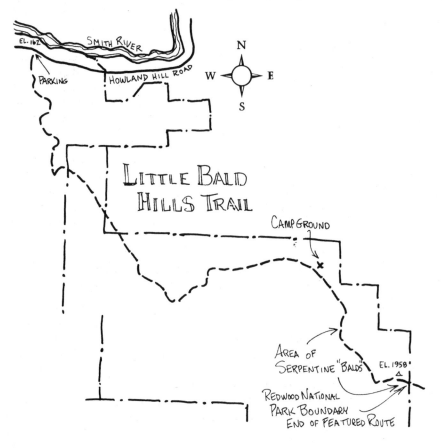

Elevation Change: 1,800 feet

Location: the northern end is at a parking area just off of mile 2.1 of the Howland Hill Road route; the trail runs southeast all the way to South Fork Road, but midway it leaves park land and enters the Six Rivers National Forest

Description: The trail begins as an almost level dirt road, winding through thick mixed forest until mile 0.5, when it begins climbing the hillside. Much of the early course is marked by vanilla leaf and deer fern, while in spring a trio of blossoms brighten the surroundings: delicate pink rhododendrons, rich magenta clintonias, and glowing gold leopard lilies. At 1.3 miles the route levels and crosses from Jedediah Smith Redwoods State Park into Redwood National Park. American brooklime, fringe cups, and alder now mark the way.

A side trail, mile 1.8, left, leads onto private property. Park officials advise against hikers entering this area.

The main route soon passes a collection of crimson columbines, which is succeeded by scatterings of Siskiyou penstemons. Western azaleas then fill the air with their spring fragrance, mile 2.2; at a grassy clearing just ahead are ocean spray and several small flowers, among them western dog violet, blue-eyed grass, Ithuriel's spear, and pussy ears. Dead Port Orford cedars, the victims of a virulent root rot, rise wraithlike from the roadside.

A stand of tall, thin Douglas-fir, mile 2.6, is supported by coffeeberry and Indian's dream (Oregon cliffbrake). The route leaves the prairie-bound roadbed at 2.8 miles, veering left into the forest. Here several "wolf" Douglas-firs are surrounded by a younger generation of conifers; among the mix are some healthy Port Orford cedars that have yet to be attacked by the fatal root fungus.

Emerging from the thick woods, the trail passes several knobcone pines at mile 3.3, picks up the roadbed briefly, and then reenters the forest. A side trail, mile 3.5, left, leads a hundred yards to the Little Bald Hills Backcountry Camp, which sits at the edge of a small prairie. The camping area is on the site of the Murphy Ranch, whose "St. Charles Hotel" served travellers for decades; a solitary apple tree, some decaying fence posts, and a small spring-fed stream are the ranch's most visible remnants.

Leaving the camp, the trail promptly departs the forest, emerging onto a stone-stippled grassland overhung by occasional Jeffrey pine and Douglas-fir; the glint of the region's characteristic serpentine rock is often apparent. After passing two-eyed violet and pussy ears, the route rejoins the roadbed, mile 3.9, and passes a succession of sun-loving flowers as it runs along the open ridge-top; first are wedge-leafed violet and spinster blue-eyed Mary, next come cream sacs and chickweed monkey flower, then California Indian pink and blue-headed gilia, and finally spreading phlox and coast flatstem onion. At mile 5.0 the trail reaches a large boundary sign and passes out of the park.

Redwood Creek Trail

Summary: This pleasant pathway follows the canyon of Redwood Creek to the Tall Trees Grove, offering occasional glimpses of the gravel-strewn streambed. Much of the route runs along old logging roads beneath a bower of alder and bigleaf maple.

Distance: 9.5 miles, one way, including the connecting route to the Tall Trees

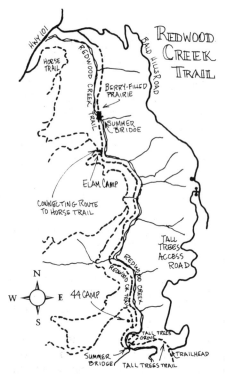

REDWOOD
CREEK
TRAIL

HWY 101
HORSE TRAIL
REDWOOD CREEK TRAIL
BALD HILLS ROAD
BERRY-FILLED PRAIRIE
SUMMER BRIDGE
ELAM CAMP
CONNECTING ROUTE TO HORSE TRAIL
TALL TREES ACCESS ROAD
N
W
E
S
44 CAMP
REDWOOD CREEK TRAIL
TALL TREES GROVE
SUMMER BRIDGE
TALL TREES TRAIL
TRAILHEAD

parking area (16.4 miles, round trip, for the Redwood Creek Trail)

Elevation Change: 200 feet

Location: the north end is at the Redwood Creek Trail parking area, reached by a short access road at mile 0.4 of Bald Hills Road; the south end is at the Tall Trees Grove parking lot

Notes: 1) The described route involves connecting with the Redwood National Park shuttle bus at the Tall Trees parking area; contact the Redwood Information Center for bus schedule and reservations. 2) The trail crosses Redwood Creek in two locations on seasonal bridges that are removed during the high water season. Hikers should check with the Redwood Information Center to determine if the bridges are in place before attempting the route.

Description: After leaving the parking area, the trail enters a mixture of redwood, alder, bigleaf maple, willow, and cascara, reaching a large park map of the route, 0.2 mile. The path emerges from the sylvan shadows, mile 0.5, running beside stretches of a blackberry-besieged prairie. At mile 1.0 a stand of Sitka spruce shades the way.

The trail skirts another meadow and then crosses Redwood Creek on a seasonal bridge, 1.7 miles; red triangles on each streambank indicate the route, but the markers may be obscured by foliage—if so, the footprints of previous hikers can serve as a guide. The path passes through a thicket of elderberry, mile 1.8, after which two small boardwalks bridge McArthur Creek. Intermittent patches of piggyback plant then crowd the pathway.

At mile 2.3 the trail ascends the hillslope, passing several very large redwoods. An unmarked side route, mile 2.6, right, presently reaches the Elam Creek Horse Camp and a junction with the Horse Trail.

Continuing upstream along the main route, a foliage-framed vista, mile 2.7, left, offers a view of an osprey nest high in a spiketop redwood; the tree stands opposite the confluence of Elam and Redwood creeks. The path then passes through a seasonally shaded corridor of alder, bigleaf maple, and piggyback plant. Within sight of the trail's three-mile marker is a large clump of California spikenard, left. After briefly running through the creekside sand at mile 3.8, the route returns to the forest; here several sizeable redwoods attract attention. The creek appears periodically through the alders, 4.4 miles, left, while salmonberry and elderberry add to the surrounding greenery.

As the route continues up the canyon, California laurel diversifies the plantlife, mile 5.4; a short distance ahead, a narrow bridge spans the deep canyon of Bond Creek. At 6.7 miles a wider bridge crosses the Forty-Four Creek gorge. On the right, 7.2 miles, a side route leads a quarter mile along an old logging road to the Forty-Four Horse Camp; the spur path continues past the camp to join the Horse Trail.

The Redwood Creek Trail proceeds amid an accompaniment of alders; second-growth conifers are dimly visible farther off the route. At mile 7.7 is the Tall Trees Overlook, which provides a view across the creek of the world's most famous redwood skyline. The path continues to follow the relict logging road until mile 8.2, where the trail turns left and drops to the creek; another summer bridge then offers access to the benchland on the stream's far side. Here the route meets the Tall Trees Loop Trail; a right turn follows this uphill to the shuttle bus connection at mile 9.5.

West Ridge-Zig Zag #2-Prairie Creek Trail Loop

Summary: Passing near three of the four largest "champion" redwoods, this rambling route circles through the center of the park; the maple-lined corridor along Prairie Creek is especially lovely in fall.

Distance: 9.0 miles, round trip, including the approach routes

Elevation Change: 600 feet

Location: the loop starts and finishes at the Elk Prairie Visitor Center, located off mile 1.1 of the Newton B. Drury Scenic Parkway

Description: The route follows the Nature Trail from the Visitor Center parking lot, promptly crossing Prairie Creek on a high wooden bridge. Turning west, the path winds through large redwoods, passing the turnoff for the Prairie Creek Trail, mile 0.1, right. Bearing left, the loop route soon turns onto the James Irvine Trail, 0.2 mile, right, following it

Mountain beaver, a.k.a. aplodontia

briefly to a junction with the West Ridge Trail at 0.3 mile, right.

Almost immediately the West Ridge Trail begins climbing on switchbacks through mature redwoods. After a brisk ascent, the path reaches the ridgetop, mile 0.8, whence it continues northward across undulating terrain. The Zig Zag Trail #1 descends to the right, 2.6 miles. The loop route turns left; in 50 yards it reaches the scenically situated "Forever" Bench, left, which offers a view of a lovely rhododendron on the hillside far below. The trail continues along the ridgetop; the slopes on both sides are covered with redwood, black huckleberry, and sword fern.

The loop route leaves the West Ridge Trail at mile 4.1, turning onto the Zig Zag Trail #2, right, and dropping into the canyon of Prairie Creek; clasping twisted stalk and leopard lily lounge be-

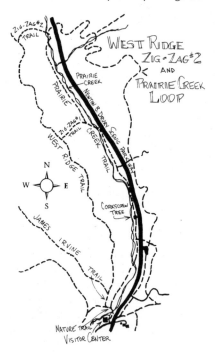

neath large redwoods on the steep descent to the canyon floor. The path levels and, at a sharp right turn, mile 4.5, the route abruptly becomes the Prairie Creek Trail. Just ahead, a stout wooden bridge rises on stairs to span the stream.

A spur trail, mile 4.6, left, soon connects with the Newton B. Drury Scenic Parkway; the main route bears right and presently crosses Prairie Creek on an unusual bridge that reaches the far bank in a series of short, descending levels. The way now runs between the creek and the nearby base of shadowy West Ridge, first passing bigleaf maple and then redwood, hemlock, and spruce. Along the way lies the park's current celebrity, the mammoth "Sir Issac Newton Tree," which was recently awarded the status of "champion" coast redwood.[1] At present, the tree's location remains unmarked. Searchers who try to find the now-famous giant are urged to tread gently if they depart from the path.

At mile 5.5 the trail bends away from the hillside and arrives at the turnoff, right, to the secluded Drury Grove. The main route continues its course beside Prairie Creek; and soon passes, across the stream, the enormous "Newton B. Drury Tree," the second-place champion redwood.

Vine maple, salmonberry, and elderberry then crowd the pathway, while alder and bigleaf maple line the nearby creekside; below the banks are a series of shimmering, shallow pools; in winter salmon may be seen here, struggling upstream towards their spawning sites.

The Zig Zag Trail #1 branches ridgeward, mile 6.0, right. Bearing left, the loop route reaches another bridge, 6.2 miles, that is situated next to a sediment monitoring station; at the eastern end of the bridge a spur route, left, connects

The contorted Corkscrew Tree

with the parkway. A large, hollow log at mile 6.5, right, offers an inviting entrance that in wet weather can be extremely slippery. Just ahead, a bridge spans Brown Creek; upstream stands the "Brown Creek Tree," number four among champion redwoods. After turning right, the route arrives at a junction, 6.6 miles; left leads promptly to the parkway, while right continues the Prairie Creek Trail.

Both bigleaf and vine maples now line the route; large redwoods loom high overhead. The three-part trunk of one maple, mile 6.9, arches over the center of the trail. A bog-bridging boardwalk announces a junction, 7.3 miles, where a spur trail branches left; as it proceeds to the parkway, this side path passes the Corkscrew Tree, an entertaining entwinement of redwood trunks that ranks as one of the parks' premier oddities.

An enormous double-trunked redwood log blocks the trail at mile 7.7; two sets of stile-like stairs offer a way over the obstacle. A short distance ahead is a side path, 7.8 miles, left, that reaches the nearby parkway and continues on the far side to the Big Tree.

The Prairie Creek Trail then crosses its namesake on yet another bridge, 8.2 miles; soon the path rises up the shaded hillside before ending, mile 8.9, at the Nature Trail. A left turn here leads to route's end at the Elk Prairie Visitor Center, mile 9.0.

Section IV

* * *

A Quick Guide to the Parks

What to Do
and Where to Find It

Listed below are descriptions and locations of important sites and activities that are found in the parks. Park visitor centers can provide further details.

Some Words of Warning

Following are a few of the main hazards found on the North Coast; for additional information contact park officials.

Poison Oak: A common shrub or vine growing in many areas of the parks, poison oak can create an itchy, pustulant rash. All parts of the plant are dangerous at all times of the year; seasonally, poison oak can be identified by its lobed, often-shiny leaves grouped in threes.

Deer Tick: These tiny critters occasionally carry Lyme disease; exercise special care when hiking through grass and brush, which are favorite tick habitats.

Roosevelt Elk: These large and unpredictable animals should be viewed only from a safe distance. Observers are cautioned to be especially careful during both calving season (May-June) and rutting season (late August-November).

Black Bear: Bears are potentially dangerous, and contact with them should be avoided. When camping, secure all food in metal "bear boxes." (Hang food from metal arches at backcountry sites.)

Vehicle Break-ins: Lock your car when leaving it; take all valuables with you.

Bicycling Hazards: Follow proper safety procedures, including the use of a helmet. All park bicycling routes are shared with other users, so exercise caution and courtesy. Most park trails and dirt roads are closed to bicycles; if in doubt about a route, check with park officials.

*Note: Many dangers and difficulties can be avoided by having a proper knowledge of park rules and regulations. For **complete** information, contact **both** national **and** state park officials.*

⊲⊳ Pets ⊲⊳

Pets and park wildlife do not mix; encounters between the two can result in disruption, illness, injury, and death. To prevent such occurrences, pets are not allowed on any park trail except the access path to Enderts Beach. When in campgrounds, pets must be restrained at all times; dogs must be on a six-foot (or shorter) leash. Park staff can provide additional details.

Park Addresses and Phone Numbers

Redwood National Park (RNP):

Headquarters
1111 Second Street
Crescent City, CA 95531
(707) 464-6101

Redwood National Park Headquarters

Redwood Information Center
(south of Orick)
(707) 488-3461

State Parks:

North Coast Redwoods District Office
600A West Clark Street
Eureka, CA 95501
(707) 445-6547

Prairie Creek Redwoods State Park
(707) 488-2171

Trinidad Sector Office (supervises the
Prairie Creek park)
15336 Highway 101
Trinidad, CA 95570
(707) 488-2041

Jedediah Smith Redwoods State Park-
Del Norte Coast Redwoods State
Park
(707) 458-3310

Hiouchi Sector Office (supervises the
Jedediah Smith and Del Norte Coast
parks)
1375 Elk Valley Road
Crescent City, CA 95531
(707) 464-9533

State Park Campground Reservations:

MISTIX
Box 85705
San Diego, CA 92138-5705
(800) 444-7275

Information Centers (i)

Five information/visitor centers are located within the parks; all provide posters, books, maps, interpretive displays, and helpful staff. **Prairie Creek Redwoods State Park** has a center next to the campground entrance station at Elk Prairie. It is open year round, while the adjacent bookstore operates during the summer and on a staff-available basis the rest of the year. The center at **Jedediah Smith Redwoods State Park** is open from Memorial Day through Labor Day; it is located in the campground next to site 55. Although **Del Norte Coast Redwoods State Park** does not have an information facility, brochures and maps can be obtained from the host at the Mill Creek Campground. **Redwood National Park** has a center at each of the three major entrances to the parks. The **Redwood Information Center** is situated near the parks' southern boundary, off Highway 101 just north of Freshwater Spit. Another site is at **Park Headquarters**, located on Second Street in Crescent City, just west of Highway 101. The **Hiouchi Ranger Station** serves those travelling on Highway 199; it is located west of Hiouchi on the north side of the highway. The Hiouchi center operates summers only, while the other two RNP centers are open all year.

Tall Trees Shuttle Bus 🚐 and Vehicle Pass 🚗

Redwood National Park operates a shuttle bus to the Tall Trees trailhead from late May through mid-September. The bus leaves the Redwood Information Center, stops at the Redwood Creek Trailhead, and then continues on to Tall Trees. By arrangement, the bus will also connect with the Dolason Prairie Trailhead on the Bald Hills Road; a $7.00 donation is requested. Contact the Redwood Information Center for schedule and details. *Note: in summer the bus often fills up early.*

Passenger vehicles may travel the steep, gravel-surfaced Tall Trees Access Road by permit; motor homes and RVs are prohibited. Permits are available at the Redwood Information Center.

🚰 Picnicking 🚱

Redwood National Park offers several free picnicking facilities; state park picnic areas require a day use fee. All sites provide tables; grills and fire rings are noted where available. Other features are indicated by the following symbols:

🚰 water   🚱 no water   🚻 restrooms

Freshwater Spit Day Use Area (RNP): on Highway 101 at the south end of the spit; grills 🚱🚻

Redwood Creek Picnic Area (RNP): on the beach between Freshwater Spit and the Redwood Information Center, approximately two miles south of Orick on Highway 101; grills 🚱🚻

Redwood Information Center (RNP): table at the start of the Wetlands Boardwalk, north of the parking area; other facilities at the main building 🚰🚻

Redwood Creek Horse Trailhead (RNP): at the Orick Rodeo grounds, end of Drydens Road, one mile northeast of Orick 🚱🚻

Redwood Creek Trailhead (RNP): at a tree-fringed parking area for the north end of the trail, on a short side route at mile 0.4 of Bald Hills Road 🚱🚻

Lady Bird Johnson Grove Trailhead (RNP): in a high-elevation redwood forest, mile 2.7 of Bald Hills Road 🚱🚻

Redwood Creek Overlook (RNP): at a ridgetop viewpoint of the creek canyon, mile 6.7 of Bald Hills Road ⊗🄵

Dolason Prairie Trailhead (RNP): in an encirclement of second-growth firs, mile 11.4 of Bald Hills Road ⊗🄵

Lost Man Creek Trailhead (RNP): near the creek in a stand of striking redwoods, a mile off Highway 101 about four miles north of Orick; grills ⊗🄵

Gold Bluffs Beach (Prairie Creek Redwoods State Park): nestled in the dunes at mile 5.2 of Gold Bluffs Beach Road; fire rings ⊗🄵

Fern Canyon Trailhead (Prairie Creek Redwoods S. P.): at the alder-shaded mouth of the canyon, mile 7.1 of Gold Bluffs Beach Road; fire rings ⊗🄵

Elk Prairie (Prairie Creek Redwoods S. P.): in the forest west of the prairie, off mile 1.1 of the Newton B. Drury Scenic Parkway; grills ⊛🄵

High Bluff Picnic Area (RNP): atop a picturesque rocky point, off mile 4.6 of Coastal Drive; grills ⊗🄵

Klamath Overlook (RNP): spectacular views of the ocean and the Klamath River from this open hillside, mile 2.3 of Requa Road ⊗🄵

Lagoon Creek (RNP): next to a lilypad-covered lagoon, about five miles north of Klamath on Highway 101 ⊛🄵

Wilson Creek (Del Norte Coast Redwoods S. P.): beside a sandy beach and near several sea stacks, about six miles north of Klamath on Highway 101 ⊗

Crescent Beach (RNP): near a lagoon off Enderts Beach Road, about two miles south of Crescent City; grills ⊛🄵

Crescent Beach Overlook (RNP): atop a rocky promontory near the end of Enderts Beach Road, approximately four miles south of Crescent City ⊗

Redwood National Park Headquarters: in a small courtyard, in Crescent City on Second Street, just west of Highway 101 ⊛🄵

Jedediah Smith Campground (Jedediah Smith Redwoods State Park): next to a beach on the Smith River, just west of Hiouchi; grills ⊛🄵

Hiouchi Ranger Station (RNP): beside a park information center, just west of Hiouchi ⊛🄵

Car Camping ▲ and RV Camping ⊕

With the exception of RNP's Freshwater Lagoon Spit, all vehicle-accessible camping is provided by the state parks; they offer both traditional campgrounds and environmental camps, the latter of which require walking a short distance from a parking area. All state camping areas have a use fee. RNP has no fee but accepts donations. All sites have potable water, restrooms, picnic tables, and fire rings unless otherwise noted; locations in bear country have metal food boxes. There are no hookups.

Freshwater Lagoon Spit (RNP): tent and RV camping in separate areas next to Highway 101

Elk Prairie Campground (Prairie Creek Redwoods S. P.): between the western edge of Elk Prairie and Prairie Creek; 75 tent and RV sites, with showers, trailer sanitation station, and handicapped access

Gold Bluff Environmental Camp (Prairie Creek Redwoods S. P.): at mile 3.2 of Davison Road; three sites, each for groups of up to eight persons—NO water, NO garbage pick up, requires a short hike from the parking area (register at the Elk Prairie Entrance Station and

Circle of second growth,
Mill Creek Campground

obtain the combination for the gate on the camp access road)

Gold Bluffs Beach Campground (Prairie Creek Redwoods S. P.): at mile 5.7 of Gold Bluffs Beach Road, in the dunes between the bluffs and the ocean; the site offers solar showers *(Note: road restrictions prohibit vehicles more than 8 feet wide and 24 feet long from reaching this area.)*

Mill Creek Campground (Del Norte Coast Redwoods S. P.): in the forested canyon bottom of Mill Creek; 145 tent and RV sites, with showers, trailer dump station, and handicapped access

Jedediah Smith Campground (Jedediah Smith Redwoods S. P.): beside the Smith River in mixed forest; 106 tent and RV sites, showers, trailer sanitation station, handicapped access

Hiouchi, Crescent City, and the Klamath area all have privately operated tent/RV campgrounds, while Orick offers RV-only camping.

Other Lodging 🛏

Motels and other indoor accommodations are available at Orick, Klamath, Klamath Glen, Requa, Crescent City, Hiouchi. The **Redwood Hostel**, located midway between Klamath and Crescent City; attracts travellers from around the world. It combines inexpensive lodging in the historic DeMartin House with superb ocean views.

Rotary Grove marker, FoothillTrail—
Prairie Creek Redwoods State Park

Hiking 🚶

The parks provide more than 70 paths and roads; round-trip distances range from less than a mile to more than 16 miles. See Section III: "Hiking Trails," (pp. 235-270) for recommended routes.

Backcountry Camps ⚊

Several longer park trails offer opportunities for overnight backpacking trips.

A multi-day hike can be plotted along the Coastal Trail, but the Klamath River interrupts the route between the Flint Ridge and Hidden Beach sections, requiring either a long detour along roads or a car shuttle.

Both Redwood National Park and Prairie Creek Redwoods State Park provide camps for backpackers; only the state park sites have a use fee, which must be paid at the Elk Prairie Entrance Station. The camps offer picnic tables, fire rings, bear boxes or food hangers, restrooms, and potable water unless otherwise noted.

Redwood Creek (RNP): camping is allowed on the gravel bars in the streambed, from 1.5 miles above the lower Redwood Creek Trailhead to a quarter mile below the Tall Trees Grove, and then again starting a quarter mile above the grove; no facilities are provided

Elk Prairie Hike & Bike Camp (Prairie Creek Redwoods S. P.): next to the main campground on the western edge of Elk Prairie

Gold Bluffs Beach Hike & Bike Camp (Prairie Creek Redwoods S. P.): on a forested bluff near the west end of the Miner's Ridge Trail, off mile 5.7 of Gold Bluffs Beach Road

Butler Creek Hike & Bike Camp (Prairie Creek Redwoods S. P.): three tent sites in an alder grove at the junction of the West Ridge Trail and the Coastal Trail; NO potable water

Flint Ridge Primitive Camp (RNP): on a hillside overlooking the ocean, near the west end of the Flint Ridge Section, Coastal Trail; 10 sites

DeMartin Primitive Camp (RNP): in the forested fringe of a hillside prairie, midway on the DeMartin Section of the Coastal Trail; 10 sites

Nickel Creek Primitive Camp (RNP): near the mouth of Nickel Creek, off the Last Chance Section, Coastal Trail; five sites, NO potable water

Little Bald Hills Horse Camp & Primitive Camp (RNP): at the site of the historic Murphy Ranch off the Little Bald Hills Trail

Horseback Riding

Equestrians will find several days' worth of riding trails within the parks; backcountry camp sites allow for extended stays. Redwood National Park offers the **Redwood Creek Horse Trails**, a system that runs along the ridges southeast of Orick; they contain four loop routes with durations and mileages as follows: three-hour loop, 6.5 miles; six-hour loop, 13 miles; one-day loop, 18.5 miles; three-day loop, 31 miles. An outfitter at the Orick rodeo grounds provides guided rides and pack trips into the area; contact the Redwood Information Center for details.

Two horse camps lie along the trail system south of Orick:

Elam Horse Camp (RNP): midway along the Horse Trail near Elam Creek

Forty-Four Horse Camp (RNP): near the southern end of the Horse Trail close to Forty-Four Creek, a short distance north of the Tall Trees Grove

RNP also maintains the **Mill Creek Horse Trail**, located southwest of Jedediah Smith Redwoods State Park on Bertsch Road, off Howland Hill Road. The **Little Bald Hills Trail**, which runs through both Jed Smith State Park and RNP lands, is open to hikers, mountain bikers, and equestrians. A trail camp on the route offers facilities for horses (see "Backcountry Camps" above).

Mountain Bicycling

The parks provide several bicycling routes of varying quality. Most serious cyclists head south for the many ridge-climbing roads in Humboldt Redwoods State Park.

Holter Ridge/Lost Man Creek Trail: The Holter Ridge section is an undulating passage through second-growth conifers; the Lost Man Creek segment is mostly steep, with lots of large redwoods in the lower canyon. Running between Bald Hills Road and Highway 101, the route is 11 miles long. A car shuttle eliminates the exerting uphill out of Lost Man Creek.

Prairie Creek Loop Trail: A 20-mile mishmash of routes, this loop at different times follows the Elk Prairie Campground entrance road, the Jogging Trail, Davison-Gold Bluffs Beach Road, the Coastal Trail, the Ossagon Trail, and the Newton B. Drury Scenic Parkway. Scenery is spectacular—Elk Prairie, Gold Bluffs, beautiful beachside alder groves, stunning stands of redwoods—but route conditions are not always congenial; obstacles include summertime dust on Davison and Gold Bluffs Beach roads, an often-flooded trail segment near Butler Creek, a staircase (on a bike route!) above Ossagon Creek, and the occasional wind-whipping Winnebago on the parkway.

Last Chance Section, Coastal Trail: The southern segment of the trail is an eerie excursion into a time warp—a faded white line intermittently appears beneath a litter of redwood needles as one wheels along the pavement of the original Redwood Highway. The route then begins a roller coaster run on a rough and often steep roadbed that even park officials advise against biking. A car shuttle between the southern trailhead and the end of Enderts Beach Road eliminates the daunting uphill return for those who follow the trail through its harrowing climax. The round-trip length is 14 miles for the entire route, or 10 miles for the saner stretch on the old highway.

Little Bald Hills Trail: Most people—including some park personnel—don't even know this is a bike route. Cyclists who somehow discover it will find a grueling initial climb, a rocky and sometimes narrow roadbed, and the possibility of encountering unsuspecting hikers and horseback riders. Round trip distance to the park boundary and back is 10 miles; a loop can be made by continuing through Six Rivers National Forest land to the trail's end at South Fork Road, and then returning by way of South Fork Road, Douglas Park Road, and Howland Hill Road to the original trailhead.

Park Roads: Other trails are not open for cycling, but certain secondary roads lend themselves to mountain bike use. The ridgetop section of **Bald Hills Road** is wide, alternately paved and graveled, and offers several stunning views of peaks and prairies; traffic is occasional but can include logging trucks. **Coastal Drive** is another gravel-pavement mix; it offers vistas of the ocean, some moderate hills, and the possibility of a partial loop via Klamath Beach Road and Alder Camp Road. **Howland Hill Road** is narrow, entirely gravel, generally muddy in winter, and frequently driven by tourists. It offsets these liabilities by passing through thick redwood forest and crossing magnificent Mill Creek.

Mountain bikers riding the Little Bald Hills Trail can utilize that route's horse

camp/primitive camp, while those taking the Prairie Creek Loop have access to the hike and bike camps at Squashan and Butler creeks (see "Backcountry Camps" above).

Fishing ⌙

The North Coast has long boasted fabulous fishing; although runs have diminished in recent years, anglers may still want to wet a line in one of several locations.

The **Klamath River** offers the best steelhead and king (chinook) salmon fishing in the state. The king run starts in late July or early August and ends in late October; silver (coho) salmon are in the river from mid-September until December. Small steelhead cruise the Klamath year round, but the big boys run only from July to December or January. Sea-run cutthroat trout are available from late fall through spring. The river mouth sees fishing activity from both boat and shore, while boats are used on the upstream riffles. The Klamath area provides a selection of fishing guides.

Farther north, the **Smith River** has a king run from September through December, silver during October and November, and then steelhead in December and January. Cutthroat and rainbow trout bite during the spring and summer along the state park section of the river.

Redwood Creek, although heavily silted by upstream logging, provides small salmon and steelhead runs. **Mill Creek** has rainbow and cutthroat trout and king salmon. Stocked trout can be caught at Lagoon Creek and in Freshwater Lagoon.

Saltwater fishing in the **Pacific Ocean** includes redtail surfperch, surf smelt, and night fish along the beaches; sea

Yuroks sun drying surf fish, mouth of Redwood Creek, 1928

trout, rockfish, cabezon, and ling cod at rocky outcrops; and salmon offshore. Charter and rental boats can be had at Crescent City, Trinidad, and Eureka.

Check at the parks' vistor centers for current information. A California fishing license is required for all types of fishing; special regulations may apply for salmon and steelhead.

Historic Sites

A number of structures, ruins, and remnants mark park areas of historical significance. Some are undesignated and difficult to locate, but they can usually be found by persistent perusers.

Orick Inn: a large roadside inn dating from the 1920s (private building, no longer open to the public)—at mile 3.0 of the Orick section of Highway 101

Old Trinidad Trail: a vestige of the 1850s pack trail, marked with orange flagging—on the Tall Trees Loop Trail, off mile 7.1 of Bald Hills Road

Sherman Lyons Ranch: still evident are an early-day barn, a more modern residence, and an outhouse of undetermined age—on Bald Hills Road at mile 9.6

Dolason Prairie Barn: part of the original, circa-1900 structure still stands on a picturesque prairie—on the Dolason Prairie Trail, off mile 11.4 of Bald Hills Road

Lyons Ranch "Home Place": an old barn, a sheep-shearers' shack, and a small family graveyard on the site of the original Lyons Ranch—at the end of Lyons Road, off mile 17 of Bald Hills Road

Lyons Ranch Historic District–Other Sites: two line shacks, two barns, and two barn remnants lie on hillslopes north of Coyote Creek—either on or

Downtown Dooleyville

reached from Lyons Road, High Prairie Road, or Rock Fork Road via Coyote Peak Road, between miles 17.7 and 18.7 of Bald Hills Road

Union Gold Bluffs Mine: old boards and debris from the southernmost of the Gold Bluffs mining operations— reached by either a side road off mile 2.6 of Davison Road or from the northern end of the Skunk Cabbage Section, Coastal Trail

Plank Road, Squashan Creek: timbers set as tracks for an old logging road— near the western end of the Miner's Ridge Trail, off mile 5.7 of Gold Bluffs Beach Road

Prairie Creek Redwoods State Park Visitor Center: a finely crafted building constructed by the Civilian Conservation Corps in the 1930s—off mile 1.1 of the Newton B. Drury Scenic Parkway

Cal Barrel Logging Camp: ruins of old buildings and trucks—at the eastern (upper) end of Cal Barrel Road, which is reached either off mile 3.9 of the Park Bypass or mile 1.5 of the Newton B.

Drury Scenic Parkway *(Note: freeway regulations restrict access to this site; contact CalTrans and/or RNP officials for further information.)*

Johnston Ranch/Amony Placer Mine/ Crothers' House: an old bottle dump, bridge remnant, mining flume, house foundation, and debris—on and near the Carruther's Cove Trail, off mile 1.1 of Coastal Drive

Radar Station B–71: two concrete block buildings that constituted a camouflaged World War II radar station—at mile 5.3 of Coastal Drive

Douglas Memorial Bridge: the southern end of a historic bridge, opened in 1926 and washed out in the 1964 flood—at mile 8.5 of the Coastal Drive side trip

Requa Inn: an old inn that still operates as a bed and breakfast—at mile 0.8 of Requa Road

Yurok Tribal Office: a finely crafted, early 1940s masterpiece, with extensive use of wood and stone; at mile 8.7 of the Klamath section of Highway 101

Yurok Loop Trail: the route passes the site of O'men, a one-time Yurok village—off mile 10.7 of the Klamath section of Highway 101

DeMartin House: the former home of a pioneer ranching family now serves as the Redwood Hostel—off mile 11.4 of the Klamath section of Highway 101

Old Redwood Highway: several miles of roadbed from the original highway—on the Last Chance Section, Coastal Trail, off mile 2.9 of the Del Norte Coast Redwoods section of Highway 101

Old County Wagon Road: an old plank road dating from the 1890s—near the eastern end of the Damnation Creek Trail, off mile 3.3 of the Del Norte Coast Redwoods section of Highway 101, and at various points along the highway

Hobbs, Wall & Company Logging Site: remains of the Del Norte Southern railroad and scattered debris—on the Hobbs, Wall Trail and Trestle Trail at the Mill Creek Campground, off mile 7.6 of the Del Norte Coast Redwoods section of Highway 101

***Emidio* Monument:** a marker and steel fragments from an oil tanker torpedoed by the Japanese during World War II—on Front Street, Crescent City

Battery Point Lighthouse: the historic harbor lighthouse is now a museum—off the end of Front Street, Crescent City

Del Norte County Historical Society Museum: many photos, exhibits, and artifacts; Sixth and H streets, Crescent City

Camp Lincoln: a house that was once officers' quarters at an 1860s military site (now a state park ranger's residence, not open to the public)—on Kings Valley Road, off mile 0.4 of Highway 199

Crescent City Plank Road: part of an early route to the inland gold mines—on the Leiffer Loop Trail, off Walker Road, off mile 2.8 of Highway 199

Peacock Ferry Site: the Crescent City Plank Road crossed the Smith River here—off Walker Road, off mile 2.8 of Highway 199

Murphy's Ranch: a spring, fence, and apple tree mark the site of this 1880s ranch and "hotel"—on the Little Bald Hills Trail, off mile 2.1 of the Howland Hill Road side trip

Old Stage Road: the remains of another early plank road—at mile 5.2 of the Howland Hill Road side trip

Wildlife Watching ⚋

Wildlife may be seen throughout the park, but the following locations offer some of the best chances for regular viewing:

Redwood Information Center: gray whales

Redwood Creek: marbled murrelets

Bald Hills: elk, raptors

Lost Man Creek: marbled murrelets

Gold Bluffs Beach: elk, gray whales offshore, tracks of various animals in the sand

Elk Prairie: elk, raccoons, marbled murrelets; various other birds at the prairie edge

High Bluff Picnic Area: gray whales

Marshall Pond: beavers, wood ducks, other birds

Mouth of the Klamath River: marine mammals

Klamath Overlook: gray whales

Lagoon at Crescent Beach: river otters, herons, waterfowl

Crescent Beach Overlook: gray whales

Gray whale

Smith River: river otters near the Jed Smith campground

See Chapter 5, "Nature's Neighborhoods," for other wildlife locations.

Plant Perusing

Sites for frequently-found flora are noted in Chapter 5, "Nature's Neighborhoods." Prime viewing areas for many plants are also listed throughout Section III, "Twenty-Five Favorite Hikes."

The parks are filled with many colorful wildflowers, many of which bloom in spring and/or early summer. Among those to watch for are: western trillium (early spring); Hooker's and Smith's fairybells, rhododendron, clintonia, and lilies (spring); redwood sorrel and monkeyflowers (spring through summer); most prairie flowers (late spring through early summer). In fall, many leafy plants provide their own color, including poison oak, bigleaf and vine maple, western burning bush, California spikenard, and dogwood. Fall and winter rains produce a many-hued array of mushrooms.

Disabled Access

Most park restrooms and some trails are wheelchair accessible; check with the visitor centers for details. Near the Elk Prairie Campground are two wheelchair paths: the Redwood Access Trail and the Revelation Trail; the latter also accommodates the visually impaired. All three state park campgrounds have sites with handicapped access.

Other Activities

Swimming: The Smith River offers several swimming sites where it passes through Jedediah Smith Redwoods State Park. A beach runs along the edge of the park campground; other beaches are reached by the access road just west of the Hiouchi Bridge and off of both Walker and North Bank roads.

Kayaking and Boating: The Smith River is a favorite of white-water enthusiasts. Redwood National Park conducts summer kayak trips on the river led by park naturalists; a $6.00 donation is requested. Reservations are made at the Hiouchi Visitor Center. Contact the park for dates and details. Kayakers, canoe and raft users, and fishing enthusiasts will find Smith River launch sites at the Jed Smith Campground and on South Fork Road between the river's main and south forks. Other put-in spots are on park land below the Hiouchi Bridge. Contact the parks for details.

Tidepool Viewing: Enderts Beach, south of Crescent City, offers good tidepool areas. RNP staff guide tidepool/seashore walks here in summer; contact the park for further information. Another tidepool site is near the northern end of the Hidden Beach Section, Coastal Trail, at False Klamath Cove.

Slug Racing: Prairie Creek Redwoods State Park is the setting for the annual "Banana Slug Derby," a summer event that determines the speediest (a very relative term) slug.

Plants:
A Selected Species List

Trees:

alder, red	*Alnus rubra*
cedar, Port Orford	*Chamaecyparis lawsoniana*
chinquapin, golden	*Castanopsis chrysophylla*
cottonwood, black	*Populus trichocarpa*
dogwood, Pacific	*Cornus nuttallii*
Douglas-fir	*Pseudotsuga menziesii*
fir, grand	*Abies grandis*
hemlock, western	*Tsuga heterophylla*
laurel, California	*Umbellularia californica*
madrone, Pacific	*Arbutus menziesii*
maple, bigleaf	*Acer macrophyllum*
oak, California black	*Quercus kelloggii*
oak, Oregon white	*Quercus garryana*
pine, Jeffrey	*Pinus jeffreyi*
pine, knobcone	*Pinus attenuata*
redcedar, western	*Thuja plicata*
redwood, coast	*Sequoia sempervirens*
spruce, Sitka	*Picea sitchensis*
tanoak	*Lithocarpus densiflora*
willow (various species)	*Salix* spp.

Shrubs:

azalea, mock	*Menziesia ferruginea*
azalea, western	*Rhododendron occidentale*
blackberry, Himalayan	*Rubus procera*
blackberry, California	*Rubus vitifolius*
blueblossom	*Ceanothus thyrsiflorus*
burning bush, western	*Euonymus occidentalis*
cascara sagrada	*Rhamnus purshiana*
coffeeberry	*Rhamnus californica*
coyote brush	*Baccharis pilularis*
currant, red flowering	*Ribes sanguineum*
elderberry, coast red	*Sambucus callicarpa*
gooseberry (various species)	*Ribes* spp.

Shrubs, continued

hazel, California	*Corylus cornuta*
honeysuckle, hairy	*Lonicera hispidula*
huckleberry, black	*Vaccinium ovatum*
huckleberry, red	*Vaccinium parvifolium*
manzanita, hairy	*Arctostaphylos columbiana*
maple, vine	*Acer circinatum*
ninebark, Pacific	*Physocarpus capitatus*
ocean spray	*Holodiscus discolor*
Oregon grape	*Berberis nervosa*
osoberry	*Oemleria cerasiformis*
poison oak	*Rhus diversiloba*
rhododendron	*Rhododendron macrophyllum*
rose (various species)	*Rosa* spp.
salal	*Gaultheria shallon*
salmonberry	*Rubus spectabilis*
snowberry	*Symphoricarpos albus*
thimbleberry	*Rubus parviflorus*
twinberry	*Lonicera involucrata*
wax myrtle, western	*Myrica californica*

Ferns:

deer fern	*Blechnum spicant*
five-fingered fern	*Adiantum pedatum*
giant chain fern	*Woodwardia fimbriata*
goldenback fern	*Pityrogramma triangularis*
Indian's dream	*Aspidotis densa*
lady fern	*Athyrium filix-femina*
leather fern	*Polypodium scouleri*
licorice fern	*Polypodium glycyrrhiza*
polypody, California	*Polypodium californicum*
sword fern	*Polystichum munitum*
wood fern, coastal	*Dryopteris arguta*
wood fern, spreading	*Dryopteris dilatata*

Flowers: (* non-native species)

alum root	*Heuchera micrantha*
aster, Chilean	*Aster chilensis*
baby blue eyes	*Nemophila menziesii*
baneberry	*Actaea rubra*
beargrass	*Xerophyllum tenax*
bedstraw, sweet-scented	*Galium triflorum*
bleeding heart, western	*Dicentra formosa*
blue dicks	*Dichelostemma capitatum*
blue-eyed grass	*Sisyrinchium bellum*
blue-eyed Mary, spinsters	*Collinsia sparsiflora*
bouncing bet *	*Saponaria officinalis*

Flowers, continued

boykinia, coastal	*Boykinia elata*
brodiaea, harvest	*Brodiaea elegans*
brooklime, American *	*Veronica americana*
buttercup, California	*Ranunculus californicus*
buttercup, creeping	*Ranunculus repens*
buttercup, western	*Ranunculus occidentalis*
cattail, common	*Typha latifolia*
clintonia, Andrews'	*Clintonia andrewsiana*
coltsfoot, western	*Petasites palmatus*
columbine, crimson	*Aquilegia formosa*
cow parsnip	*Heracleum lanatum*
cream sacs	*Orthocarpus lithospermoides*
daisy, seaside	*Erigeron glaucus*
delphinium, coast	*Delphinium decorum*
evening primrose, beach	*Camissonia cheiranthifolia*
false lily-of-the-valley	*Maianthemum dilatatum*
false Solomon's seal, fat	*Smilacina racemosa*
false Solomon's seal, thin	*Smilacina stellata*
fairybell, Hooker's	*Disporum hookeri*
fairybell, Smith's	*Disporum smithii*
farewell-to-spring	*Clarkia amoena*
fetid adders tongue	*Scoliopus bigelovii*
firecracker flower	*Dichelostemma ida-maia*
fireweed, red	*Epilobium angustifolium*
flax, western blue	*Linum perenne*
foxglove *	*Digitalis purpurea*
fringe cups	*Tellima grandiflora*
gilia, blue-headed	*Gilia capitata*
ginger, wild	*Asarum caudatum*
gnome plant	*Hemitomes congestum*
harebell, California	*Asyneuma prenanthoides*
hound's tongue, western	*Cynoglossum grande*
Indian paintbrush (various species)	*Castilleja* spp.
Indian pipe	*Monotropa uniflora*
inside-out flower, northern	*Vancouveria hexandra*
iris, Douglas'	*Iris douglasiana*
Ithuriel's spear	*Brodiaea laxa*
Jupiter's beard *	*Centranthius ruber*
lady's tresses, hooded	*Spiranthes romanzoffiana*
lily, leopard	*Lilium pardalinum*
lupine, broad-leaved	*Lupinus latifolius*
lupine, bush*	*Lupinus arboreus*
lupine, miniature	*Lupinus bicolor*
lupine, riverbank	*Lupinus rivularis*
milkmaids	*Dentaria californica*
mission bells	*Fritillaria lanceolata*
monkeyflower, chickweed	*Mimulus alsinoides*

Flowers, continued

monkeyflower, seep-spring	*Mimulus guttatus*
monkeyflower, sticky	*Mimulus aurantiacus*
monkeyflower, toothed	*Mimulus dentatus*
morning glory, beach	*Calystegia soldanella*
nettle, stinging *	*Urtica dioica*
nightshade, white *	*Solanum nodiflorum*
onion, coast flatstem	*Allium falcifolium*
orchid, calypso	*Calypso bulbosa*
orchid, rattlesnake	*Goodyera oblongifolia*
penstemon, Siskiyou	*Penstemon anguineus*
phacelia, Bolander's	*Phacelia bolanderi*
phlox, spreading	*Phlox diffusa*
piggy-back plant	*Tolmiea menziesii*
pink, California Indian	*Silene californica*
pond-lily, yellow	*Nuphar polysepalum*
poppy, California	*Eschscholzia californica*
pussy ears	*Calochortus tolmiei*
sand verbena, beach	*Abronia umbellata*
sand verbena, yellow	*Abronia latifolia*
sea rocket *	*Cakile maritima*
shooting stars, Henderson's	*Dodecatheon hendersonii*
Siberian candyflower	*Montia sibirica*
silvertop, beach	*Glehnia leiocarpa*
silverweed *	*Potentilla anserina*
sorrel, redwood	*Oxalis oregana*
spikenard, California	*Aralia californica*
starflower, Pacific	*Trientalis latifolia*
stonecrop	*Sedum spathulifolium*
strawberry, beach	*Fragaria chiloensis*
strawberry, wood	*Fragaria californica*
sunflower, woolly	*Eriophyllum lanatum*
tansy, dune	*Tanacetum douglasii*
trail plant	*Adenocaulon bicolor*
trillium, giant	*Trillium chloropetalum*
trillium, western	*Trillium ovatum*
twisted stalk, clasping	*Streptopus amplexifolius*
vanilla leaf	*Achlys triphylla*
violet, redwood	*Viola sempervirens*
violet, smooth yellow	*Viola glabella*
violet, two-eyed	*Viola ocellata*
violet, wedge-leaved	*Viola cuneata*
violet, western dog	*Viola adunca*
wild cucumber	*Marah oreganus*
windflower	*Anemone deltoidea*
wintergreen, white-veined	*Pyrola picta*
wood nymph	*Moneses uniflora*
yerba de selva	*Whipplea modesta*

Wildlife:
A Selected Species List

Birds:

auklet, Cassin's
auklet, rhinoceros
blackbird, Brewer's
blackbird, red-winged
bluebird, western
brandt
bufflehead
bunting, lazuli
bushtit
canvasback
chat, yellow-breasted
chickadee, black-capped
chickadee, chestnut-backed
coot, American
cormorant, Brandt's
cormorant, double-crested
cormorant, pelagic
cowbird, brown-headed
creeper, brown
crossbill, red
crow, American
dipper, American
dove, mourning
dowicher, long-billed
dowicher, short-billed
duck, ring-necked
duck, ruddy
duck, wood
dunlin
egret, cattle
egret, great
egret, snowy
finch, house

finch, purple
flicker, northern
flycatcher, dusky
flycatcher, olive-sided
flycatcher, western
gadwall
godwit, marbled
goldfinch, American
goose, Canada
grebe, eared
grebe, horned
grebe, pied-billed
grebe, western
grosbeak, black-headed
grouse, ruffed
guillemot, pigeon
gull, Bonaparte's
gull, California
gull, glaucous-winged
gull, Heermann's
gull, mew
gull, western
harrier, northern
hawk, red-shouldered
hawk, red-tailed
hawk, rough-legged
hawk, sharp-shinned
heron, black-crown night
heron, great blue
heron, green-backed
hummingbird, Allen's
hummingbird, Anna's
hummingbird, rufous
jaeger, parasitic

Birds, continued

jaeger, pomarine
jay, gray
jay, scrub
jay, Steller's
junco, dark-eyed
kestrel, American
killdeer
kingbird, western
kingfisher, belted
kinglet, golden-crowned
kinglet, ruby-crowned
kite, black-shouldered
kittiwake, black-legged
longspur, Lapland
loon, common
loon, Pacific
loon, red-throated
martin, purple
meadowlark, western
merganser, common
murre, common
murrelet, ancient
murrelet, marbled
nighthawk, common
nuthatch, red-breasted
oriole, northern
osprey
owl, common barn
owl, great horned
owl, long-eared
owl, northern pygmy
owl, northern saw-whet
owl, short-eared
owl, spotted
owl, western screech
oystercatcher, black
pelican, brown
pewee, western wood
phalarope, red
phalarope, red-necked
phoebe, black
pigeon, band-tailed
pintail, northern
pipit, water

plover, black-bellied
plover, semipalmiated
puffin, tufted
quail, California
quail, mountain
rail, Virginia
raven, common
robin, American
sanderling
sandpiper, least
sandpiper, pectoral
sandpiper, spotted
sandpiper, western
scaup, greater
scaup, lesser
scoter, surf
scoter, white-winged
shoveler, northern
shrike, northern
siskin, pine
snipe
sora
sparrow, chipping
sparrow, fox
sparrow, golden-crowned
sparrow, Lincoln's
sparrow, savannah
sparrow, song
sparrow, white-crowned
surfbird
swallow, bank
swallow, barn
swallow, cliff
swallow, northern rough-winged
swallow, tree
swallow, violet-green
swan, tundra
swift, Vaux's
tanager, western
teal, blue-winged
teal, cinnamon
teal, green-winged
tern, Caspian
tern, common
thrush, hermit
thrush, Swainson's

Birds, continued

thrush, varied
towhee, rufous-sided
turnstone, black
turnstone, ruby
vireo, Hutton's
vireo, solitary
vireo, warbling
vulture, turkey
warbler, hermit
warbler, MacGillivray's
warbler, Nashville
warbler, orange-crowned
warbler, Townsend's
warbler, Wilson's
warbler, yellow
warbler, yellow-rumped
whimbrel
widgeon, American
willet
woodpecker, acorn
woodpecker, downy
woodpecker, hairy
woodpecker, pileated
wren, Bewick's
wren, house
wren, marsh
wren, winter
wrentit
yellowlegs, greater
yellowlegs, lesser
yellowthroat, common

Mammals:

bat, big brown
bat, red
bat, silver-haired
bear, black
beaver
bobcat
chipmunk, Allen's
chipmunk, Siskiyou
chipmunk, Townsend
coyote
deer, black-tailed

dolphin, common
dolphin, Pacific white-sided
elk, Roosevelt
fox, gray
harvest mouse, western
jumping mouse, Pacific
mink
mole, California
mole, Pacific
mole, Townsend
mountain beaver
mountain lion
mouse, California
mouse, deer
myotis, California
myotis, little brown
otter, river
pocket gopher, valley
porcupine
porpoise, Dall's
porpoise, harbor
rabbit, brush
raccoon
sea lion, California
sea lion, northern
seal, harbor
shrew, marsh
shrew, Pacific
shrew, Trowbridge
shrew, vagrant
shrew-mole
skunk, spotted
skunk, striped
squirrel, California ground
squirrel, Douglas'
squirrel, northern flying
squirrel, western gray
vole, California
vole, Oregon
vole, red tree
vole, Townsend
vole, white-footed
weasel, longtail
whale, finback
whale, gray
whale, killer

Mammals, continued

woodrat, bushy-tailed
woodrat, dusky-footed

Reptiles:

alligator lizard, northern
alligator lizard, southern
fence lizard, northwestern
garter snake, coast
garter snake, common
garter snake, northwestern
garter snake, Oregon
gopher snake, Pacific
king snake, California mountain
pond turtle, northwestern
racer, western yellow-bellied
rattlesnake, northern Pacific
ringneck snake, northwestern
skink, western

Amphibians:

bullfrog
frog, California red-legged
frog, foothill yellow-legged
frog, northern red-legged
newt, northern rough-skinned
newt, red-bellied
salamander, arboreal
salamander, black
salamander, brown
salamander, California slender
salamander, clouded
salamander, Del Norte
salamander, Pacific giant
salamander, painted
tailed frog
toad, boreal
toad, western
treefrog, Pacific

Fishes:

lamprey, Pacific
salmon, king (chinook)
salmon, silver (coho)
steelhead
trout, coastal cutthroat

Invertebrates:

slug, banana

Notes

Chapter 1. Redwoods: Sawed and Saved

1. Paul A. Zahl, "Finding the Mt. Everest of All Living Things," *National Geographic*, July 1964: 37.

2. Ibid.: 37,40.

3. U. S. Congress. House. Committee on Public Lands. *Letter from the Secretary of the Interior: California Redwood Company*. 50th Cong., 1st sess., 1888. Ex. Doc. 282, 2. The Secretary's letter describes the fraud in detail and summarizes the actions taken on 352 suspect timberland claims. Of these, 177, or just over half, had either been cancelled, were in the process of being cancelled, or were still being investigated; most of the rest (167) had, by then, already been patented and were referred to the Attorney General for court action (with little result). The remaining eight entries were deemed legitimate.

4. Agent Smith was rewarded for his integrity by being removed from his job. A later agent, B. F. Bergin, amassed the evidence for the cancellations.

5. "A Fraud on the Government," *New York Times*, April 5, 1886, 2.

6. "Laws not Enforced," *New York Times*, April 20, 1886, 4.

7. Susan R. Schrepfer, *The Fight to Save the Redwoods: A History of Environmental Reform 1917-1978* (Madison: University of Wisconsin Press, 1983), 186.

Chapter 2. Tribes of the Tall Trees

1. Jack Norton, *Genocide in Northwestern California* (San Francisco: the Indian Historian Press, 1979), 54-55. The report quotes contemporary Tolowa leader Loren Bommelyn, who reviewed the account that appears here.

2. The story is based on: Robert Spott and A. L. Kroeber, "Yurok Narratives," *University of California Publications in American Archaeology and Ethnology*, vol 35 (1943): 158-164. Reprint, New York: Kraus Reprint Corporation, 1965. Beeb White, a descendant of Flounder's, reviewed the current version.

3. Robert Spott, "Address," *Transactions of the Commonwealth Club of California*, vol. XXI no. 3: 133-4.

Chapter 3. Northcoast Newcomers

1. Andrew Mason Prouty, *More Deadly than War! – Pacific Coast Logging 1827–1981*. (Ph. D. Thesis, University of Washington, 1982), 345-6.

2. Ibid., 216-7.

Chapter 4. Earth, Water, and Weather

1. Peggy Coons, "Crescent City's Destructive Horror of 1964" (Del Norte Historical Society files, Photocopied), 3-5.

Chapter 7. Orick Area

1. Much of the Big Diamond story is based on an account by Elmer Hufford in: Savina Barlow, editor, *Oreq-ʷ: Orick Then and Now.........*, 59-60.

Chapter 8. Side Trip: The Bald Hills

1. John Carr, *Pioneer Days in California,* (Eureka, CA: Times Publishing Company, 1891), 102.

2. Ibid, 103-104.

3. One source indicates that the picture is actually of Willie Childs, but her age at the time (she would have been perhaps 60) makes this implausible.

Chapter 9. Side Trip: The Gold Bluffs

1. Walter Van Dyke, "Early Days in Klamath," *Overland Monthly,* vol. XVIII: 176.

2. A. W. Chase, "Gravel Deposit of Gold Bluffs," *American Journal of Science,* 3d ser., 7 (Jan-Jun 1874) 382.

Chapter 18. Side Trip: Howland Hill Road

1. Arthur W. Anderson, quoted in "Thrill Trip Says Tourist," *Del Norte Triplicate Bicentennial Edition,* July 6, 1976: 124.

2. The American Forestry Association maintains a listing of current champions in its "National Register of Big Trees." The rating system is based upon the total of three measurements: a) circumference of the tree, in inches, at 4½ feet above ground level; b) vertical height of the tree to the nearest foot; c) average diameter of the tree's crown to the nearest foot.

Chapter 21. Moderate Meanders

1. This bridge style is strengthened on both sides by triangular trusses; each truss has two diagonal pieces attached to a center upright, or "king" post.

Chapter 23. Terrific Treks

1. The four largest champions were measured and named by the "Big Tree Boys," Ron Hildebrant and Michael Taylor. According to their calculations, the "Dyerville Giant," in Humboldt Redwoods State Park, had been *both* the champion *and* tallest coast redwood until it fell to the ground in March 1991.

A Selected List of Sources

Many sources were consulted in preparing this book. The following list selects those which either provided substantial information or which expand significantly on accounts contained in the text. Many of the more obscure items can be found at: the Humboldt County Collection, Humboldt State University, Arcata; the Humboldt County Room, Humboldt County Main Library, Eureka; the Indian Action Council Library, Eureka.

General

California Department of Parks and Recreation. *Inventory of Features for Jedediah Smith Redwoods S. P., Del Norte Coast Redwoods S. P., Prairie Creek Redwoods, S. P.* 1982.

Dolezal, Robert J. *Exploring Redwood National Park.* Beaverton, OR: The Touchstone Press, 1974.

Hewes, Jeremy Joan. *Redwoods: the World's Largest Trees.* Rand McNally & Company, 1981.

Rohde, Jerry, and Gisela Rohde. *Humboldt Redwoods State Park: The Complete Guide.* Eureka, CA: Miles & Miles, 1992.

Human History: Indians

Baker, Marc Andre. "The Ethnobotany of the Yurok, Tolowa, and Karok Indians of Northwest California." Master's thesis, Humboldt State University, 1981. Photocopy.

Bommelyn, Loren. 1993. Tolowa. Typescript.

Drucker, Philip. "The Tolowa and Their Southwest Oregon Kin." *University of California Publications in American Archaeology and Ethnology* 36:4 (1937): 221-300.

DuBois, Cora A. "Tolowa Notes." *American Anthropologist* 34:2 (1932): 248-262.

Goddard, Pliny Earle. "Chilula Texts." *University of California Publications in American Archaeology and Ethnology* 10:7 (1914): 289-389.

———. "Notes on the Chilula Indians of Northwestern California." *University of California Publications in American Archaeology and Ethnology* 10:6 (1914): 265-288.

Gould, Richard A. "Tolowa." In *Handbook of North American Indians* Vol. 8, edited by Robert. F. Heizer. Washington: Smithsonian Institution, 1978.

Heffner, Kathy. *Following the Smoke: Contemporary Plant Procurement by the Indians of Northwest California.* Eureka, CA: Six Rivers National Forest, 1984.

Heizer, Robert F., and M. A. Whipple, eds. *The California Indians: A Source Book,* 2nd ed. Berkeley: University of California Press, 1971.

——. *The Destruction of the California Indians.* Santa Barbara: Peregrine Smith, 1974.

——, ed. *They Were Only Diggers.* Ramona, CA: Ballena Press, 1974.

Kroeber, A. L. *Handbook of the Indians of California.* Bureau of American Ethnology, Smithsonian Institution, Bulletin 78, 1925. Reprint, New York: Dover, 1976.

Kroeber, A. L., and S. A. Barrett. "Fishing among the Indians of Northwestern California." *Anthropological Records* 21:1. University of California, 1960.

Kroeber, A. L., and E. W. Gifford. "World Renewal: A Cult System of Native Northwest California." *University of California Publications in Anthropological Records* Vol. 13: 1-156. Reprint, Millwood, NY: Kraus Reprint Co., 1976.

Lake, Robert G. Jr. *Chilula: People from the Ancient Redwoods.* Washington: University Press of America, 1982.

Moratto, Michael J. *An Archaeological Overview of Redwood National Park.* Publications in Anthropology, no. 8, Tucson: National Park Service, Western Anthropological Center, Cultural Resources Management Division, 1973.

Pilling, Arnold A. "Yurok." In *Handbook of North American Indians,* Vol. 8, edited by Robert F. Heizer. Washington: Smithsonian Institution, 1978.

Spott, Robert, and A. L. Kroeber. "Yurok Narratives." *University of California Publications in American Archaeology and Ethnology.* vol. 35 (1943): 142-256. Reprint, New York: Kraus Reprint Corporation, 1965.

Thompson, Lucy. *To the American Indian.* Berkeley: Heyday Books, 1991.

Transactions of the Commonwealth Club of California 21, no. 3 (June 1926): 101-152

Wallace, William J. "Hupa, Chilula, and Whilkut." In *Handbook of North American Indians,* Vol. 8, edited by Robert F. Heizer. Washington: Smithsonian Institution, 1978.

Waterman, T. T. "Village Sites in Tolowa and Neighboring Areas." *American Anthropologist* 27: 528-543.

———. "Yurok Geography." *University of California Publications in American Archaeology and Ethnology* 16:5 (1920): 177-314. Reprint, New York: Kraus Reprint Corporation, 1965.

Articles were also consulted in *News from Native California*.

Several individuals provided direct information: Loren Bommelyn, Kenny Childs, Albert Gray, Mary Gray, Axel Lindgren (who offered accounts about Willie Childs and Billy Childs), Chris Peters, Richard Ricklefs, Francis "Beeb" White, and Sylvia "Jackie" White.

Human History: Whites

Barlow, Savina, editor. *Oreq-ʷ: Orick Then and Now*.......... Historical Committee of Orick Chamber of Commerce, 1984.

Bearss, Edwin C. *Redwood National Park: Del Norte and Humboldt Counties.* Department of the Interior, National Park Service, 1969.

Bledsoe, A. J. *History of Del Norte County.* Eureka, CA: Humboldt Times Print/Wyman & Co., 1881.

Burdick, George. *Klamath: River Angling Guide.* Portland, OR: Frank Amato Publications, 1989.

Coons, Peggy. N.d. Crescent City's Destructive Horror of 1964. Del Norte Historical Society files. Photocopy.

Coy, Owen C. *The Humboldt Bay Region 1850-1875.* Los Angeles: California State Historical Association, 1929. Reprinted, Eureka, CA: Humboldt County Historical Society, 1982.

Del Norte Triplicate Bicentennial Edition. Crescent City, CA: July 6, 1976.

Fountain, Susie Baker. *Papers.* 120 vols. Arcata, CA: Humboldt State University, 1967

Grosvenor, Melville Bell. "World's Tallest Tree Discovered." *National Geographic*, July 1964: 1, 8–9.

History of Humboldt County, Calif. San Francisco: Wallace W. Elliott & Co., 1881.

McBeth, Frances Turner. *Lower Klamath Country.* Berkeley: Anchor Press, 1950.

Melendy, Howard Brett. "One Hundred Years of the Redwood Lumber Industry, 1850–1950." Ph. D. diss., Stanford University, 1954. Photocopy.

Prouty, Andrew Mason. *More Deadly Than War!: Pacific Coast Logging 1827–1981.* Ph. D. diss., University of Washington, 1982. Photocopy.

Schrepfer, Susan R. *The Fight to Save the Redwoods: A History of Environmental Reform 1917–1978.* Madison, WI: University of Wisconsin Press, 1983.

Shinn, Charles Howard. "Land of the Redwoods." In *West of the Rocky Mountains,* edited by John Muir. Philadelphia: Running Press, 1976.

Smith, Esther Ruth. *The History of Del Norte County, California.* Oakland: the Holmes Book Company, 1953.

Stanton, Kathleen, Susie Van Kirk, and Ann King Smith. *Home Place: An Historic Resources of the Coyote Creek Lands, Redwood National Park, Humboldt County, California.* National Park Service. Redwood National Park. Photocopy.

There Really Was......a Klamath County! 1851–1874. Fortuna, CA: Redwood Genealogical Society, n.d.

Turner, Dennis W. *Place Names of Humboldt County, California: A Compendium 1542–1992.* Eureka, CA: Eureka Printing Company, Inc., 1993.

U. S. Congress. House. Committee on Public Lands. *Letter from the Secretary of the Interior: California Redwood Company.* 50th Cong., 1st sess., 1888. Ex. Doc. 282.

U. S. War Department. *The War of the Rebellion.* Series I. Vol. 51, pt. I. 1897.

Zahl, Paul A. "Finding the Mt. Everest of All Living Things." *National Geographic,* July 1964: 10–51.

In addition, articles were consulted in the following periodicals.

Newspapers: *Arcata Union, Crescent City Herald, Del Norte Record, Del Norte Triplicate, Ferndale Enterprise, Humboldt Standard, Humboldt Times, Humboldt Times-Telephone, New York Times, Times-Standard, Western Watchman*

Journals: *Del Norte County Historical Society Bulletin, Humboldt Historian*

A number of local residents provided direct information: Don Andreasen, Savina Barlow, Blanche Blankenship, Victor Crutchfield, Janice Dore, Helen Happ, Thelma Hufford, Florence Kring, Ora Leazer, Charles Lindgren, Ruby McNamara, Glen Nash, Mary Phillips Peacock, Thomas Peacock, Cheryl Seidner, Bill Watson, and Francis "Beeb" White.

Natural History: Birds

Dawson, William Leon. *The Birds of California.* 3 vols. San Diego: South Moulton Company, 1923.

Lemmon, Robert S. *Our Amazing Birds.* New York: American Garden Guild and Doubleday & Company Inc., 1952.

Peterson, Roger Tory. *Western Birds.* 3d ed. Boston: Houghton-Mifflin Company, 1990.

Stokes, Donald and Lillian Stokes. *Bird Behavior.* 3 vols. Boston: Little, Brown and Company, 1979, 1983, 1989.

Strachan, Gary. *Birds of the Redwoods.* Orick, CA; North Coast Redwoods Interpretive Association, 1988.

Natural History: Flowers

Niehaus, Theodore F. *Pacific States Wildflowers*. Boston: Houghton Mifflin Company, 1976.

Parsons, Mary Elizabeth. *The Wild Flowers of California*. San Francisco: California School Book Depository, 1930.

Rickett, Harold William. *Wildflowers of the United States*. Vol. 5, *The Northwestern States*. New York: The New York Botanical Garden/McGraw-Hill Book Company, n.d.

Ross, Robert A., and Henrietta L. Chambers. *Wildflowers of the Western Cascades*. Portland OR: Timber Press, 1988.

Spellenberg, Richard, *The Audubon Society Guide to North American Wildflowers: Western Region*. New York: Alfred A. Knopf, 1979.

Watts, Phoebe. *Redwood Region Flower Finder*. Berkeley: Nature Study Guild, 1979.

Natural History: General

Hickman, James C. *The Jepson Manual: Higher Plants of California*. Berkeley: University of California Press, 1993.

Kricher, John C., and Gordon Morrison. *Ecology of Western Forests*. Boston: Houghton Mifflin Company, 1993.

Lyons, Kathleen, and Mary Beth Cooney-Lazaneo. *Plants of the Redwood Region*. Boulder Creek CA: Looking Press, 1988.

Mathews, Daniel. *Cascade-Olympic Natural History*. Raven Editions, 1988.

Plants of the Redwoods. Orick, CA: North Coast Redwoods Interpretive Association, 1988.

Wernert, Susan J., ed. *North American Wildlife*. Pleasantville, N. Y.: Reader's Digest, 1982.

Whitney, Stephen. *Western Forests*. New York: Alfred A. Knopf, 1985.

Whittlesey, Rhoda. *Familiar Friends: Northwest Plants*. Portland OR: Rose Press, 1985.

Wildlife of the Redwoods. Orick, CA: North Coast Redwoods Interpretive Association, 1988.

Natural History: Mammals

Barker, Will. *Familiar Animals of North America*. New York: Harper & Brothers, 1951.

Burt, William H. and Richard P. Grossenheider. *Mammals*. 3d ed. Boston: Houghton Mifflin Company, 1976.

Calhane, Victor H. *Mammals of North America.* New York: The Macmillan Company, 1961.

Caras, Roger A. *North American Mammals.* New York: Meredith Press, 1967.

Wrigley, Robert E. *Mammals in North America.* Winnipeg: Hyperion Press Limited, 1986.

Natural History: Trees, Bushes, and Ferns

Caufield, Catherine. "The Ancient Forests." *The New Yorker.* May 14, 1990: 46–84.

Elias, Thomas S. *Field Guide to North American Trees.* rev. ed. Danbury CT: Grolier Book Clubs Inc., 1989.

Grillos, Steve. *Ferns and Fern Allies.* Berkeley: University of California Press, 1966.

Keator, Glenn. *Pacific Coast Berry Finder.* Berkeley: Nature Study Guild, 1978.

Keator, Glenn, and Ruth M. Heady. *Pacific Coast Fern Finder.* Berkeley: Nature Study Guild, 1981.

Pavlik, Bruce M.; Pamela Muick; Sharon Johnson; and Marjorie Pepper. *Oaks of California.* Los Olivos CA: Cachuma Press and the California Oak Foundation, 1991.

Peattie, Donald Culross. *A Natural History of Western Trees.* Boston: Houghton Mifflin Co., 1953.

Petrides, George A., and Olivia Petrides. *Western Trees.* Boston: Houghton Mifflin Co., 1992.

Index

Left to right: Jerry Rohde, Gisela Rohde, Larry Eifert

In 1972, Jerry and Gisela met in the San Bernardino Mountains of Southern California and they have been enjoying the outdoors together ever since. The Rohdes relocated to Humboldt County in 1979 and began hiking the North Coast's forests, mountains, and shorelines. Among the first areas they explored were the lands of Redwood National and State Parks.

Gisela, who took to the trails of her native Germany at age two, is now employed at the Humboldt State University Library. She is a self-taught naturalist, and an avid gardener, jogger, and cyclist. Jerry is a full-time writer; he was previously the coordinator for a network of environmental organizations. He has written a column about local history for southern Humboldt's *Redwood Record* and is a board member of the Humboldt County Historical Society.

The Rohdes live in the woods east of Clam Beach with their cat, Shinto. Their home is adjacent to the site of the Strawberry Creek railroad trestle that appears on page 16 of the book.

Disciplined by his family in both nature and art, Larry Eifert has spent the past twenty years painting and learning about coastal redwoods. The Eifert Gallery in Ferndale exhibits Larry's original paintings; his yearly calendar project features his essays and images of nature.

Commissioned by some of America's finest national parks, including Mammoth Cave, Yosemite, and Badlands, Larry has painted murals that serve both as art and as interpretation of nature. Each year countless people enjoy his popular images of these "last great places" as posters, prints, jigsaw puzzles, and book covers.

Larry has served on several interpretive association boards of directors, including the Redwood Natural History Association. To publicize Redwood National Park, he has provided the park with art and graphics, and taught at its summer field seminars. *The Distinctive Qualities of Redwoods*, written and illustrated by Larry, is now in its third edition; it explains the unique attributes of these great trees.